The Oder-Neisse Boundary and Poland's Modernization

Z. Anthony Kruszewski

foreword by
Morton A. Kaplan

The Praeger Special Studies program—
utilizing the most modern and efficient book
production techniques and a selective
worldwide distribution network—makes
available to the academic, government, and
business communities significant, timely
research in U.S. and international economic, social, and political development.

The Oder-Neisse Boundary and Poland's Modernization
The Socioeconomic and Political Impact

PRAEGER SPECIAL STUDIES IN INTERNATIONAL POLITICS AND PUBLIC AFFAIRS

Praeger Publishers   New York   Washington   London

PRAEGER PUBLISHERS
111 Fourth Avenue, New York, N.Y. 10003, U.S.A.
5, Cromwell Place, London S.W.7, England

Published in the United States of America in 1972
by Praeger Publishers, Inc.

Library of Congress Catalog Card Number: 74-159411

Printed in the United States of America

To the memory of Janusz, whose unfailing faith in me was an obligation, a challenge, and a determinant of standards to be emulated and cherished as a guide for all time.

FOREWORD
Morton A. Kaplan

The West is aware of the transfer of German territory to Poland, but is comfortably unfamiliar with the forced human dislocations that accompanied it. This relocation is a veritable major resource for social science analysis, as well as one of the more dramatic events of postwar history. The 4.5 million Poles who moved westward, thus taking the place of forcibly displaced Germans, were young and rural. The area into which they moved was urbanized and industrialized. The transformation of the Poles in their new surroundings and the impact of this transformation upon the new Poland are of the utmost importance in understanding modern Poland.

The analysis of this problem required a scholar with a thorough knowledge of the relevant languages, access to the materials, a background in economics and sociology as well as politics, the patience to bring order to a mass of disparate materials and statistics, and the analytical capacity to carry out a serious interdisciplinary study. If Professor Kruszewski does not employ many of the abstruse categories of political or economic development, his book is a serious contribution to its understanding. It perhaps would not be going too far to suggest that careful studies of this kind are more valuable than a number of the methodological treatises with which we have been inundated lately.

The author is indebted to so many scholars and institutions on both sides of the Atlantic Ocean that it would be virtually impossible to enumerate all those who contributed directly or indirectly to making this project possible.

Without the encouragement, guidance, and support of some scholars, however, this study would not have been completed. Its complexity would have prevented it from being finished. In particular, the following scholars were sources of inspiration and intellectual sustenance for the author: Morton Kaplan, Arcadius Kahan, Bert Hoselitz, and Chauncy Harris of the University of Chicago; Hans Morgenthau of the University of Chicago and the City University of New York; Hugh McLean of the University of California at Berkeley; Philip Wagner of Simon Fraser University; Stanislaw Wellisz of Columbia University; and Alicja Iwanska of the State University of New York at Albany.

The Polish academic institutions and social scientists extended their advice and help to the author in the most cordial fashion during his research in that country. This was a conditio sine qua non since obviously a topic of this kind could not have been attempted without extensive field research. Also, Polish archives in England opened their doors to the author and enabled him to include in this study excerpts from previously unpublished World War II Polish classified governmental documents.

To all the individuals and groups mentioned above goes the author's gratitude for sharing his trials and tribulations. Errors of commission and omission are, of course, his sole responsibility.

Financial support from The Polish American Academic Association of Chicago and from The Kosciuszko Foundation of New York provided research help when it was most needed, and a grant from The Research Institute of The University of Texas at El Paso enabled this study to appear in book form.

The manuscript was typed and retyped expertly and with dedication by a veritable jewel among students—turned temporary secretary—Alicia Holguin.

To my old friend B. Andrew Mudryk go my thanks for help in preparation of cartographic materials without which many of the geographical descriptions found in this study would have remained abstract.

The author's wife June deserves much more than stereotyped thanks. Her input into the study ranged from crash nonstop typing of many early versions of the manuscript through expert editorial and bibliographical help and advice to, and above all, psychological solace, so needed in times of scholarly frustrations. Her devotion is responsible for the conclusion of this work and is deeply cherished.

CONTENTS

LIST OF TABLES

LIST OF MAPS

GLOSSARY

The first column lists place names used in the text; they are Polish place names unless otherwise indicated (G=German; R=Russian). These exceptions are listed in the first column since they appear in such forms in the text in quotations or relate to the present territory of the USSR.

Babimost—Bomst
Bay of Gdansk—Danziger Bucht
Bober (G)—Bobr
Boleslawiec—Bunzlau
Braniewo—Braunsberg
Choszczno—Arnswalde
Danzig (G)—Gdansk
Drawsko—Dramburg
Drogobych (R)—Drohobycz
Elblag—Elbing
Gdansk—Danzig
Glogow—Glogau
Gorzow—Landsberg
Gorzowskie Holendry—Chwalowice
Gubin—Guben
Jelenia Gora—Hirschberg
Kaliningrad (R)—Konigsberg
Kleinitz (G)—Klenica
Kolobrzeg—Kolberg
Konigsberg (G)—Kaliningrad
Kostrzyn-Kustrin
Koszalin—Koslin
Krosno—Krossen
Kurzig (G)—Kursko
Legnica—Liegnitz
Leknica—Lugknitz
Lobes (G)—Lobez
Lvov (R)—Lwow
Mazuria—Masuren

Miedzyrzecz—Meseritz
Nowa Sol—Neusalz
Neisse (G)(Western, Gorlizer, Lusatian)—Nysa Luzycka
Neisse (G)(Eastern, Glatzer)—Nysa Klodzka
Oder (G)—Odra
Olawa—Ohlau
Olsztyn—Allenstein
Opole—Oppeln
Piensk—Penzig
Queis (G)—Kwisa
Radnitz (G)—Radnica
Santok—Zantoch
Skwierzyna—Schwerin
Slupsk—Stolp
Stettin (G)—Szczecin
Swinemunde (G)—Swinoujscie
Szczecin—Stettin
Turoszow-Turchau
Vilna (R)—Wilno
Vistula Lagoon—Frisches Haff
Walbrzych—Waldenburg
Warmia—Ermeland
Wroclaw—Breslau
Zagan—Sagan
Zary—Sorau
Zielona Gora—Grunberg

The Oder-Neisse Boundary and Poland's Modernization

**MODERNIZATION
AND POLAND'S
WESTWARD SHIFT:
BASIC ELEMENTS
OF CAUSALITY**

THE PROBLEM: RESEARCH INTO THE UNDERLYING
CAUSES OF POLAND'S MODERNIZATION

This study analyzes the underlying causes of Poland's rapid
modernization, a phenomenon not yet fully researched and described
in Western scholarly literature. It is concerned especially with the
bases for processes of modernization, which can be traced largely
to problems associated with the 1945 changes in both the eastern and
western borders of Poland and with the migration of Poles into the
new boundaries of the new homogenous state. These changes amounted
to a westward shift of the seventh largest European nation-state, an
unprecedented event in modern history. The socioeconomic consequences of such a dramatic and drastic national transformation are
unique, but in Western literature they are seldom mentioned, far less
discussed fully.

By contrast, many studies have been made to characterize the
changes wrought in postwar West Germany by the mass migration
of refugees and expellees. This difference prompted an official U.S.
government publication to comment in 1954:

Loss of life and the acquisition of the new territories
vacated by the Germans afforded the Polish Government
a unique opportunity to reallocate its human resources.
One regrets that the Polish authorities have not released
information to other countries regarding the steps taken
to meet the new problems. . . . Who were the people who
moved into these new areas? What were their characteristics? What had been their previous occupational

experience? Questions such as these cannot be answered
or can be answered only in part.[1]

Lack of data on the subject even in the late 1950's and early
1960's prevented any serious analysis of these questions. The basic
sources, such as the materials of the Polish national census of 1950,
were never published fully.* Only in the early 1960's did the Central
Statistical Office of Poland begin to publish the comparative data from
both the national censuses of 1950 and 1960 and make them available
for analysis by Polish social scientists.

Unfortunately, the books and monographs that appeared in
Poland during the 1960's and began to explore the subject have all
had two common traits that largely distort true analysis of the situation and to some extent undermine scholarly value:

1. Since these books have been published in Poland, they tend
to overemphasize the positive role of the Communist Party and its
organs in the formative years of the new society of the western territories.

2. They underemphasize or altogether omit the positive role
of the Catholic Church as the only unifying force and formal organization of the masses of strangers settling in the area.

In several instances known to the author, in manuscripts
about to be published the passages dealing with the role of the Church
had to be omitted or sharply curtailed. Thus, in order to properly
analyze the role of the Church as a unifying factor—an element of
extreme importance in the formation of new society in the Oder-Neisse
territories after 1945, and, ironically the least documented element—
we have had to rely on a few unpublished primary sources, interviews
with clergymen and local residents, and some material published in
articles. Consequently, it is at best a sketchy presentation of the
problem.

---

*The author obtained a copy of the mimeographed edition
("exclusively for official use only") of materials on the origin of the
population, which was never printed. After protracted negotiations,
this information was acquired by convincing the authorities that in
the West any serious analysis of such a vital problem starts with the
basic sources and that, therefore, such basic sources cannot be classified.

Last but not least, there is a problem in comparing Polish and German data. The developmental approach is used to describe an area that has always been an integrated part of a centrally administered state. Thus, one is faced with difficulty in separating out the prewar German data for this particular area to compare them with current Polish data. Furthermore, in order to properly document the destruction and rebuilding of the area, it is necessary to use two standards for comparison of data: the current data must be compared with the prewar and, again, with the postwar data (which reflected the total wartime destruction of the Oder-Neisse territories). Current nomenclature is used throughout this study, according to the recommendations of the American Geographical Society. The glossary supplies equivalent place names. The concept of nationality as used in the study pertains to the ethnic and sociocultural definition current in Central and Eastern Europe.

This study seeks to explore the consequences of demographic shifts in Poland and their impact on the political and social structure of the Polish nation. It assesses the socioeconomic effects of the shift of the national territory of a medium-sized nation—a shift that is unique in modern history—and its implications for the international relations of East-Central Europe. The author was inspired to examine this subject by Jiri Kolaja, the Czech-born American sociologist who outlined some of those implications as follows:

> Dramatic history of the last decade furnished new experiences and introduced new elements into the national personalities of both [Polish and Czech] nations. Let us only consider the fact that six million Poles—majority of whom stem from the eastern rural areas of the country—were settled in the industrialized regions on the Oder and the Neisse and in Silesia. Sooner or later this fact has to influence the Polish psyche. The history of industrialization of other countries supplies us with examples which support this thesis. There is no reason to suppose that the Polish case will be different. As a consequence it seems also that the "gentry-landowning" ideal will be transformed.[2]

How little these phenomena are really known in the West, even among the leading political scientists, is fully illustrated by a passage in a new edition of one of the best and most popular political science texts currently used on American college campuses. Robert A. Dahl of Yale University, in the second edition (1971) of his book, Modern Political Analysis,[3] quotes Bruce M. Russett[4] (the author of a

number of pioneering behavioral reference works and sources in
political science) and classifies Poland as having "fifty percent or
more of the labor force employed in agriculture."[5] This statement
is outdated by some twenty years and reflects the results of the Polish
national census of 1950.[6]

The 1950 census was made at the end of the period of post-World
War II rebuilding and obviously does not reflect contemporary realities. Still, such statements as the one cited above are reprinted in
1971 and used to educate college students. The time-lag and lack of
Western knowledge about the realities of the rapid modernization and
industrialization of Poland since 1945 could not be more glaring, especially in view of the fact that the recently released results of 1970
Polish national census indicate that only 29.5 percent of Poles derive
their livelihood from agricultural pursuits (see Chapter 3, Table 3).

THE STUDY: ASSUMPTIONS AND METHODS

This study has a twofold aim: (1) to prove that the rapid modernization and drastic transformation of the Polish social structure
and economy that have occurred since World War II can be traced to
the boundary changes and resulting migrations and (2) to partially
fill the gap in the literature on the subject that has appeared in English-
speaking countries.

The study attempts: (1) to collect data on post-World War II
migrations in Poland, hitherto scattered or unavailable in the United
States and (2) to assess the effects of the postwar boundary shifts
and subsequent migrations on Poland's society and economy in
general and on the newly created society in the Polish western territories in particular.

We consider that the boundary shifts of the eastern and western
frontiers provided Poland with a much more viable territorial base
and enabled it to reallocate its human and natural resources to
afford their full use.[7] Thus, the territorial shifts and migrations
that created the new homogenous Polish state are as important in
the study of the socioeconomic modernization of that nation as the
Communist-directed transformation of its economy.[8]

We also assume that the rapid industrialization of Poland would
have been delayed or hampered if it had not been for Poland's new
territorial and economic bases as restructured after the Potsdam
decisions of 1945.

This assumption stems from the analysis of the ill-developed and relatively backward economy of prewar Poland, in which industrial development was perennially hampered by the existence of an under-employed agricultural labor force (estimated variously at five to eight million) in the villages. This factor alone precluded any progress in the economic development of the country and unduly delayed the mechanization of agriculture. It also hindered any increase in Poland's productivity and a better allocation of human resources. Furthermore, industry, which was weak and heavily dependent on foreign capital, was unable to absorb the surplus agricultural labor.

The drastic postwar territorial and population shifts enabled Poland to strengthen its economy and provided Poland with new econo-mic resources. This was accomplished by the incorporation of the much more industrialized territories east of the Oder-Neisse into the Polish body politic. These areas were emptied of their former inhabitants but endowed with productive facilities. At the same time, Poland lost 46 percent of its prewar area, only a fraction of whose population was transferred into the new Polish boundaries. The economic losses in the east were mainly agricultural: the only econo-mically significant resources mined in the east were oil, potash, and ozokerite. The eastern territories that were lost to the USSR had a much lower productive output than the western and central provinces of pre-1939 Poland.

Thus, the shift of boundaries in 1945 afforded the Polish govern-ment a unique opportunity to make drastic economic reallocations. It enabled Poland to transfer surplus underemployed agricultural labor to the towns and villages of the western territories, dramatically resolving the basic economic problem of the pre-1939 economy. Furthermore, it accelerated the urbanization of Poland by doubling its urban population.

At the same time, since the industrial output of the incorporated areas was roughly equal to the total industrial output of pre-1939 Poland, postwar Poland theoretically had doubled its industrial capa-city. Thus, even if the war losses in industry are considered to have temporarily reduced Polish industrial output (within the new frontiers) by half, Poland had emerged with a much stronger economic frame-work. We assume that this in turn made possible the rapidity of Poland's postwar reconstruction, the further growth in its industrial capacity, and the allocation of the agricultural surplus labor to the new territories.

We shall try to assess the overall effects of the territorial changes and subsequent migrations on the newly created society of the Oder-Neisse territories. We shall analyze the demographic elements that contributed to the formation of that society and the developmental processes affecting the economic structure of the area. At all points it is assumed that the migratory movements connected with the incorporation of the Oder-Neisse areas have affected the economy and demography of Poland as a whole, and these links will be shown.

Furthermore, by discussing at length the historical developments and political decisions responsible for the territorial shifts, we shall demonstrate the connection between political developments and the scale of postwar migrations. It is assumed that the postwar frontier changes were consciously determined by the Great Powers in order to provide Poland with a stronger political and economic structure within the realities of the postwar balance of power.

We also assume that the socioeconomic results of the postwar migrations have deeply affected Polish society at large and accelerated its modernization.[9] Finally, it will be demonstrated that the changing social and economic patterns affect the future viability of the Polish state and thus influence the international relations of East-Central Europe.

NOTES

1. U.S. Bureau of the Census, The Population of Poland, Series P-90, No. 4 (Washington, D.C.: U.S. Government Printing Office, 1954), p. 41.

2. Jiri Kolaja, "Polityczne konsekwencje cech narodowych," Kultura (Paris), No. 11/61 (1952), pp. 77-78.

3. Robert A. Dahl, Modern Political Analysis, 2nd. ed. (Englewood Cliffs, N.J.: Prentice-Hall, 1971).

4. Bruce M. Russett, "Inequality and Instability: The Relation of Land Tenure to Politics," World Politics, Vol. XVI (April 1964), pp. 442-54.

5. Dahl, op. cit., Table 10, p. 71.

6. Rocznik Statystyczny, 1970, Vol. XXX (Warsaw: Glowny Urzad Statystyczny Polskiej Rzeczypospolitej Ludowej, 1970), Tables 15 and 16, p. 40.

7. David E. Apter, The Politics of Modernization (Chicago: The University of Chicago Press, 1965).

8. Lucian W. Pye, Aspects of Political Development (Boston: Little, Brown and Company, 1966); Robert T. Holt and John E. Turner, The Political Basis of Economic Development (Princeton, N.J.: D. Van Nostrand Company, 1966).

9. Jason L. Finkle and Richard W. Gable, Political Development and Social Change (New York: John Wiley & Sons Inc., 1966).

2

HISTORICAL BACKGROUND
AND POLITICAL FRAMEWORK
OF THE POSTWAR
POPULATION MIGRATIONS

The delimitation of the Polish state after 1945 was determined by political decisions made by the three Great Powers (the United States, Great Britain, and the USSR) during the course of World War II rather than by agreements between the Polish government and the governments of Germany and the USSR. The postwar borders differed drastically from those of prewar Poland: both western and eastern frontiers were shifted westward by approximately 150 miles.[1] Pre-1939 Poland was a multinational state with over 30 percent of its population belonging to minority groups.[2] The border changes and migrations after the war transformed Poland into a national state with 98 percent of its population made up of Poles.[3]

Because wartime decisions made by the three Great Powers changed the frontiers of Poland, causing population exchanges and postwar migrations, it is necessary to provide a historical review of the political framework in which those wartime decisions were reached. Analysis of different boundary variants of both western and eastern frontiers is needed to demonstrate how changes in the demarcation of those borders affected the size of the postwar migrations. In addition, the claims and positions of the powers directly concerned in the establishment of Poland's new frontiers must be summarized.

ORIGIN OF THE POST-1945 EASTERN FRONTIER

The new eastern frontier of Poland was outlined and de facto approved by the three Great Powers at the Teheran Conference of November 28-December 1, 1943, without the knowledge or participation of the Polish government.[4] The discussions on the outline of the future Polish-USSR border were recapitulated in Marshal Stalin's message to Prime Minister Winston Churchill, dated March 23, 1944, a copy of which was sent to President Roosevelt. Stalin wrote:

> I totally disagree with you. I must point out that at Teheran you, the President and myself were agreed that the Curzon Line was lawful.
>
> At that time you considered the Soviet Government's stand on the issue quite correct, and said it would be crazy for representatives of the Polish emigre Government to reject the Curzon Line. But now you maintain something to the contrary.[5]

The so-called Curzon Line of 1919 was never demarcated because the outcome of the Polish-Russian war of 1919-21 was favorable to the Poles. The Treaty of Riga of March 18, 1921, ended that war and established the Polish-Soviet border much farther to the east. The latter frontier was given general recognition through the decision of the Council of Ambassadors on March 15, 1923.

On October 26, 1944, Polish Prime Minister Stanislaw Mikolajczyk wrote to Roosevelt seeking his support for a change in the Curzon Line that would keep the city of Lvov and the oil fields of Drogobych in Poland.[6] In his answer of November 17, 1944, Roosevelt agreed to intercede with Stalin, through Ambassador Averill Harriman, to save Lvov for Poland. However, the Polish government felt that the acceptance of such a modification of the Curzon Line would jeopardize the city of Vilna in the north and other areas to the east of the Curzon Line that it absolutely refused to cede to the USSR.[7] The Polish government therefore rejected the mediation by outvoting Mikolajczyk's Peasant Party, which favored this final attempt to change the Curzon Line. Since the majority in the Polish government felt that only the postwar Polish parliament could vote any changes in Poland's boundaries, Mikolajczyk resigned his post as prime minister.

The Polish government wanted, realistically if extra-legally, to retain at least part of the eastern territories. The government

therefore proposed a demarcation line to the east of both Vilna and
Lvov to serve as a temporary dividing line of both administrations
until the Polish nation could be consulted in elections.[8] This was
refused by the USSR, which insisted on the Curzon Line as the final
border.[9]

Because of the Polish government's refusal to grant approval for
mediation, no attempt was made at that late date to change the Curzon
Line even partially; in any case, the prospect for success was not altogether certain in view of the prior agreement of the Western powers
at Teheran to the thus-defined Curzon Line.[10] However, there are
indications that some frontier concessions by the USSR might have
been possible if a stronger political pressure had been exerted by
the Western allies. Such sentiments prevailed even among the Polish
Communists of the Lublin Committee, as evidenced by materials now
available.[11] There is also an unverified report that Stalin considered
the Lvov problem even in informal discussions with Polish government
circles (see Appendix A).[12]

THE CURZON LINE: ITS EFFECT ON
THE ANTICIPATED MIGRATIONS

Mikolajczyk's final attempt to retain at least the city of Lvov
and the oil fields of Drogobych for Poland through Roosevelt's support
would have meant shifting the southern segment of the Curzon Line
defined as "Line A" to "Line B," which was originally suggested as a
border between Poland and the Free Ukrainian State in East Galicia[13]
(see Appendix A). The failure to achieve that change in the present
Polish eastern frontier caused the migration of the Polish population
concentrated in the city of Lvov (66 percent of the population was
made up of Poles) and the surrounding area.[14] The failure to win
from the USSR even limited changes in the new eastern border, which
was established along the line least favorable for Poland, maximized
the number of Poles (3.8-4.2 million) who had to decide whether to
remain in their homes and become Soviet citizens or opt for Poland
and move to within its new boundaries.[15] The extent of this migration,
and of wartime deportation losses to the USSR, is indicated by the
number of Poles living in the Lvov area at present (about 100,000)
as shown in current Soviet and Ukrainian sources.[16]

The population estimates for 1960 indicated the presence of
more than three million former inhabitants of the eastern territories
and their children within the present borders of Poland.[17] This figure
represented 39.6 percent of the population of the western areas when
they were acquired by Poland under the Potsdam Agreement of 1945.

Although some persons in this group did not actually settle in the western territories but rather in central Poland (for example, early transferees in the autumn of 1944 and spring of 1945), their addition to the already overcrowded villages of central Poland contributed to the compensatory migratory movement of the population of central Poland to the west. The acquisition of the western territories solved the problem of where to settle these three million persons. If no extension of the western border had occurred while the eastern border was being imposed on the Polish nation, the resettlement would have been impossible because of the overcrowding of the central areas.

THE ORIGIN OF TERRITORIAL COMPENSATION

The extension of the Polish border to the Oder-Neisse line should be reviewed briefly. This line, although deeply rooted in Polish history and a goal of various political groups and leaders,[18] was the product of a plan to shift the Polish state westward. It was conceived and executed by the wartime alliance of the United States and the Soviet Union, largely without the knowledge and completely without the consent of the Polish government or any freely elected Polish legislative body. It is evident that so great a shift of the western border would not have been possible without the claims that the USSR made against almost half the territory of Poland (the ally in whose defense the Western Powers went to war), the subsequent terrible ordeal of the Polish nationals during World War II, and the total destruction of the Polish economy by the Nazis.[19]

Those three factors gave rise to the "compensation idea" of indemnifying Poland for what it lost territorially and economically as a result of the war and its aftermath. The extension of Poland "in the North and West" (the words used at the Teheran Conference) would provide it with adequate economic resources for reconstruction and create a more viable economic and political base for postwar Poland. It also would give Poland additional territory to resettle Poles who had lost their homes in the east because of the imposition of the Curzon Line. Thus, the establishment of the Polish western border along the Oder-Neisse rivers is inexorably linked with the incorporation of 46 percent of Poland's prewar territory by the Soviet Union and the decision of the three Great Powers to transfer German population from Poland to Germany.[20]

FLIGHT AND TRANSFER OF GERMANS

More than any other decision, the decision to transfer German population from Poland to Germany made possible the westward extension of the territory of Poland. Despite the differences among the Allies about the extent of the new territorial acquisitions of Poland, the Allied Powers of World War II agreed unanimously to the principle of the transfer of the German population from the territory assigned to Poland.[21] The German population transfer plan enacted by the Allied Commission for Germany on November 20, 1945,[22] authorized the transfer from Poland of 3.5 million Germans living there. This solidified the boundary solution along the Oder-Neisse line, despite the fact that the United States and the United Kingdom are still withholding de jure recognition of that border.

Of the 3.5 million Germans estimated to be in the territory of postwar Poland, the Polish government actually transferred 2.3 million between 1946 and 1949.[23] According to German estimates (there are no statistics available for that chaotic postwar period), the Polish government expelled or authorized the departure of 650,000 Germans in the period between the German military surrender on May 8, 1945, and the first months of 1946, when organized transfers were set in motion under the schedule approved by the Allied Commission for Germany on November 20, 1945.[24] Eventually, the "reuniting of families" scheme of 1955-59 removed virtually all the Germans remaining in postwar Poland.[25]

The latter group was also composed to a large extent of ethnic Poles who were German citizens before the war. They either decided to join their families in West or East Germany or took the long-delayed opportunity for emigration. The total number of Germans who left the territory of Poland from the time the Eastern front rolled over that area can be estimated at about 3.2 million people. This is the total number of persons who were classified, or for various reasons classified themselves, as Germans and were expelled from the western territories or were later allowed to leave Poland.

All other surviving members of the prewar German community in the Oder-Neisse territories, estimated at about 3.6 million (the total number of former German inhabitants of the Oder-Neisse areas present in Germany on January 1, 1949, was estimated by the American Bureau of the Census at 6.2 million),[26] either fled those areas before

the retreat of the German Army or were evacuated by order of the
Nazi authorities. That evacuation and chaotic retreat in the battle
zone caused huge losses among the population (for reasons of morale,
the evacuation was purposely delayed by Nazi officials until the last
minute). German sources give some description of those losses, the
extent of which is impossible even to estimate.[27] Further losses
were incurred in the bombing and shelling of the evacuation transports
by the Soviet Army and during the Nazis' desperate defense of the
cities in the area, some of which were defended to the end of the war
in Europe (Wroclaw until May 8, 1945; Glogow until April 1, 1945;
and Kolobrzeg until March 18, 1945). Despite the partial evacuation
of the German population, civilian losses in those beleaguered cities
were huge.[28]

Since both the flight and the evacuation—which bordered on
panic—occurred in the latter part of January 1945 under extremely
severe climatic conditions, the toll of lives lost assumed frightful
proportions.[29] Those losses were compounded by the swiftness of
the Soviet offensive and the savage fighting for strongly fortified
centers, some of which changed hands several times (for example,
Gubin and Kostrzyn changed hands seven times each) and were virtually
destroyed. The German population fleeing to safety suffered especially
severe losses in the area of Wroclaw and on the Bay of Gdansk, where
refugees and members of the retreating German army drowned by
the thousands while trying to escape the Soviet encirclement by flight
across the frozen Vistula Lagoon, which was repeatedly bombed,
and in the evacuation ships sunk off shore.

The heavy losses suffered during the military operations in the
Oder-Neisse territories and the chaotic flight of up to 50 percent
of the surviving population greatly simplified border solutions in the
area. Before the losses and flight were estimated, the drawing of a
new eastern border of Germay was thought to involve the transfer
of 6 to 7 million persons. Churchill spoke of those figures in connection with the boundary shift as early as 1944.[30] However, as
shown in Table 1, the actual transfer involved about 3 million Germans rather than the 7.6 million residing in the area in 1939 [31] (of 8.9
million area residents in 1939, 1.3 million were ethnic Poles).

The decision to transfer the Germans and to authorize the
settlement of Poles (especially those from the former eastern territories of Poland) stabilized the border, regardless of the varying
opinions of the World War II Allies about the outline of the western
extension of Poland.

TABLE 1

Transfer of Germans from Poland, 1945-50

Year	Number of Germans Transferred from Poland	
Summer 1945 through autumn 1945	approx.	650,000
February through December 1946		1,632,562
1947		538,324
1948		42,740
1949		61,449
1950	approx.	59,000
Total	approx.	2,984,075

Sources: Polish Central Office of Statistics data; Gotthold Rhode, Die Ostgebiete des Deutschen Reiches (Wurzburg: Holtzner-Verlag, 1955), p. 131.

POLISH BOUNDARY CLAIMS IN THE WEST
DURING WORLD WAR II

The German invasion of Poland aimed to destroy the existence
of any Polish state. In view of the extent of the Polish catastrophe,
the policy of total destruction of the Polish nation[32] produced thoroughly unexpected results. There was a prompt revival of far-reaching
Polish territorial claims in preparation for the hoped-for victory.[33]
The territorial goals simultaneously formulated by the resistance
movement and the Polish government in London varied but little.

All political parties, both in Poland and in the exiled government,
were united in their desire to see a greatly shortened Polish-German
frontier, a frontier that would include Polish-speaking territories of
pre-1937 Germany, that would be more defensible, and that would
give Poland broader access to the sea. The demands officially advanced
by the Polish government in exile and its clandestine press organs in
Poland essentially repeated the claims advanced by the Polish delegation to the Versailles Conference of 1919,[34] but the organs of the
National Party both in Poland and in exile in London pressed for the
Polish western border on the Oder-Neisse.

The arguments advanced for the Oder-Neisse claims were
based mainly on security considerations:

> As early as 1940 the claim to Oder-Neisse areas as both
> historically and politically justified was for the first time
> discussed in the Polish Underground press published in
> Nazi-occupied Warsaw and advocated by the "Salamander
> Society," the war-time resistance organization of the pre-
> war National-Radical Party.[35]

The lead article in the December 15, 1942, issue of the National
Party organ published in London, Mysl Polska, stated explicitly that
the chief principle governing the Polish western border delimitation
in future peace negotiations (unlike the ethnic and plebiscite principles
espoused by the Versailles Peace Conference of 1919) should be the
"principle of expulsion and security considerations."[36] The National
Party press in Poland and England essentially advanced the theory of
the western expansion of the postwar Polish state as a solution that
would constitute adequate compensation and enable Poland to recover
from its crushing economic losses. It would help prevent future
aggression from the west by redistributing economic power and by
shortening the Polish-German frontier from 1,912 to 460 kilometers.[37]

That program of frontier extension did not anticipate any dimi-
nution of Polish territory in the east. All the political parties in
exile and in Poland were firm in defense of the 1939 eastern border
with the USSR.[38] Furthermore, in the later war years even the limited
program of western frontier revision advanced by the Polish government in exile in London (East Prussia, Opole Silesia, and part of
Western Pomerania) was affected by the growing realization that the
Soviet border claims had the support of the Western Allies. Thus,
the Polish western border claims were formulated in such a way as
to not prejudice the defense of the eastern territories of Poland against
Soviet claims. The future extension of the territory in the west was
considered as compensation for economic and population losses sustained during the war and as a security requirement, rather than as
compensation for the loss of the territories east of the Curzon Line
(see Appendix A).

The Allied political decision to shift simultaneously both Poland's
western and eastern frontiers, and to transfer the Germans living in
the areas to be given to Poland, made an extension of the western border
of Poland to the Oder-Neisse rivers possible and feasible in terms of
the ethnic disentanglement of the Poles and Germans living in the
border lands. In the final analysis, the decisions of the three Great
Powers were responsible for the extent of the postwar territory of
the Polish state. A short review of the American, British, and Soviet
positions on that issue is thus in order. A somewhat brief review of
the French position is also interesting because of its differences with
the American and British views.

THE UNITED STATES POSITION
ON THE ISSUE OF POLISH BORDERS

The United States position on the question of Poland's future
western border in the closing days of World War II is best summarized
in the hitherto unpublished document dated March 9, 1945, prepared
by the Research and Analysis Branch of the Office of Strategic Services and entitled <u>Postwar Poland: Economic and Political Outlook</u>.[39]

This confidential position paper, issued after the Yalta Conference, covers the views of the American government on political and
economic matters concerning Poland (the document is extensively
quoted in Appendix B). The American government was in favor of
strengthening the economic structure of Poland mainly through the
incorporation of the Upper Silesian industrial basin into Poland to
enable Poland to accelerate postwar rebuilding and much-needed
economic reforms.

Although the present Polish-German boundary along the Oder-Neisse line was mentioned in this position paper, it was a political alternative, initially rejected by the American delegation to the Potsdam Conference. Later it was accepted as a compromise solution, as a part of the "package deal" involving the Soviet concessions on German reparations.[40] The American agreement to the extension of the Polish frontier to the Oder and the Eastern Neisse was considered a maximum concession. The United States was not willing to assign to Poland the territory between both the Neisse rivers, mainly to avoid enlarging the already extensive program of population transfers. Those transfers were officially endorsed by the United States government in a letter from President Roosevelt to Prime Minister Mikolajczyk dated November 17, 1944. The letter stated:

> If the Polish Government and people desire in connection with the new frontiers of the Polish State to bring about the transfer to and from territory of Poland of national minorities, the United States Government will raise no objection and as far as practicable will facilitate such transfer.[41]

The extension of Polish territory to the Oder-Lusatian Neisse line was, in the opinion of the American delegation to the Potsdam Conference, considered too ambitious for the absorptive capacity of the war-ruined Polish economy and society.[42] The final concession was made on July 30, 1945, when the issue of German reparations was linked with that of the Polish-German border. Although final American assent was subject to "final determination" at the future peace conference with Germany, the "package" decision involving the Oder-Neisse line was considered to be practically irreversible in view of the population transfer provisions included in that agreement.[43]

Of the powers present at Potsdam, the American delegation was the last to accept the Oder-Lusatian Neisse line as part of the "package," and it actually did so after the Poles were ready, because of the consistent American opposition, to modify their border demands slightly. That concession, transmitted to the United States delegation on July 30, 1945, in the final days of the Potsdam Conference, would have amended Poland's new western border to run along the Oder-Bober-Queis river line, thus substituting, for the southern segment of the Oder-Lusatian Neisse line, the Bober-Queis rivers line, which flow parallel to the Lusatian Neisse, about twenty miles east. However, the offer appears to have reached the American delegation after it had finally agreed to include the Oder-Lusatian Neisse line in the "package."[44]

If the Polish counterproposal had been considered, postwar Poland would not have had the extensive brown coal deposits of the Turoszow coal basin across the Lusatian Neisse near Zittau, East Germany. That area, now fully developed by the Poles, produces 16 million tons of brown coal annually.[45] Furthermore, the glass works near Piensk and Leknica along the Neisse and the well-developed light and textile industry in and around the town of Zary near the border would have been included in East Germany. Thus, a classical quirk of fate—the tardy delivery of the Polish counterproposal—was decisive in the final outline of the current German-Polish border.[46]

THE BRITISH POSITION ON THE
ISSUE OF POLISH BORDERS

The British government was the host of the Polish government in exile in London, its chief ally, and the sponsor of the Polish forces fighting in the West during World War II. Hence, Great Britain was involved in the Polish boundary negotiations for the longest time and was most directly concerned with that problem. The Polish-British Treaty of August 25, 1939, stipulated the defense of Polish territory against invasion by a foreign power. Article 1 of that treaty was mutually interpreted as the guarantee of the existing Polish-German border. In view of the events following the 1939 German invasion of Poland, the British government supported the Polish government position on the postwar changes of the western frontier of Poland. The changes advocated by the Poles were based primarily on military considerations and improving the defensibility of the new postwar frontier by shortening its length. The British position on Polish acquisitions in the west basically coincided with the stated border demands made throughout the war by the Polish government (i.e., East Prussia and Opole Silesia and the shortening of the western border).[47]

Thus, the British government acceded to the idea of western territorial extension by the Poles even before the Soviet annexation of eastern Poland had to be reconciled with British political commitments on behalf of Poland. It was only then that Churchill formulated the territorial "compensation theory" in regard to Poland. He stated it explicitly on April 15, 1943, and was the first to attempt to find a solution to the conflicting Polish and Soviet positions on the eastern borders of Poland.[48]

To induce the Polish government to shift its position on the eastern border, the British government modified its support of

moderate annexation by Poland to include all the territories east of
the "Oder Line." The British government stated its new position in
the so-called "Cadogan letter" sent under the signature of Sir Alexander
Cadogan, then undersecretary of state. The letter, dated November 2,
1944, reads:

> The Prime Minister, after consultations with the Cabinet,
> has now directed me to give you the following replies. . . .
> You asked in the first place whether, even in the event of
> the United States Government finding themselves unable
> to agree to the changes in the western frontier of Poland
> foreshadowed in the recent conversations in Moscow, His
> Majesty's Government would still advocate these changes
> at the Peace Settlement. The answer of His Majesty's
> Government to this question is in the affirmative. Sec-
> ondly you enquired whether His Majesty's Government
> were definitely in favour of advancing the Polish frontier
> up to the line of the Oder, to include the port of Stettin.
> The answer is that His Majesty's Government do consider
> that Poland should have the right to extend her territory
> to this extent. . . . Finally you enquired whether His
> Majesty's Government would guarantee the independence
> and integrity of the new Poland. To this the answer is
> that His Majesty's Government are prepared to give such
> a guarantee jointly with the Soviet Government. If the
> United States Government could see their way to join also,
> that would plainly be of the greatest advantage, though His
> Majesty's Government would not make this a condition of
> their own guarantee in conjunction with that of the Soviet
> Government.[49]

In conjunction with the "compensation theory," it should also be
noted that, toward the end of the World War II, the United States
government also considered these extensive shifts of the Polish
frontiers as territorial compensation. In his letter to Mikolajczyk
of November 17, 1944, Roosevelt stated:

> In regard to the future frontier of Poland, if mutual agree-
> ment on this subject including the proposed compensation
> for Poland from Germany is reached between the Polish,
> Soviet, and British Governments, this Government would
> offer no objection.[50]

The transfer of the remaining German population from the Oder-
Neisse territories, which was largely completed in 1945-47, should

be considered together with the similar transfer of Poles from the former eastern territories who opted for Poland, also largely completed in those years. These movements were foreshadowed in the speech dealing with the problems of postwar Polish frontiers made by Churchill on December 15, 1944, in the British House of Commons. He said:

> The Poles are free so far as Russia and Great Britain are concerned, to extend their territory at the expense of Germany to the West. . . . Thus they gain in the west and north territories more important and highly developed than they lose in the east. . . . The transference of several millions of people would have to be effected from the east to the west or north and the expulsion of the Germans, (because that is what is proposed—the total expulsion of the Germans) from the area to be acquired by Poland in the west and north. For expulsion is the method which, so far as we have been able to see, will be the most satisfactory and lasting. There will be no mixture of populations to cause endless trouble as in Alsace-Lorraine. A clean sweep will be made. I am not alarmed at the prospect of the disentanglement of populations, nor am I alarmed by these large transferences, which are more possible than they ever were before through modern conditions. . . . Nor do I see why there should not be room in Germany for the German population of East Prussia and of the other territories I have mentioned. After all, 6 million or 7 million Germans have been killed already in this frightful war, into which they did not hesitate, for a second time in a generation to plunge all Europe.[51]

Thus, the British delegation to the Potsdam Conference (having already publicly accepted the new eastern border of Poland along the Curzon Line) was prepared to agree to the new western border of Poland on the Oder and Eastern Neisse as de facto territorial compensation for the areas lost in the east to the USSR. Under pressure from the Soviet delegation and in view of the united stand on the issue by the delegation of the Polish provisional government of national unity (which was composed largely of Communists but also included some former members of the Polish government in exile in London, such as Stanislaw Mikolajczyk and Stanislaw Grabski),[52] the British governmental delegation (led by Prime Minister Clement Attlee) agreed to assent to the Oder-Western Neisse Line in return for Soviet concession on the reparations issue.[53] In its decision, the British delegation preceded the United States delegation.

The Anglo-American concession on the border issue was reluctantly granted. As a result, there was a lack of commitment by the United States and Great Britain to support that line at the future peace conference, whereas both Western Powers were committed to support Article V of the Potsdam Communiqué transferring the Konigsberg area of former East Prussia to the Soviet Union.

By analyzing the Potsdam negotiations on the new Polish western border, one could demonstrate that the only basic problem at issue between the Western Powers and Poland (supported by the USSR) was the territory of Silesia between the Western and Eastern Neisse rivers.[54] Although they were originally prepared to give Poland less territory at Potsdam, neither Western Power questioned the Oder line.[55]

THE FRENCH POSITION ON THE
ISSUE OF POLISH BORDERS

The French Government, although a nonparticipant in the Potsdam Conference, did recognize the agreement as binding on France. It had shared, with the governments of the United States and Britain, the view that the final delimitation of the Polish western border would be made in the future peace treaty with Germany, as specified by the Potsdam Agreement:

> In conformity with the agreement on Poland reached at the
> Crimea Conference, the three heads of Government have
> sought the opinion of the Polish Provisional Government
> of National Unity in regard to the accession of territory
> in the north and west which Poland should receive. The
> President of the National Council of Poland and members
> of the Polish Provisional Government of National Unity
> have been received at the conference and have fully pre-
> sented their views. The three heads of Government re-
> affirm their opinion that the final delimitation of the
> Western frontier of Poland should await the peace settle-
> ment. The three heads of government agree that, pending
> the final determination of Poland's western frontier, the
> former German territories east of a line running from
> the Baltic Sea immediately west of Swinemuende, and
> hence along the Oder River to the confluence of the West-
> ern Neisse River and along the Western Neisse to the
> Czechoslovak frontier, including that portion of East

Prussia not placed under the administration of the Union of
Soviet Socialist Republics in accordance with the understanding reached at this conference and including the area
of the former Free City of Danzig, shall be under the
administration of the Polish state and for such purposes
should not be considered as part of the Soviet zone of
occupation in Germany.[56]

However, the French Government, in the statement of President
Charles DeGaulle on March 25, 1959, made it clear that it considers
the present boundary along the Oder-Western Neisse as permanent.[57]
It thus subscribes to the point of view held by the Soviet government.

THE SOVIET POSITION ON THE
ISSUE OF POLISH BORDERS

The Soviet government, as chief architect of the westward shift
of postwar Poland, was interested in supporting the Polish claims to
the Oder-Neisse line as the future boundary. Thus, the fulfillment of
Polish territorial aspirations was conceived mainly as a political
device to divert Polish public opinion from (1) the annexation by the
USSR of the former eastern territories and (2) the subsequent migration
of a large percentage of the Polish inhabitants of the former eastern
territories into postwar Polish territory.[58] The firm support given
by the Soviet Union to Poland's western border aspirations also was
designed to provide Poland's Communist government with popular
appeal to the masses, as the spokesman for the Polish national interest.

Thus, the simultaneous shift of the borders of postwar Poland was
considered by the Soviet government as adequate territorial compensation for the losses sustained in the east, although such an argument
was never voiced officially and is now being vehemently denied.[59]
The official position proclaims that the eastern areas were transferred to the USSR on an ethnographic basis. However, the Soviet
ethnographic atlas published in 1964, which reflects the status quo
twenty years after the transfer of eastern Poles, shows that the Vilna
area remains ethnographically Polish. It thus disproves the USSR
claims advanced at the time of the wartime conferences that there
was an ethnographic basis for the transfer of certain parts of eastern
Poland.[60]

In reality, the transfer of eastern Poland to the USSR was largely
a confirmation of the Nazi-Soviet partition of the Polish state in the
treaties of August 23 and September 29, 1939. Ethnographic considerations had little to do with the original delimitation of the Ribbentrop-

Molotov line, which was to have run along the rivers Narew-Bug-Vistula and San, thus leaving to Russia the ethnically Polish areas of the provinces of Lublin and parts of Warsaw. The swift advance of the Germans by September 17, 1939, when the Soviet Union agreed to march in, subsequently caused slight modifications of that line, leaving Lublin province to Nazi Germany and Lithuania to the USSR.* By placing the changed borders along the river Bug instead of the Vistula, the USSR reduced the number of Poles in its part of annexed areas of Poland to a minority, although a sizable one (4.2 million out of 11.6 million).

Only then was an ethnographic argument advanced as a rationalization for annexation. Until the German attack on the Soviet Union on June 22, 1941, the policy of the Soviet government was based strictly on the stipulations of a secret appendix to the German-Soviet Agreement of August 23, 1939, that "each party will refrain from reconstituting of the Polish state."[61] Thus, the Ribbentrop-Molotov line of September 28, 1939, was considered as final.

After it was attacked by the Nazis, the Soviet Union recognized, under British prodding, the Polish government in exile in London and acknowledged the legal existence of the Polish state. Although the subsequent Polish-Soviet treaty of July 30, 1941, stated that "all the German-Soviet agreements lost their validity," the Soviet government never abandoned its claims to the Ribbentrop-Molotov border line, as amended, which largely coincided with the Curzon Line of 1919. The Soviet government merely waited for an opportune moment to press this claim.

During his first meeting with the Polish prime minister, General Wladyslaw Sikorski, Stalin unsuccessfully attempted to reopen the question of the Polish-Soviet boundary.[62] While discussing Polish postwar extensions in the west, he did not endorse any particular line. General statements about the need for Poland to "obtain a wider Baltic coast and recover Germanized areas in the west" were often repeated. They were not translated into any concrete proposals that the Soviet Union promised to support when the Polish-German delimitation occurred.[63] Stalin discussed the Polish western border issue with Roosevelt, Churchill, and Eden, but indecisively and not specifically. In the earlier phases of the war, only East Prussia was under discussion.[64]

---

*This was modified by a treaty signed in Moscow on September 29, 1939.

Only after the military turning point was reached at Stalingrad did the future Soviet government policy become evident. The formation, in March 1943, of the Union of Polish Patriots, a Polish political body in the Soviet Union that placed itself in opposition to the Polish government in London (still recognized as such by the USSR), marked the beginning of the new phase in Polish-Soviet relations. The Union of Polish Patriots was composed mainly of Communists. They openly advocated that Poland abandon the eastern provinces (as inhabited by a non-Polish majority) and recover areas in the west (Germanized throughout the centuries). They called for recreation of an ethnically homogenous "Poland of Boleslaw the Wry-mouth" which in the twelfth century, as Poland does today, stretched from the Oder-Neisse Rivers in the west to the Bug River in the east.[65] To offset the Polish losses in the east, the Soviet Union made its first indirect move in support of such a large-scale territorial extension of Poland. The de facto compensation theory was thus formulated.

The "Oder Line" was discussed as the western limit of Poland during the Teheran Conference, even before the Soviet government openly advanced its own territorial claims.[66] In 1944, when the Soviet Union officially demanded the Curzon Line border, it also began supporting the Oder-Neisse line. Since the cession of the eastern territories involved 46 percent of prewar Poland, the Soviet government knew that no smaller acquisition of territory in the west would be acceptable to Polish public opinion.

At this point it can only be surmised (in view of the lack of access to the documents, which remain in Soviet archives) that the Soviet government also hoped to create permanent Polish-German enmity through such a territorial shift. The Soviet Union's open advocacy of the Western Neisse and Oder at the Yalta and Potsdam Conferences resulted in the compromise solution of that issue.[67] However, analysis of the negotiations on the issue shows that if it had not been for the Western Neisse claim—which was resisted by the West—other sectors of the new border would have been endorsed by all the Great Powers without reservations.[68]

The Western Neisse claim was pressed not only by the Communists but also by former Prime Minister Mikolajczyk. He pleaded with Western leaders at Potsdam to accept that extension of the new border. He wanted to prevent Poland's total dependence on Soviet support for the frontier (vis-à-vis Germany). Knowing also that the east was irrevocably lost, he wanted to stabilize the western frontier and obtain strong Western endorsement for it in any postwar settlement.[69] Paradoxically enough, the Soviet government's position on the border was identical with that of non-Communist Polish public opinion. Through the lack of de jure recognition of the Oder-Neisse frontier by the United States and the United Kingdom, the Soviet government had thus obtained a powerful political lever in Poland. It has been using it successfully ever since.

The lack of official recognition of the Oder-Neisse frontier by the German Federal Republic has allowed until recently the Soviet Union to assume the role of sole defender of Polish-assigned territory against German claims. This issue, more than any other, has secured the orthodoxy, at the polycentric stage of development of communism, of the Polish leadership and the Polish government structure. Among the Eastern European states, Poland has had the most to lose from any open break with the Soviet Union. This shadow over the Polish leadership partially explained the rigidity in political and economic thinking and the considerably slower tempo of reforms in Poland under Wladyslaw Gomulka. Even Rumania and Hungary, hitherto rigid in internal outlook, have recently reorganized their economies much more extensively. (This phenomenon has recently been analyzed extensively in Western reports.)

It is a moot question whether the Polish government, itself based on one-party rule and lacking broad public support—as evidenced by bloody riots in the Baltic coast ports of Gdansk, Szczecin, Gdynia, and other coastal towns which led to the change of national leadership— would really wish to see the "German issue" in Polish politics irre-vocably removed.

It is perhaps significant that the riots occurred almost exclusively in the western territories (with the exception of Gdynia) a week after the official recognition of the Oder-Neisse boundary by West Germany. Perhaps the population was mindful that no threat exists any longer from that quarter. No doubt, the youthfulness of cities like Szczecin (the youngest large city in Poland) played a role in these volatile and tragic events as was noted by a leading American journal.[70]

At present, the Polish Communist Party is fully exploiting the support given to Poland by the USSR on the border issue and pointing out the lack thus far of full support from the West, where Polish public opinion has traditionally placed its faith.

NOTES

1. F. W. Putzger, Historischer Weltatlas, 83rd ed. (Bielefeld: Velhagen and Klasing, 1961), p. 116.

2. Glowny Urzad Statystyczny Rzeczypospolitej Polskiej, Maly Rocznik Statystyczny, 1939, Vol. X (Warsaw, 1939), Table 17, p. 23. (Cited hereafter as Maly Rocznik Statystyczny, 1939.)

3. U. S. Bureau of the Census, The Population of Poland, Series P-90, No. 4 (Washington, D. C.: U.S. Government Printing Office, 1954), p. 79.

4. U. S. Department of State, The Conferences of Malta and Yalta (Washington, D.C.: U. S. Government Printing Office, 1955), p. 205.

5. Ministry of Foreign Affairs of the USSR, Correspondence Between the Chairman of the Council of Ministers of the USSR and the Presidents of the U.S.A. and the Prime Ministers of Great Britain During the Great Patriotic War of 1941-1945, Vol. II (Moscow: Foreign Languages Publishing House, 1957), p. 133

6. Wladyslaw Pobog-Malinowski, Najnowsza Historia Polityczna Polski 1864-1945, Vol. III (London: B. Swiderski, 1960), p. 807.

7. Ibid., p. 814.

8. Ibid., p. 754.

9. TASS Agency statement, January 17, 1944; Dziennik Polski i Dziennik Zolnierza (London), January 18, 1944, p. 1.

10. Foreign Relations of the United States: Diplomatic Papers, The Conferences at Cairo and Teheran 1943 (Washington, D. C.: U.S. Government Printing Office, 1961), pp. 603-4.

11. Jerzy Putrament, Pol wieku (Warsaw: Czytelnik, 1962).

12. Tadeusz Rozmanit, "Czy Mikolajczyk zaprzepascil Lwow?" Horyzonty (Paris), Vol. X, No. 107, pp. 55-65.

13. Encyclopaedia Britannica, Vol. XVIII, article entitled "Poland" (1967), p. 133.

14. Maly Rocznik Statystyczny, 1939, op. cit., Table 33, p. 37.

15. U. S. Bureau of the Census, op. cit., p. 34; Henryk Kopec, "Zjawiska Demograficzne towarzyszace zmianom granic Polski," in Problemy Ogolne Akcji Osadniczo-Przesiedlenczej (Warsaw, 1946), Table 5, p. 19.

16. Ukraine: A Concise Encyclopaedia, Vol. I (Toronto: University of Toronto Press, 1963), p. 232; Atlas Narodov Mira (Moscow: Akademia Nauk SSSR, 1964), pp. 14-15.

17. Joanna Kruczynska, et al., Polska Zachodnia i Polnocna (Poznan: Wydawnictwo Zachodnie, 1961), p. 328.

18. A. Lewicki and J. Friedberg, Zarys historii polskiej (London: Wydawnictwo Swiatowego Zwiazku Polakow z Zagranicy, 1947), pp. 80-83.

19. W. Cienkowski, et al., Straty Wojenne Polski w latach 1939-1945 (Poznan: Wydawnictwo Zachodnie, 1962), pp. 41-45.

20. Polish Embassy Press Office, Poland, Germany and European Peace: Official Documents 1944-1948 (London, 1948), p. 115. (Cited hereafter as Poland, Germany and European Peace.)

21. Speech by Prime Minister Winston Churchill in the House of Commons, December 15, 1944, on the results of the Polish-Soviet-British negotiations regarding the transfer of German minorities from Poland to Germany.

22. Poland, Germany and European Peace, op. cit., p. 115.

23. Glowny Urzad Statystyczny Rzeczypospolitej Polskiej, Rocznik Statystyczny, 1950, Vol. XIV (Warsaw, 1951), Table 7, p. 22. (Cited hereafter as Rocznik Statystyczny, 1950.)

24. Gotthold Rhode, Die Ostegebiete Des Deutschen Reiches, 2nd ed. (Wurzburg: Holzner-Verlag, 1955), p. 131.

25. S. Waszak, "The Number of Germans in Poland in the Years 1931-1939 Against the Background of German Losses in the Second World War," Polish Western Affairs, Vol. I (1960), p. 246-90.

26. U.S. Bureau of Census, op. cit., p. 41.

27. Johannes Kaps, Die Tragedie Schlesiens 1945-46 in Dokumenten unter besonderer Berucksichtigung des Erzbistums Bzeslau (Munich: Christ Unterwegs, 1952-53), pp. 52-55.

28. Ibid., p. 125.

29. Ibid.

30. Speech by Churchill, op. cit.

31. Rhode, op. cit., p. 131.

32. 1946 Nuremberg trial records numbered L-03 and 1014-PS.

33. Wojciech Wrzesinski, "Przyczynki do problemu wschodnio-pruskiego w czasie II wojny swiatowej," Komunikaty Mazursko-War-minskie (Olsztyn), No. 1 (1965), p. 100.

34. Marian Seyda, Poland and Germany and the Post-War Recon-struction of Europe (New York: Polish Information Center, 1943); Ministerstwo Obrony Narodowej, Fakty i zagadnienia polskie (London, 1944).

35. Ibid.; Wrzesinski, op. cit., p. 100; "Nasze cele wojenne," Szaniec (Warsaw), December 20, 1940, p. 3; Tadeusz Bielecki, "Zagadnienia glowne," Mysl Polska (London), December 15, 1942, pp. 581-82.

36. Bielecki, op. cit., pp. 581-82; "Nasze cele wojenne," loc. cit., p. 3.

37. Ibid.

38. Ministerstwo Obrony Narodowej, op. cit., pp. 153-63.

39. U. S. Office of Strategic Services, Research and Analysis Branch, Postwar Poland: Economic and Political Outlook (Washington, D. C., 1945, mimeographed).

40. Herbert Feis, Between War and Peace: The Potsdam Con-ference (Princeton, N. J.: Princeton University Press, 1960), p. 262.

41. Poland, Germany and European Peace, op. cit., p. 108.

42. Wlodzimierz T. Kowalski, ZSRR a granica na Odrze i Nysie Luzyckiej 1941-1945 (Warsaw: Wydawnictwo MON, 1965).

43. Feis, op. cit., pp. 260-69.

44. Ibid., p. 261.

45. Glowny Urzad Statystyczny Polskiej Rzeczypospolitej

Ludowej, Rocznik Statystyczny, 1970, Vol. XXX (Warsaw, 1970), Table 53, p. 173.

46. Feis, op. cit., p. 261.

47. Seyda, op. cit.

48. Edward Raczynski, W sojuszniczym Londynie (London: Polish Research Centre, 1960), pp. 169-70.

49. Poland, Germany and European Peace, op. cit., p. 105-6.

50. Ibid., p. 107.

51. Great Britain, Parliamentary Debates (Commons), Vol. CMVI (1944) 1484.

52. Feis, op. cit., p. 229.

53. Ibid., p. 262.

54. Ibid., p. 261.

55. Ibid.

56. Protocol of the Proceedings of the Berlin Conference, August 2, 1945, as quoted in Feis, op. cit., pp. 348-49.

57. Le Monde (Paris), March 27, 1959.

58. Rocznik Statystycany, 1950, op. cit., Table 8, p. 22; K. Pruszynski, "Wobec Rosji," Wiadomosci Polskie (London), October 4, 1942, p. 3.

59. Kowalski, op. cit., p. 12.

60. Atlas Narodov Mira, op. cit., p. 16.

61. Instytut Historyczny imienia Generala Sikorskiego, Documents on Polish-Soviet Relations 1939-1945, Vol. I, 1939-43 (London: Heinemann, 1961).

62. Ibid., pp. 244-46.

63. Stanislaw Kot, Listy z Rosji do Generala Sikorskiego (London: Sklad Glowny Jutro Polski, 1955), pp. 211-12.

64. Cordell Hull, The Memoirs of Cordell Hull, Vol. II (London: Hodder and Stoughton, 1948), p. 1167.

65. Pruszynski, op. cit.

66. R. E. Sherwood, The White House Papers of H. Hopkins, Vol. II (London: Eyre & Spottiswoode, 1949), p. 776.

67. U. S. Department of State, Historical Office, The Conference of Berlin: The Potsdam Conference, 1945, Vol. II (Washington, D. C.: U. S. Government Printing Office, 1960), pp. 480, 1150-51.

68. Feis, op. cit., p. 260.

69. Ibid., pp. 209, 230.

70. The Christian Science Monitor, February 17, 1971.

3

DEMOGRAPHIC ELEMENTS
THAT CONTRIBUTED
TO THE FORMATION
OF THE NEW SOCIETY
IN THE WESTERN TERRITORIES

The post-World War II socioeconomic structure of Poland was virtually predetermined by two basic factors: (1) the westward shift of Poland's ethnic and national territory and (2) the Communist-directed industrialization of the country. Both set in motion a chain of events of tremendous proportions that completely changed the Polish social structure and economy. Thus, the image of a predominantly agricultural and rustic Poland of over thirty years ago has become outdated.

The changes that developed in the immediate postwar years were primarily effected by the following factors:

1. Over 4.5 million predominantly rural persons transferred to the newly acquired and more industrialized western territories, which were emptied of their former inhabitants under the terms of the Potsdam Agreement of 1945.

2. The fact that, as a result of the mass migration of peasants to urban areas, cities that had been virtually destroyed—for example, over 70 percent of Warsaw and Wroclaw had been destroyed, as had about 50 percent of Szczecin, Poznan, Gdansk, and Bialystok[1]—and depopulated quickly recovered their economic importance and population. (The urban population in Poland more than doubled within the 24 years following the end of World War II—see Table 2.[2])

TABLE 2

Population of Poland by Sex and Urban-Rural
Distribution, Selected Years, 1931-69

Year	Total	Male	Female	Urban		Rural	
				Percentage		Percentage	
				Thou-sands	% of Total	Thou-sands	% of Total
1931	32,107	15,619	16,488	8,731	27.4	23,185	72.6
1946	23,930	10,954	12,976	7,517	31.8	16,109	68.2
1950	25,008	11,928	13,080	9,605	39.0	15,000	61.0
1960	29,776	14,404	15,372	14,206	48.3	15,200	51.7
1969	32,671	15,877	16,794	16,829	51.5	15,842	48.5

Sources: Glowny Urzad Statystyczny Polskiej Rzeczypospolite Ludowej, Rocznik Statystyczny, 1965, Vol. XXV (Warsaw, 1965), Table 1, p. 13, and Rocznik Statystyczny, 1970, Vol. XXX (Warsaw, 1970), Table 2, p. 21.

GENERAL EFFECTS OF THE MIGRATIONS
ON POLISH SOCIETY

Analysis of the size of ethnically Polish urbanized population in
the censuses of 1931 (the last before World War II) and 1960 reveals
that the mass migrations and postwar industrialization caused a far-
reaching transformation of the Polish countryside. In 1931, roughly
75 percent of the ethnically Polish population lived in villages[3] (the
proportion was nearly the same in 1939), while in 1969 half the Polish
nation lived in cities. The industrial revolution and urbanization in
Poland are even more apparent in the statistics relating to the growing
nonagricultural employment of the population (see Table 3).[4]

The migration caused by the shift of frontiers had an urbanizing
effect on the predominantly rural migrants, more than half of whom
settled in the cities. The migration of peasants to cities located
elsewhere in the country paralleled the external movements and
western colonization. Since 1946, the rural proportion of Poland's
population has decreased,[5] despite an annual natural increase in the
rural population of 10.8 to 19.1 percent (see Tables 4 and 5).

Furthermore, the migration of 4.5 million Poles to the Oder-
Neisse territories had a profound effect on the economy and population
of those areas, which were heavily destroyed during World War II
(over 54 percent of the cities and 27.5 percent of the villages were
destroyed). The migrants were mostly young pioneers in the marriage-
able age group who brought with them the demographic pattern of large
families. This caused the birth rate in those areas to increase above
the already high average for the rest of the country (see Table 6).[6]
The youthful age of the earlier migrants caused a demographic explosion
in the Oder-Neisse area in the 1950's and early 1960's, and this enormous population growth is now having its full impact in the increased
social mobility of the newly created society. The destruction caused
in those areas by the war and its chaotic aftermath were heavy. The
damage was substantially increased by the planned dismantling of
industrial equipment and municipal facilities by Soviet authorities
and the wholesale removal of such materials as war booty.

Nevertheless, the housing and living conditions to be found in
the Oder-Neisse area were still much better then in the Nazi-ravaged
remainder of Poland. That area's great economic capacity, the
necessity of its reconstruction, and its relatively good housing conditions provided the migrants with better opportunities for economic
advancement and much more social mobility than the places of their

TABLE 3

Population by Main Source of Maintenance,
Selected Years, 1921-70

Specification	Thousands				Percentage of Total				
	1921	1931	1950	1960	1921	1931	1950	1960	1970
Total									
Total	27,177[a]	32,107[a]	25,008[a]	29,776[a]	100.0	100.0	100.0	100.0	n.a.
Earning livelihood from work	24,758[b]	29,049[b]	23,618	27,502	97.6[b]	91.0[b]	96.0	93.5	n.a.
Outside agriculture	8,004	9,915	12,021	16,258	31.6	31.0	48.9	55.3	n.a.
Industry	3,184	4,057	5,138	7,343	12.6	12.7	20.9	25.0	n.a.
Construction	341	421	1,181	1,859	1.3	1.3	4.8	6.3	n.a.
Transport and communications	813	1,014	1,268	1,785	3.2	3.2	5.2	6.1	n.a.
Commodity turnover	1,468	1,529	1,328	1,427	5.8	4.8	5.4	4.9	n.a.
Education, science, and culture	229	318	547	819	0.9	1.0	2.2	2.8	n.a.
Public health, social welfare, and physical culture	67	191	290	546	0.3	0.6	1.2	1.8	n.a.
Other sectors	1,902	2,385	2,269	2,479	7.5	7.4	9.2	8.4	n.a.
In agriculture	16,754	19,134	11,597	11,244	66.0	60.0	47.1	38.2	29.5
Supported from sources other than earnings[c]	509	929	996	1,904	2.0	2.9	4.0	6.5[d]	n.a.

Of Which Economically Active and Supported from Sources Other Than Earnings

Specification	Thousands				Percentage of Total				
	1921	1931	1950	1960	1921	1931	1950	1960	1970
Total	13,532	15,006	13,175	15,341	100.0	100.0	100.0	100.0	n.a.
Economically active	13,238[e]	13,622[e]	12,404	13,908	97.8[e]	90.8[e]	94.2	90.7	n.a.
Outside agriculture	2,994	4,045	5,388	7,362	22.1	27.0	40.9	48.0	n.a.
Industry	1,160	1,635	2,328	3,238	8.6	10.9	17.7	21.1	n.a.
Construction	105	149	519	791	0.8	1.0	3.9	5.1	n.a.
Transport and communications	237	289	469	673	1.7	1.9	3.6	4.4	n.a.
Commodity turnover	458	627	644	738	3.4	4.2	4.9	4.8	n.a.
Education, science, and culture	111	167	308	505	0.8	1.1	2.3	3.3	n.a.
Public health, social welfare, and physical culture	37	108	169	350	0.3	0.7	1.3	2.3	n.a.
Other sectors	886	1,070	951	1,067	6.5	7.2	7.2	7.0	n.a.
In agriculture	10,244	9,577	7,016	6,546	75.7	63.8	53.3	42.7	n.a.
Supported from sources other than earnings[c]	245	491	771	1,433	1.8	3.3	5.8	9.3	n.a.

Notes: n.a. = not available

[a] Total does not include: in 1921—1,801,000 persons (including 1,482,000 inhabiting the area not covered by the census); in 1931—191,000 persons; in 1950—394,000 persons; in 1960—370,000 persons.

[b] Unemployed persons and their dependent family members were not included as follows: in 1921—109,000 persons (0.4 percent of the population); in 1931—1,938,000 persons (6.1 percent of the population).

[c] Scholars, retired, etc., and their dependents and, in 1960, recipients of life annuities.

[d] Of which, 0.2 percent recipients of pensions in agriculture.

[e] Not including unemployed: in 1921—49,000 persons (0.4 of total economically active and having a source of maintenance other than earnings); in 1931—893,000 persons (5.9 percent of total economically active and having a source of maintenance other than earnings).

Sources: Concise Statistical Yearbook of Poland, 1970 (Warsaw: Central Statistical Office, 1970), Table 13, p. 26 (data from general censuses); preliminary data for 1970 general census, as published in Contemporary Poland, Vol. V, No. 4 (1971), p. 21.

TABLE 4

Estimated Population Structure by Main Source of
Maintenance, Selected Years, 1960-68
(percentage distribution)

| | | Main Source of Maintenance | | | | | | |
| | | Nonagricultural Labor Sector | | | Agricultural Labor | | Nonemployment Source of Living | |
Specification	Total	Total	Socialized	Nonsocialized	Total	Portion on State Agriculture	Total	Portion Composed of Pensioners
1960								
Total	100.0	55.3	52.1*	3.2	38.2	3.4	6.5	5.1
Economically active and possessing nonemployment source of living	52.2	25.1	26.6*	1.5	22.2	1.2	4.9	3.6
Dependent family members	47.8	30.2	28.5*	1.7	16.0	2.2	1.6	1.5
1965								
Total	100.0	58.5	55.3	3.2	33.8	3.7	7.7	6.2
Economically active and possessing nonemployment source of living	55.0	27.9	26.4	1.5	21.3	1.4	5.8	4.4
Dependent family members	45.0	30.6	28.9	1.7	12.5	2.3	1.9	1.8
1967								
Total	100.0	58.8	55.6	3.2	33.1	4.0	8.1	6.6
Economically active and possessing nonemployment source of living	56.3	29.3	27.7	1.6	20.9	1.5	6.1	4.6
Dependent family members	43.7	29.5	27.9	1.6	12.2	2.5	2.0	2.0
1968								
Total	100.0	59.0	55.8	3.2	32.7	4.2	8.3	6.8
Economically active and possessing nonemployment source of living	57.0	30.0	28.4	1.6	20.7	1.6	6.3	4.8
Dependent family members	43.0	29.0	27.4	1.6	12.0	2.6	2.0	2.0

Note: Data for 1960 from general census as of December 6, data for 1965, 1967, and 1968 are estimates describing approximate proportions as of December 31.

*Including types of economy not elsewhere classified.

Source: Concise Statistical Yearbook of Poland, 1970 (Warsaw: Central Statistical Office, 1970), Table 14, p. 27.

TABLE 5

Agricultural and Nonagricultural Population by
Voivodship, Selected Years, 1950-68

Specification	Percentage Outside Agriculture				Percentage in Agriculture			
	1950*	1960	1966	1968	1950*	1960	1966	1968
Poland	52.9	61.6	66.5	67.3	47.1	38.4	33.5	32.7
Urban areas	92.8	94.3	95.0	95.2	7.2	5.7	5.0	4.8
Rural areas	22.8	31.1	38.0	38.4	77.2	68.9	62.0	61.6
Warsaw City	97.9	98.3	98.5	98.5	2.1	1.7	1.5	1.5
Krakow City	95.6	97.0	97.3	97.5	4.4	3.0	2.7	2.5
Lodz City	98.3	98.5	98.6	98.6	1.7	1.5	1.4	1.4
Poznan City	97.9	98.1	98.3	98.4	2.1	1.9	1.7	1.6
Wroclaw City	97.4	97.8	98.1	98.2	2.6	2.2	1.9	1.8
Bialystok	27.2	37.5	44.1	45.0	72.8	62.5	55.9	55.0
Bydgoszcz	55.1	61.0	65.0	65.8	44.9	39.0	35.0	34.2
Gdansk	71.7	76.6	79.7	80.6	28.3	23.4	20.3	19.4
Katowice	86.7	90.0	91.0	91.2	13.3	10.0	9.0	8.8
Kielce	31.6	42.9	50.7	51.4	68.4	57.1	49.3	48.6
Koszalin	41.7	55.0	61.2	62.1	58.3	45.0	38.8	37.9
Krakow	38.0	51.4	57.3	58.3	62.0	48.6	42.7	41.7
Lublin	24.1	33.2	40.6	42.0	75.9	66.8	59.4	58.0
Lodz	39.0	48.1	54.6	45.5	61.0	51.9	45.4	44.5
Olsztyn	41.7	50.2	55.6	56.3	58.3	49.8	44.4	43.7
Opole	58.5	64.9	68.8	69.3	41.5	35.1	31.2	30.7
Poznan	48.1	55.3	60.6	61.2	51.9	44.7	39.4	38.8
Rzeszow	27.5	41.3	48.2	49.7	72.5	58.7	51.8	50.3
Szczecin	59.3	67.6	72.3	73.2	40.7	32.4	27.7	26.8
Warszawa	38.0	46.9	53.6	55.3	62.0	53.1	46.4	44.7
Wroclaw	60.0	68.3	73.2	73.5	40.0	31.7	26.8	26.5
Zielona Gora	52.3	64.0	69.0	69.9	47.7	36.0	31.0	30.1

Note: For 1950 and 1960, data based on general censuses; for 1966 and 1968, estimates as of December 31, based on the results of studies of structure of rural population and of population of selected towns and settlements. Breakdown by main source of maintenance. In the total number of population, the following are not included: in 1950—394,500 persons, in 1960—369,800 persons.

*Administrative Division as of January 1, 1962.

Source: Concise Statistical Yearbook of Poland, 1970 (Warsaw: Central Statistical Office, 1970), Table 15 p. 28.

TABLE 6

Birth Rate in Poland, 1950–59
(births per thousand)

Area	1950	1951	1952	1953	1954	1955	1956	1957	1958	1959
Poland	30.7	31.0	30.2	29.7	29.1	29.1	28.1	27.6	26.3	24.7
Western territories	40.8	40.3	38.9	37.7	36.8	36.7	34.8	33.9	32.1	29.6
Other provinces	27.7	28.2	27.6	27.2	26.6	26.7	25.8	25.6	24.3	23.1

Source: Demographic Research Section (Department XIII), Central Statistical Office of Poland.

origin. These factors in turn tended to affect the already high birth rate. They also accelerated the reconstruction of the area and brought its population, now exclusively Polish, to 8.9 million in 1971, which represented 100 percent of the area's 1939 population (see Table 7).

The second migratory wave, from the villages to the cities in the country as a whole (which reached its peak in the early 1950's), occurred during the period of intensive building activity (for example, during this period Warsaw was rebuilt and the Nowa Huta steel mill near Cracow and the new town of Nowe Tychy in Silesia were built). Although the new construction did not keep pace with the need for reconstruction and the ever increasing demand for housing by the migrants, the overcrowded conditions of the Polish cities were still better than the backward housing conditions in the villages (see Table 8).

Nevertheless, partially because of those migratory movements and the increased rate of construction, the average density per room in Polish villages decreased between 1950 and 1966. However, in the city, the high birth rate and migrations tended to offset the much higher rate of new construction, and density was hardly affected.[7] However, the 1966 averages hide some significant disproportions, especially between rural housing conditions in eastern and southern areas of contemporary Poland (i.e., Kielce and Lublin regions) and the more advanced north-central and western areas (i.e., Poznan and Gdansk).[8] Despite the fact that reserves of rural labor are nearly depleted in some regions of the country, the migratory trends toward the cities continued unabated, contributing about 50 percent of Poland's average yearly increase of 250,000 in urban population.

It is estimated that the Polish villages of the central and south-eastern regions still possess a large surplus labor force because of their dwarf-farm structure, which hinders economic output and the intensification of agricultural production. Hence, the recent migratory movements to urban centers play a part in correcting the historical heritage of backward agricultural structure in those regions, a structure that stems from the nineteenth-century policy of the partitioning powers, Russia and Austria-Hungary. The migratory movements relieve the population pressures of the traditional Polish village and at the same time improve the existing economic structure of very small, and often scattered, farm plots.

It is also important that, as was the case in the population migrations to the western areas, the rural migrants brought to the contemporary Polish cities their high birth-rate demographic pattern.

TABLE 7

Population of the Oder-Neisse Areas,
Selected Years, 1939-71[a]
(thousands)

Voivodship	1939	1946	1950	1969	1971
Bialystok[b]	125.9	36.9	70.6	115.3	—
Olsztyn[b]	966.5	351.8	610.1	882.6	—
Gdansk[b]	694.1	354.2	500.9	829.3	—
Koszalin	810.4	585.1	528.0	789.8	—
Szczecin	1,014.9	307.5	517.0	895.6	—
Poznan[b]	85.6	36.9	48.0	80.4	—
Zielona Gora	918.6	337.7	559.0	883.4	—
Wroclaw	2,646.5	1,768.8	1,736.0	2,511.2	—
Opole	1,066.7	792.2	809.0	1,045.9	—
Katowice[b]	556.2	468.6	588.5	691.1	—
Total	8,885.4	5,039.7	5,967.1	8,724.6	8,904.6

[a]Areas in Oder-Neisse administrative region as of December 31, 1969.
[b]Share of the province's population in Oder-Neisse areas only.

Sources: 1939, Statistisches Jahrbuch fur das Deutsche Reich 1941/42, figures for May 17, 1939, national census, extrapolated for the above area; 1946, Materialy Informacyjne Biura Studiow Osadniczo-Przesiedlenczych, fasc. 1 (Krakow, 1946), pp. 12-14; 1950, Narodowy Spis Powszechny z dnia 3 grudnia 1950 (Warsaw, 1952, mimeographed), pp. 82-84; 1969, Glowny Urzad Statystyczny Polskiej Rzeczypospolitej Ludowej, Rocznik Statystyczny 1970, Vol. XXX (Warsaw, 1970), Table 5, pp. 23-31; 1971, author's estimate for June 30, 1971, based on areas natural rate of growth.

TABLE 8

Average Density per Room, Selected Years, 1950-70

Area	Average Number of Persons per Room			
	1950	1960	1966	1970
Poland	1.75	1.66	1.53	1.37
Urban	1.55	1.53	1.41	1.31
Rural	1.95	1.80	1.66	1.43
Warsaw-City	1.91	1.58	1.37	n.a.
Krakow-City	1.77	1.63	1.48	n.a.
Lodz-City	1.93	1.78	1.49	n.a.
Poznan-City	1.67	1.55	1.44	n.a.
Wroclaw-City	1.32	1.45	1.35	n.a.
Bialystok	1.94	1.73	1.58	n.a.
Urban	1.61	1.60	1.46	n.a.
Rural	2.07	1.79	1.65	n.a.
Bydgoszcz	1.66	1.64	1.54	n.a.
Urban	1.52	1.58	1.48	n.a.
Rural	1.79	1.70	1.61	n.a.
Gdansk	1.46	1.50	1.42	n.a.
Urban	1.41	1.48	1.38	n.a.
Rural	1.54	1.55	1.52	n.a.
Katowice	1.64	1.50	1.39	n.a.
Urban	1.55	1.44	1.36	n.a.
Rural	1.98	1.70	1.49	n.a.
Kielce	2.54	2.19	1.95	n.a.
Urban	1.96	1.83	1.62	n.a.
Rural	2.77	2.36	2.13	n.a.
Koszalin	1.19	1.35	1.32	n.a.
Urban	1.09	1.33	1.32	n.a.
Rural	1.26	1.37	1.33	n.a.
Krakow	2.22	1.94	1.74	n.a.
Urban	1.72	1.63	1.46	n.a.
Rural	2.42	2.09	1.89	n.a.
Lublin	2.31	2.03	1.80	n.a.
Urban	1.93	1.80	1.54	n.a.
Rural	2.42	2.12	1.91	n.a.

Area	Average Number of Persons per Room			
	1950	1960	1966	1970
Lodz	2.13	1.90	1.69	n.a.
Urban	1.81	1.75	1.55	n.a.
Rural	2.30	1.98	1.77	n.a.
Olsztyn	1.42	1.55	1.50	n.a.
Urban	1.37	1.55	1.45	n.a.
Rural	1.44	1.55	1.53	n.a.
Opole	1.37	1.31	1.24	n.a.
Urban	1.25	1.28	1.22	n.a.
Rural	1.43	1.33	1.25	n.a.
Poznan	1.68	1.62	1.51	n.a.
Urban	1.49	1.54	1.42	n.a.
Rural	1.78	1.66	1.57	n.a.
Rzeszow	2.33	2.02	1.80	n.a.
Urban	1.73	1.61	1.45	n.a.
Rural	2.53	2.19	1.96	n.a.
Szczecin	1.17	1.34	1.31	n.a.
Urban	1.11	1.31	1.31	n.a.
Rural	1.26	1.39	1.31	n.a.
Warsaw	2.14	1.91	1.72	n.a.
Urban	1.83	1.72	1.53	n.a.
Rural	2.29	2.01	1.84	n.a.
Wroclaw	1.23	1.39	1.33	n.a.
Urban	1.19	1.38	1.38	n.a.
Rural	1.26	1.40	1.28	n.a.
Zielona Gora	1.15	1.31	1.27	n.a.
Urban	1.12	1.35	1.33	n.a.
Rural	1.17	1.29	1.21	n.a.

Note: n.a. = not available

Sources: Glowny Urzad Statystyczny Polskiej Rzeczypospolitej Ludowej, Rocznik Statystyczny 1970, Vol. XXX (Warsaw, 1970), Table 5, p. 380; data for 1970 from preliminary results of the 1970 general census as published in Contemporary Poland, Vol. V, No. 4 (1971), pp. 21-22.

This is the chief cause of a rare phenomenon observed in the period between the 1950 and 1960 censuses: the natural increase rate of the cities (13 percent) and that of the villages (16 percent) are only slightly different.

In connection with such demographic consequences of the internal migrations, one must consider the psychological effects of the population losses during the World War II (over 6 million, or 17.2 percent of the total 1939 population of Poland), which destroyed 90 percent of Polish Jewry (3 million) and threatened the very existence of the Polish nation. These losses undoubtedly contributed to the unprecedented high postwar birth rate, which ranged from 16 percent in 1946 to 19.5 percent in 1955,[9] thus adding one-half million people annually to Poland's population. During those years, Poland had the highest birth rate of any European country with the exception of Albania. In 1957, however, the Polish birth rate began to diminish, reaching the low of 8.2 percent in 1969.[10] By that time, Poland already had made up its shattering war losses, and in 1960 one-third of Poland's population (about 10 million persons) was composed of children under fifteen years of age.

TRANSFERS WITHIN THE NEW TERRITORY OF POLAND: ANALYSIS OF MAJOR GROUPS

Although the final delimitation of the western border of Poland was left to the future peace treaty, there is virtually no doubt that the bargain struck at Potsdam had elements of finality in its basic stipulations, despite the misgivings of the Western Powers[11] and the legal interpretations of that border arrangement that were subsequently promoted during the Cold War. The following were significant indications of the permanency of the new borders:

1. The lack of any restrictions whatsoever imposed on the administering authority—Poland—in regard to its jurisdiction and authority in its newly-acquired territories east of the Oder-Neisse rivers.[12]

2. The provision for the transfer of all the Germans still residing in the territory of the new Poland, implemented by the agreement of the Allied Control Commission for Germany on November 20, 1945[13] (this provision was especially significant).

Poland re-emerged from World War II within the area bounded by the Oder-Neisse line in the west and the Curzon Line in the east. Under wartime agreements among the Great Powers, this territory

was to be the home of the Polish nation. Poles living outside these
limits were to be transferred to that area and settled, primarily in
the new western territories. The Poles to be transferred included
large numbers of the following groups: (1) Poles who were cut off by
the new Polish-Soviet border; (2) emigrants who had gone abroad in
search of work in the previous decades; (3) Polish minorities outside
Poland; and (4) Poles who were either deported for forced labor or
imprisoned in the concentration and prisoner of war camps in Germany
or joined (via various routes) the wartime emigration to England,
Western Europe, the Middle East, and overseas areas.

These diverse groups were to form the immigrant portion of the
new population of the Oder-Neisse territories, joining the Polish-
speaking people autochthonous to the area. They were expected to
remain in the area and become citizens of the new Poland.

Furthermore, Polish planners and economists considered that
the new areas to be acquired by Poland in the west would be able to
provide jobs and housing for the economically redundant portion of
Poland's population, which was composed of millions of landless rural
members of the proletariat[14] and underemployed farmers barely able
to feed their families from so-called "dwarf farms" of under five
hectares (which comprised 64.2 percent of all farms[15]). In view of
the weakness of the Polish investment structure and the slow growth
of Poland's industrial capacity, before World War II, such members
of the surplus rural labor force stopped moving to the cities in large
numbers.

The pre-1939 unemployment in the cities (456,000 in 1938[16])
and the worldwide drop in prices for agricultural products contributed
to the grave economic situation of the Polish villages. Furthermore,
the structural imbalance inherent in Polish industry, crafts, and
commerce—characterized by a multitude of small and inefficient units—
itself called for reform. Since too large a portion of the urban population depended for its livelihood on small marginal industrial and
business enterprises,[17] a more economic redistribution of the existing
urban labor force was urgently needed. Hence, there was little or no
chance for the landless Polish peasants to migrate to towns en masse.

PREWAR MIGRATORY TRENDS
AND RURAL OVERCROWDING

Overseas and European migration (primarily to the United States,
Argentina, Canada, and France[18]) provided the only outlet through

which the peasants, for whom there was no work in their native villages and little work in the cities, could escape the abject poverty of the overcrowded countryside.[19] The mass underemployed redundant labor in the villages was considered the key economic problem of pre-1939 Poland. This problem was virtually insoluble in the short run because of the situation in the Polish urban centers and the existing industry and business structure. Poland's capital formation rate was slow.[20] The modest industrial expansion begun in 1936 through the creation of a new industrial center in the most overcrowded rural section of southern Poland could, at best, provide only a partial solution to the pressure of rural labor.

The ambitious long-range (18 years) industrial and economic development plan for the so-called Central Industrial Region (COP) could not yield immediate results. It only provided enough industrial jobs to cover the population's natural yearly increase.[21] Since the plan was interrupted by the outbreak of World War II, it is impossible to assess its potential effectiveness in alleviating the heavy burden of Poland's rural overcrowding. In view of the slow rate of native capital formation, we must also indicate that, in the years preceding World War II, the outflow of foreign capital from Poland was larger than the inflow.[22] Hence, in attempting to reform its economic structure, Poland had to rely on its own woefully inadequate capital resources. In essence, this was the dilemma the Polish planners confronted. They shared a general consensus that no solution could be found without the use of more drastic social measures. However, the Polish Parliament resisted such measures (as with regard to agricultural reform in the years 1918-25).[23]

The westward border shift imposed on Poland after World War II, and the terrible population losses Poland incurred during more than five and one-half years of Nazi occupation, drastically affected the demographic and social structure of Poland as it emerged from the war. The border shift removed from Poland most of the national minorities whose presence had caused repeated political and social tensions.[24] The limited human resources of the Polish cities were still further weakened by the fact that the huge war losses fell largely on the town populations because of the Nazi policies of genocide toward the Jews and decimation of the Polish elite.[25]

The population losses prompted the total realignment of Poland's postwar social and economic structure. Thus, the postwar rural-urban migrations were superimposed on the migrations caused by the changes in the country's frontiers. The population groups transferred from outside the Polish postwar frontiers were mostly settled in the new areas acquired by Poland in the west. The rural population had suffered much smaller losses than that of the towns under the Nazi terror, and the rural birth rate was, surprisingly enough, relatively unaffected by the war (it declined from 23.2 percent in 1939 to 18.6 percent in 1942).[26] This was partly due to the Nazi policy of selectivity in the recruitment of women for forced labor (hence, pregnancy was a protective device). After the war, the rural migrants not only replaced the portion of the urban population that had been wiped out by the war but also supplied the largest segment of the migrants to the newly settled Oder-Neisse areas (2.9 million or 49.1 percent of the total).[27] This fact is probably the best illustration of the magnitude of the agricultural overcrowding problem in pre-World War II Poland.

EASTERN POLES: THEIR CHARACTERISTICS AND MIGRATION HISTORY

The wholesale Polish population migrations that accompanied the westward shift of Polish ethnic and national territory irrevocably affected Poles from the east of the Curzon Line (the present border with the Soviet Union) who decided to relocate within the new western territories of Poland. There, they were to receive the equivalent of the property they lost to the USSR by deciding to leave their former homes.[28] On the eve of World War II, the Polish population of the prewar eastern territories was estimated at between 3.5 million and 4.2 million, depending on the criteria used to determine Polish nationality.[29]

In the eastern territories, which had a nationally intermixed population, one could use the religion or the mother tongue as an index in determining nationality. These two questions, among others, were asked in the Polish national census of December 9, 1931. If one interpolates these figures to reflect the estimated strength of the Poles in that population as of August 31, 1939 (the last day before World War II began in the area), there were in the Polish eastern territories 3.5 million Catholics (which in this region was synonymous with being Polish) as well as 4.2 million persons who considered Polish their native language. Since the religious index can be considered more realistic, one may interpolate and assume that there were about 3.8 million Poles in the eastern territories of 1939 Poland on the eve of World War II.[30]

The Scientific Council for the Problems of the Recovered Territories, an advisory body of scholars, was organized by the Polish Ministry of Public Administration on July 30, 1945. It was attached

to the Bureau for Colonization and Resettlement Studies in Cracow
and asked to discuss and execute a comprehensive plan for the settlement of the newly acquired western territories. The Council planned
on the assumption that it would be necessary to resettle 3.8 million
Poles within the new borders of Poland. Furthermore, although
statistics were completely lacking at that date, the Council made a
fairly realistic estimate of the number of Polish Jews who survived
the Nazi holocaust (it estimated surviving Jews as 350,000 of the
approximately 3.5 million Jews in Poland in 1939).[31] The Council
also anticipated that an undetermined number of Poles from the prewar Polish minority of the USSR would opt for and settle in Poland.
Many of these Poles were serving in the Polish army originally formed
in the USSR under the auspices of the Soviet government, as a counter-
balance to the Polish army under the British Command, or working
for the Soviet-sponsored government of the new Poland which essentially developed from the political institutions established by the Polish
Communists in the USSR and in Poland during the war.

Those were at best educated guesses, attempts to assess the
number of potential settlers of the new territories. Considering the
total destruction of government institutions and the lack of statistics
in the postwar chaos, the Council could only estimate the prospective
resettlers. Although its figures were accurate, the number of actual
resettlers did not come up to expectations. Of the estimated 3.8
million eastern Poles (as of August 31, 1939), only about 2.2 million
were found within the borders of the new Poland in the 1950 national
census. To the estimated 1.6-million absolute discrepancy, one
must add the estimated natural increase in that group of the population for 1939-50[32] and subtract the number who remained in the
east and the war losses. The war losses included: (1) casualties
incurred by the eastern Poles under the Nazi occupation in 1941-44;
(2) losses associated with the advance and retreat of the German
armies in battles of 1941 and 1944; (3) substantial losses caused
by the Soviet secret police terror in 1939-41 against the "enemies
of the state" through mass executions in jails; (4) losses resulting
from deportation of over one million ethnic Poles into the interior
of the USSR.

Less than half of those deported survived the terror and the
extremely difficult wartime conditions in the deportation camps, the
climate, and the epidemics. Of the survivors, 117,000 left the USSR
during the war with General Anders' army for the Middle East,[33]
while the rest joined General Berling's Communist-organized army
or returned to Poland after the war. For obvious reasons, Communist
government publications—for that matter, books published in

contemporary Poland—generally try to avoid this subject. One seldom finds estimates of the number of surviving deportees in Russia,[34] and deaths are attributed almost exclusively to the wartime hardships in the USSR and not to the terror.

The proceedings of subsequent sessions of the Council show that the choice of opting for Poland was offered only to persons of Polish and Jewish extraction who could prove with documents that they were residents of Poland as of September 17, 1939 (the date the Soviet armies crossed, in accordance with the German-Soviet pact of August 23, 1939, the eastern border of Poland in pursuit of their agreement to divide the Polish territory).[35] In the discussions during Council sessions, some scholars stressed that the required proof of residence posed an obstacle that many Poles could not surmount because of the loss of government records and the destruction of homes and churches where baptismal records were kept. Thus, a sizable proportion of people who requested transfer could not obtain it.[36] Furthermore, members of the older generation were hesitant to leave their homes and immovable property, which often had been in their families for generations or centuries.

Thus, a pattern emerged in which families divided. The older generation often remained in the eastern territories now within the USSR, whereas the younger generation opted for transfer. This was especially true in the Vilna region in the northeast (the Soviet ethnographic atlas published in 1964 shows the Polish ethnic territory in the region stretching, according to the Soviet census taken in January 1959, virtually without interruption from the present Polish border between Bialystok and Grodno to the Western Dvina river).[37] Despite the 1944-49 transfers of Poles from the region and the subsequent migration in 1955-59,[38] the current ethnic composition of the area is nearly identical to that shown by the eminent Polish geographer E. Romer in his prewar atlas.[39]

The transfers considerably weakened Polish strength in the northeast regions and changed the ethnic composition of some areas (in 1931, the city of Vilna had 126,000 Catholics, mostly Poles[40]; in 1970, according to the recently released Soviet census results, Vilna had about 68,000 Poles, representing 18.3 percent of the city's population[41]). However, a decisive proportion of Poles decided to remain in the area after 1945 or could not leave because of the lack of documents or for other reasons. The Soviet census of 1959 showed approximately 750,000 Poles living in the Lithuanian and Belorussian republics.[42] (The 1954 Soviet ethnographic atlas indicated that the Poles were living in compact areas, mostly in the prewar Polish

territory.) The recently released Soviet census of 1970 shows fewer
Poles in both republics (385,000 in Belorussia-mostly in Grodno and
Minsk regions, and 240,000 in Lithuania).[43]

The decision to remain in the southeast areas of prewar Poland,
now incorporated into the Ukrainian SSR, was seldom taken. The
number of Poles enumerated in the Ukrainian SSR in the Soviet census
of 1970 (295,000) should be illustrated with the maps in the Soviet
ethnographical atlas,[44] since, as indicated, the majority of them are to
be found in the interior of the Ukraine rather than in the border area
as might have been expected. It is clear that the Poles enumerated
in the Ukraine are mostly members of the prewar Polish minority
living behind the 1939 Polish-Soviet border, who survived the wholesale deportations to Kazakhstan and Siberia and wartime ravages.
(Deportees and their descendants currently form a sizable Polish
community in Northern Kazakhstan and Western Siberia, with about
53,000 in Kazakhstan and 118,000 in Russia.[45]

In 1970, some 1,167,000 Poles were reported as living in the
USSR; despite natural increase, this figure is significantly less than
the 1,380,000 Poles living in the USSR in 1959.[46] It can be estimated
that fewer than half of these Poles were members of the prewar
Polish minority in the USSR.[47] Thus, one can safely assume that
at least 750,000 Poles living in the Soviet Union are those who decided
to remain in the area after the border changes of 1945, and their
descendants. However, this estimate does not take into consideration
the progressive denationalization of the Soviet Poles; for example,
whereas in 1959 46 percent gave Polish as the language they spoke
at home, in 1970 only 32.5 percent did so.[48]

The difference between the relatively unchanged Polish ethnic
area in the northeast of the former eastern territories and the virtually complete elimination of the Polish ethnic area in the southeast
around the city of Lvov and east of it in the Tarnopol region[49] can be
easily explained by reference to the history of inter-ethnic group
relations in the respective areas. Whereas the Polish-Lithuanian
antagonism was politically motivated but of relatively recent origin
(turn of the century), the Polish-Ukrainian feud was of long standing
(continuously since at least 1848 and beginning with the sociopolitical
Cossack conflicts of the early seventeenth century). There was little
historical Polish-Belorussian antagonism.[50]

The clash of political orientation that occurred during World
War II between the Poles and the Ukrainians, and the nationalistic
excesses that wiped out scores of Polish villages,[51] caused Poles

(after attempts at self-defense) to panic and flee the countryside for the relative safety of the towns and cities.[52] This was especially true in Volhynia and in the Lvov area, where the Poles sought to escape the pogroms organized by the Ukrainian nationalists during the Nazi occupation[53] or were motivated by fear of the approach of the Soviet administration. The extent of this unofficial and unrecorded migration, which took place over a period of months and, in some instances, years,[54] is indicated by the fact that the 1950 census recorded over 600,000 more former residents of eastern Poland than were officially transferred through the Polish-Soviet repatriation machinery established for that purpose (see Table 9).

The unorganized and uncounted westward trek of Poles from the eastern provinces—amounting to 30 percent of the transferred eastern Poles, as verified by the 1950 census figures—took place from 1942 to autumn 1944. On November 9, 1944, special agreements were signed by the Polish Committee of National Liberation with the governments of three Soviet republics bordering on Poland (Lithuania, Belorussia, and the Ukraine)[55] as to the transfer of the Polish and Jewish population domiciled in the areas behind the Curzon Line, but forming part of pre-1939 Poland, to the territory of Poland within its new borders (which, incidentally, were still undecided at that time).[56]

Approximately 1,945,000 persons initially registered for transfer under those agreements,[57] but only 76 percent actually left for Poland. It should be noted that many people who decided to remain in their old homes in the east in 1945 or could not prove their pre-1939 domicile were allowed to move to Poland in 1956-59, when a special convention concerning repatriation was signed and the regulations were relaxed following the June-October 1956 political upheaval, which removed the Polish Stalinist leadership.

The organized transfer of the Polish population opting for Poland into the part of Poland east of the Vistula river began in the autumn of 1944, while transfers into newly liberated parts of the country and the western territories immediately adjacent to Poland's prewar western border began in the spring of 1945.

SETTLERS FROM CENTRAL POLAND: THEIR CHARACTERISTICS AND MIGRATION HISTORY

The Oder-Neisse area was half empty and destroyed when wrested from the German army. New settlers began to stream into it almost as soon as the front moved away. Spontaneous, and later

TABLE 9

Transfer of Poles from the USSR, 1944-49

Year	Total	From Lithuania	From Belorussia	From the Ukraine	From Other Areas
1944	117,212	0	0	117,212	0
1945	723,488	53,899	135,654	511,377	22,058
1946	644,437	123,443	136,419	158,435	226,140
1947	10,801	671	2,090	76	7,964
1948	7,325	0	0	74	7,251
1949	3,420	0	0	0	3,420
Total	1,506,683	178,013	274,163	787,674	266,833

Source: Glowny Urzad Statystyczny Rzeczypospolitej Polskiej, Rocznik Statystyczny, 1950, Vol. XIV (Warsaw, 1951), Table 8, p. 22.

organized, waves of colonists from the overcrowded villages of central
Poland began to move into the newly acquired western territories of
Poland. Whereas the transfer of the Polish population from behind
the Curzon Line was virtually completed by 1947,[58] the colonization
of the new western territories by the mostly rural population from
central Poland continued through 1949.

Although the migrants from central Poland generally were rural,
they also included the populations of small towns in central Poland,
who were searching for better opportunities, and the inhabitants of
some large cities destroyed by the war, including Warsaw, Poznan,
Bialystok, and Grudziadz.[59] Furthermore, that wave of colonization
carried with it the population of villages and towns totally destroyed
during the battles of the second part of 1944 (July 1944-January 1945)
in the broad strip of land running across Poland roughly along the
rivers Narew, Vistula, and Wisloka. Since the villages along that
line were of wooden construction, they practically ceased to exist in
the "battle of the bridgeheads" during the 1945 winter offensive of
the Soviet army. This territory, which remained largely demolished,
mined, and flooded long after the offensive had rolled over the area,[60]
had to be evacuated, and the majority of its population was transferred
to the western areas. Apart from the pressure of the redundant agricultural labor force in the overcrowded villages of central Poland,[61]
there were other reasons for the mass migratory movements that
materialized in the 1945-49 period; in view of war losses and urbanization, the experts at the first session of the Council had doubted
that the migrations would approach the levels they actually reached.[62]

The rural population surplus available for migration in both
directions—to the cities in the central area and to the western territories—was much larger than originally anticipated. The rural birth
rate during the war compensated for the losses to a much larger
extent than initially estimated.[63] Moreover, the concentrated propaganda effort of the modern state in inducing the rural underemployed
to migrate was elaborate and effective.[64] All the peasants in the
central areas were exposed to such propaganda through organized
campaigns. Lecturers toured the villages and described the government settlement plans for the newly acquired territories in the west.
All the mass communication media—radio, press, and posters—were
used to convince people to migrate.

The westward migration of the surplus population of Polish
villages in 1945 and after followed the long-established tradition of
such movements. That tradition of "western" migratory movements
was very strong in the village. Since the second part of the nineteenth

century, the surplus agricultural labor in the Polish villages had been forced by the high birth rate (too high for home industry to absorb it) to migrate to either American or German industry.[65]

These historical migratory trends westward to industry followed similar trends in German history, known as the Ostflucht and Landflucht, whereby the German population of the Prussian Eastern Provinces (roughly corresponding to the Oder-Neisse areas plus provinces of Poznan and parts of Pomerania recovered by Poland in 1919) migrated to large urban areas, such as Berlin, the Saxon cities, or farther west to the Ruhr industrial area.[66] Thus an acute shortage of labor existed in the agriculture of what was then East Prussia. This void was filled by the Polish surplus labor.

At the beginning of World War I, as many as 800,000 foreign workers (mostly Polish) were permanently or seasonally employed in the agriculture of the "Prussian East."[67] Furthermore, the industrial force of Upper Silesia was composed of Polish-speaking workers native to the area. There was also a considerable influx of Polish workers from across what were then the Austrian and Russian frontiers (from Galicia and the Kingdom of Poland) into Silesia.

These movements were temporarily stopped or checked after World War I, when the Polish migratory flows somewhat changed their direction to go toward the voivodships of Poznan and Pomerania in the eastern territories (to replace Germans opting for Germany)[68] and to France (when the United States Immigration Act of 1924 and the quota system were put in force). However, the migrations to Germany then assumed the new form of a seasonal harvesting migration which also often resulted in rural settlement.[69] Poles bought up the border farms sold by Germans migrating west until this practice was prohibited by the German government just before 1939.

Thus, the political decisions allocating the Oder-Neisse territories to Poland and opening up settlement possibilities there followed a historical migratory pattern of previous decades, a pattern for which Polish peasants were psychologically prepared and conditioned by tradition.[70] The political decisions of Potsdam drastically accelerated that traditional westward migratory trend.

RE-EMIGRANTS AND THEIR CONTRIBUTION
TO THE NEW SOCIETY

Another significant demographic element in the present population of the Oder-Neisse areas is made up of re-emigrants who

returned to Poland after the war from countries abroad where they
had migrated in search of work or been born of Polish parents.
According to the 1950 census, their number is not large (152,200).[71]
However, since most of them were molded in their work habits by
more advanced technological societies (such as France, Germany, and
Belgium), their influx was definitely a positive addition to various
sectors of the economy in the western territories. Since the re-
emigrants brought with them special skills in mining and industry,
they often settled in compact groups. Thus, the returned miners
from France and Belgium (who left Poland, for the most part, after
World War I) settled mostly in the Upper and Lower Silesian coal
fields.[72]

It is significant to note that many of the re-emigrants ceased
to work at their trades after returning to Poland because they were
offered civic and Party jobs (which was the case, for example, of
Edward Gierek, the present First Secretary of the Polish United
Workers Party). This was the result of the fact that their return
from France (and Belgium) was to a large extent organized by the
Communist Party, which had considerable influence among the Polish
industrial workers in the Pas de Calais region of France.[73] The
high mining skills of the overwhelming majority of these miners and
workers who remained at their trades enabled Poland to resume
exploitation of the Lower Silesian Coal Basin, which was difficult to
work, requiring special skills that would have taken a newly recruited
force years to acquire. The occupational characteristics of re-
emigrants from Belgium were similar to those of re-emigrants from
France.

The skills of the re-emigrants from Germany were more varied.
Many had lived in Germany for a generation or two. There were
industrial workers, as well as farmers who brought with them the
superior farming methods so sorely needed in the agriculture of the
western territories. The skills of this important group could be used
as a model for the newly emerging society. They settled in both
towns and villages, mostly in Lower Silesia and Szczecin.[74]

The sole almost exclusively agricultural group of re-emigrants
was comprised of Poles from Yugoslavia who decided to return to
Poland in 1945 after their villages had been completely destroyed or
severely damaged. The Polish farmers from Rumania made their
decision to return in similar circumstances.[75] These farmers settled
in compact groups in the villages of Lower Silesia, which they had
selected in advance through their delegates. The Poles from
Yugoslavia settled in a few villages and agricultural cooperatives

in the same area. The scattering of other re-emigrants made their qualititive contribution to the pool of skills urgently needed in the western territories, but their number was too small to change the overall population structure.

The vigorous campaign to induce more emigrants to return to Poland from abroad foundered on two basic premises:

1. The majority of the emigrants, already materially established in the highly developed Western societies (especially in France), were reluctant to return to the conditions offered by Poland in the western territories, even though those conditions were relatively favorable. Even more important to the immigrants was the fact that Poland, at that time, was already being integrated into a drastically different political and social system, and the western territories, which were burdened with tremendous wartime destruction and accompanying dislocations, could offer only limited personal security.

2. Both France and Germany needed the skills of the highly trained Polish miners and steelworkers; as a result, governmental and business pressures were exerted to dissuade the potential re-emigrants from returning to Poland.

In France, the need for the skills of the Polish workers prevented a large migratory movement. In Western Germany, the occupying British authorities in the Ruhr were reluctant, for economic and political reasons (most of the Poles there were German citizens), to issue permits for emigration and soon suspended them altogether. The only opportune moment for emigration came immediately after World War II. The delay and subsequent Communist takeover of Poland effectively destroyed any chance of future mass returns. Thus, the Polish colony in Germany remained there.[76] Later returns to Poland were based on individual decisions, and only a few emigrated.[77]

Special political circumstances overrode the emotional, patriotic, and economic reasons for a mass return of Polish emigrants from Western Europe, a return that was realistically anticipated by the creation of favorable economic opportunities in the western areas and eagerly sought.[78] The only opportunity for Poland to repatriate most of its former citizens from Western Europe was ruined, primarily by the postwar political circumstances due to the sharp ideological split evident as early as 1946 and by the ominous socio-political situation in Poland. A mass return of Poles from overseas was never anticipated because of the distance involved, the high standard of living in the Americas, and the relatively small percentage of first-generation emigrants still surviving.[79]

MINORITY GROUPS SETTLED IN THE
WESTERN TERRITORIES

In 1947, after General Swierczewski, Commanding Officer of the second Polish Army, had been ambushed and killed by the partisans of the Ukrainian Insurgent Army (UPA) at Baligrod in the southeast corner of contemporary Poland, the Polish government, unable to control the Ukrainian resistance by other means, dispatched security forces and detachments of the Polish army to crush the UPA forces. It was decided to resettle and disperse the remaining Ukrainian population living in the southeast area of Poland (about 170,000) in the western territories.[80] This drastic move (code name: "Operation W") was taken to undercut the support given by Ukrainian civilians to the UPA forces.

Only some of those resettled returned after 1957, when official permission was granted. It should also be noted that the Ukrainian minority in contemporary Poland is only a small part of the pre-1939 Ukrainian population located west of the Curzon Line (800,000). Most of the Ukrainians residing in Poland opted for the USSR in 1945,[81] and some were forcibly transferred there by the Polish authorities. Polish-Ukrainian relations after 1945 were extremely tense, despite official denial of such national animosities.

Apart from the group of Ukrainians transferred to the western territories in 1947 in "Operation W," there are only a few other minority groups in the Oder-Neisse areas. There are some Belorussians, Lithuanians, and Russians who either mixed with Poles to leave the eastern territories or had intermarried with them.[82] There was also a small group of Germans (about 3,000) who stayed in the area after the evacuation, flight, expulsion, and postwar transfers of Germans.[83] This residue was all that remained of the prewar German population of the Oder-Neisse areas. Since 1960, most of these Germans have emigrated, largely to West Germany.

The Jews are (after the Ukrainians) the second largest minority group in the western territories (in Eastern Europe, Jews are classified as a nationality group). Some came from the east and some migrated to the west from central Poland. Approximately 10,500 Jews lived in the area before 1967, accounting for one-third of the Jewish population of contemporary Poland.[84]

The 30,000 Jews in Poland in 1967 were the tragic remnant of the second largest (about 3.5 million) Jewish community in the world prior to 1939. Of the 300,000 to 350,000 survivors of the Nazi holocaust, less than 10 percent could adapt themselves to life in the surroundings in which their families had been annihilated. Vestiges of anti-Semitism, crudely exploited for political purposes immediately after the war by Polish Communists and Nationalists alike, also played a crucial role in the decision to emigrate made by 90 percent of the survivors.

The tragic remant of Polish Jewry was further decimated by Jewish emigration from Poland in 1968-69 caused by the euphemistically called "anti-Zionist" campaign waged by the Party with blessing of its Central Committee's Education Department, as fully documented by a racist and, ironically, un-Marxist article published in the leading literary journal. Its symptomatic importance has been overshadowed only by recent changes in leadership.[85]

Scattered small groups of other nationalities, such as Gypsies and Czechs, have also settled in the western areas. Large groups of Greeks and Macedonians, political refugees of the Greek civil war of 1944-48 (about 10,000), settled in the western territories after the defeat of the Communists in Greece.[86] In the mid-1960's the sum total of all national minorities was only 170,000 of the Oder-Neisse area's population of 8.3 million.

ORGANIZED SETTLEMENT AND PLANNING

The resettlers from central Poland and the eastern Poles are the major components of the new society in the Oder-Neisse area. Large-scale migrations of these two groups were handled by a special government office, the State Repatriation Office (PUR). PUR was originally established to organize transport for the 2.2 million repatriates from the west (mostly wartime slave laborers, emigrees, concentration camp inmates, and ex-prisoners of war and soldiers)[87] and those from the east who had opted for Poland (1.5 million were transferred by organized transport).

Since its activities concerning the transfer of the eastern Poles actually involved their settlement in the newly acquired western territories, PUR was later eased into handling all phases of the colonizing of those areas by resettlers from central Poland. The "western" phase of repatriation also involved the settlement of some repatriates in the Oder-Neisse area, especially those whose homes

were behind the eastern border or in the towns or villages that had
been destroyed during the war. All told, in 1944-49 PUR handled the
repatriation of some 4 million persons, not including the resettlers
from central Poland.[88]

The formal plan for the settlement of the western territories
was elaborated by the Scientific Council for the Problems of the
Recovered Territories at its first session in Cracow, from July 30
to August 1, 1945. Before its formal acceptance, the plan was discussed by the Council in seminars at the University of Cracow and
during its session, when differing opinions about some elements of
the plan were taken into consideration. After its adoption by the
Council, the plan was transmitted to the Ministry of Public Administration. The Ministry in turn issued instructions to all administrative
organs involved in the settlement of the Oder-Neisse areas to imple-
ment the Council's plan.[89]

The Soviet-sponsored Lublin government, at that time unrecog-
nized by other Allies, ruled Poland unimpeded during the crucial
period of the Nazi retreat from the territories west of the Vistula,
which they held until January 1945, and from the Oder-Neisse areas,
which were soon to be assigned to Poland in Potsdam. Thus, it was
only when the Provisional Government of National Unity took office
on June 28, 1945 (after the war in Europe had ended), that a somewhat broader political base and wider national interest were taken
into account. The Scientific Council for the Problems of the Recovered
Territories was formed within a month. This body probably should
have been formed immediately after the liberation of Cracow at the
end of January.

The delay in its formation, due to political considerations,
introduced an element of unregulated or haphazardly improvised
settlement in the Oder-Neisse territories during most of 1945. The
Council's plan, transmitted by the Ministry of Public Administration,
did not reach all its agents until the end of the year or even later
in some cases as was revealed during the Council's second session in
Cracow.[90]

The greatest discrepancies in the planned settlement of the
rural settlers occurred when resettlers from fertile areas in central
Poland were placed on sandy soil in the west (or resettlers from
sandy soil areas in central Poland were placed on fertile soil in the
west) before the Council's plan became known to the governmental
organs responsible for resettlement.[91] These errors were compounded by the spontaneous influx of the land-hungry rural population

across the prewar 1939 western frontier of Poland almost immediately following the retreat of the German army. The influx assumed flood-like proportions in the spring of 1945. Since it was spontaneous, it did not conform to the goal of optimal utilization of land by which settlers would be transferred into environmental conditions corresponding to their old habitats.

The spontaneous settlement worked on the first-come, first-served basis, and the colonists were allocated farms accordingly. The waves of settlers came primarily from the border areas along the 1939 frontier of Poland, where the farmers had direct knowledge of the quality of land and farming conditions. Migrants from the border Mazovian regions streamed north to populate the southern districts of what had been East Prussia, farmers from the Pomeranian border districts crossed into what had been German Pomerania, and the Poznanians migrated west into former East Brandenburg and southwest into Lower Silesia. This phenomenon is known in Polish sociological literature as a "neighborly" migratory movement.[92]

Although these movements were unorganized, they nevertheless partially corresponded, coincidentally, to the optimal migratory pattern advocated in the rural settlement plan later elaborated by the Scientific Council for the Problems of the Recovered Territories. The plan called for a group settlement scheme that would direct migrants to farming conditions similar to those they had previously known. They would have been directed into the western areas roughly corresponding to the same latitude. Thus, the plan called for the Poles from the Vilna region in the northeast to be transferred, if possible, into former East Prussia and Pomerania, since the climatic and farming conditions there are somewhat similar to those in the Vilna region. Similarly, Poles from the southeast (Poles formed only a slight minority of the population south of the Niemen River and east of the Bug River) were to be transferred to Silesia and East Brandenburg.[93]

The execution of the plan was facilitated by the fact that the communications network in the areas in question, and especially the railroad system, connected the points of departure with the receiving areas.[94] Moreover, the leading railroads involved had been repaired almost immediately after the German retreat and temporarily converted to the broad gauge, since they had carried logistical supplies to the Soviet Army in Germany, precisely in the directions planned for the migrations. Thus, the realities of the transfer of the eastern Polish population by and large coincided with the settlement plan elaborated by the Council, and that part of the settlement of the new

areas in the west proceeded relatively swiftly (until 1946), although at
a huge cost in human inconvenience, sacrifice, and misery.[95] The
colonization of the western areas by the overflowing population from
central Poland proved a much longer process (it lasted until 1949),
subject to much more administrative error and mismanagement,
as well as difficulties caused by the previous spontaneous migratory
movements, which forced many corrections or complete changes in
the settlement plan.

THE EMERGING SETTLEMENT PATTERN

Two major population elements, the "eastern" and the "central"
(which together comprised about 80 percent of the population in the
western territories) should be studied more closely for a settlement
pattern, which emerged with the completion of the mass migratory
movements in 1949. This pattern now provides the basic structure
of the society of Poland's western territories.

The national census of 1950 was taken immediately after migratory movements within the new borders of Poland subsided and the
population settlement pattern stabilized. It enables us to assess the
composition of the new society in the Oder-Neisse territories as to
origin of population in each voivodship (see Table 10).[96]

Further study conducted by the Institute of Geography of the
University of Warsaw, using materials of the Central Office of Statistics, traces the origin of the population of the western territories within
each administrative district (powiat).[97] In the Oder-Neisse territories
in 1950, colonists from central Poland constituted 49.1 percent of the
population; repatriates from both the east and the west, 29.5 percent;
and natives to the area (so-called autochthons), 19.6 percent.

In view of the migratory trends described above, the following
population structure has emerged: the voivodships of Szczecin, Koszalin, Zielona Gora, and Wroclaw were populated mainly by repatriates
and resettlers; the autochthons formed a small percentage there. The
repatriates formed a large group only in the provinces of Zielona
Gora and Wroclaw, part of Poznan, and Szczecin. The resettlers from
central Poland dominated almost all of the Oder-Neisse areas apart
from Mazuria and Upper Silesia, settling in the provinces of Szczecin,
Koszalin, part of Gdansk, Olsztyn, part of Poznan, Zielona Gora, and
Wroclaw. Partly comparable data for 1947, when the first transfer
from the east was almost completed, show us that the composition of
the new society in the Oder-Neisse territories changed greatly between
1947 and 1950.[98]

TABLE 10

Origins of the Oder-Neisse Population in 1950

Province	Total (Thousands)	Autochthons		Resettlers from Central Poland		Repatriates and Eastern Poles		Other or Unknown	
		Thousands	Percentage	Thousands	Percentage	Thousands	Percentage	Thousands	Percentage
Bialystok*	70.6	4.8	6.8	56.7	80.4	8.3	11.7	0.8	1.1
Olsztyn*	610.2	111.3	18.2	352.1	57.7	137.3	22.5	9.5	1.6
Gdansk*	500.8	57.4	11.6	334.9	66.8	97.8	19.5	10.7	2.1
Koszalin	518.4	49.5	9.5	333.3	64.4	126.0	24.3	9.6	1.8
Szczecin	529.3	16.7	3.2	344.1	65.0	160.5	30.3	8.0	1.5
Poznan*	49.3	2.9	5.8	30.4	61.6	15.5	31.5	0.5	1.1
Zielona Gora	560.6	18.1	3.2	290.4	51.8	244.7	43.7	7.4	1.3
Wroclaw	1,698.9	97.5	5.7	901.8	53.1	677.7	39.9	21.9	1.3
Opole	809.5	437.7	54.1	158.1	19.5	188.3	23.3	25.4	3.1
Katowice*	588.6	369.1	62.7	114.7	19.5	93.6	15.9	11.2	1.9
Total	5,936.2	1,165.0	19.6	2,916.5	49.1	1,749.7	29.5	105.0	1.8

*Only that part of the province in the Oder-Neisse area.

Source: Leszek Kosinski, Pochodzenie terytorialne ludnosci Ziem Zachodnich w 1950r. (Warsaw: Instytut Geografii PAN, 1960), p. 8.

Thus, the colonization movement from central Poland, which continued until 1949, greatly reinforced the first spontaneous wave of migrants of 1945. As a result, the resettlers from central Poland achieved a dominant role in the newly formed society in most of the western areas, with the exception of Upper Silesia.

THE AUTOCHTHONS

Most of members of the so-called autochthonous group, the only nonimmigrant population element in the new society of the Oder-Neisse territories, are bilingual (Polish and German) but speak Polish dialects at home. Their social and economic contributions will be discussed at length in Chapters 4 and 5. Here we will analyze their distribution and influence on the population structure of the western areas. Their strength, according to the Polish statistical analysis made in 1919 by E. Romer of the University of Lvov, was 1,236,000.[99] This figure was basically derived from an analysis of the Prussian school census of 1911, which corrected the allegedly biased Prussian census of 1910. It was confirmed by the leading German demographer, Ludwig Bernhard.[100] The figure derived from the school census obviously did not reflect national loyalties, which were heavily influenced by such considerations as economic ties and pressures, political traditions, administrative pressures, and outright Germanizing attempts.[101] (We should also note that Silesia, Warmia, Gdansk, and parts of the pre-1939 western borderlands had ceased to be political parts of Poland between the fourteenth and eighteenth centuries, and even earlier in the case of Pomerania.

Thus, the tenacity with which a large segment of the population retained its Polish speech and customs is surprising in view of the official policy of Germanization and the settlement of Germans in the area.[102] The Germans based their estimates of the Polish-speaking population in the Oder-Neisse territories on official population censuses.[103] Romer pointed out, however, that even the figures of the last pre-World War I Prussian censuses (both population and school) were adjusted and subordinated to political and state goals. The figures for minorities in the subsequent censuses of 1925, 1933, and 1939 were even more drastically reduced. Contemporary German sources admit to those falsifications directly (Ludwig Bernhard) or indirectly by using the 1925 figures because they are the least distorted (see Table 11).[104] One American source estimates the realistic figure to be about a million ethnic Poles in these areas.[105]

The figure for the so-called autochthonous population of the Polish western territories corresponds very closely to the figure

TABLE 11

East German Population by Mother Tongue, 1925

Area	Population (Thousands)	German Citizens (Thousands)	Mother Tongue								
			Only German		German and One Other		Only Polish		Only Mazurian		Other	
			Thousands	Percentage	Thousands	Percentage	Thousands	Percentage	Thousands	Percentage	Thousands	Percentage
Ostpreussen	2,256	2,234	2,117	94.8	53	2.4	19	0.8	42	1.9	3	0.1
Pommern[a]	1,632	1,612	1,606	99.6	3	0.2	3	0.2	0	0.0	0	0.0
Grenzmark												
Posen-Westpreussen	333	330	317	96.0	5	1.5	8	2.5	0	0.0	0	0.0
Brandenburg[b]	640	630	625	99.2	3	0.5	2	0.3	0	0.0	0	0.0
Niederschlesien	3,132	3,076	3,038	98.8	16	0.5	2	0.1	0	0.0	20[c]	0.6
Oberschlesien	1,379	1,360	811	59.6	392	28.8	151	11.1	0	0.0	6	0.5
East Germany	9,372	9,242	8,514	92.1	472	5.1	185	2.0	42	0.5	29	0.3

[a]Stettin and Koslin provinces.

[b]Estimate (about 50 percent of the population of Frankfurt province, a subdivision of Brandenburg).

[c]There were about 16,700 persons whose mother tongue was Wendish.

Source: Statistik des Deutschen Reichs, Band 401, as quoted in Bruno Gleitze, Ostdeutsche Wirtschaft (Berlin: Duncker and Humbolt, 1956), p. 152.

estimated by Romer in 1919 for the Polish-speaking population of the area.[106] However, the figures represent a different group of people because of postwar dislocations and the evacuation of an estimated three-fourths of the 400,000 Polish-speaking Mazurians and Warmians (in what had been East Prussia) who never returned home after 1945.

Furthermore, we must also take into account the progressive denationalization through the abandonment of the Polish language between 1910 and 1945. There are obviously no reliable official statistics published on the subject, but one may assess the complexity of the situation from the progressive falsification of the official figures on minorities. However, the German authorities had a growing need to gauge the nationality problem correctly for their own internal and confidential use.

This is manifest in the secret study commissioned by the Bund der Deustchen Osten and summarized by H. Rogmann in a document discovered after the war in the Wroclaw archives and subsequently published by Stefan Golachowski.[107] Rogmann, on the basis of the language used in church ceremonies, estimates the number of Polish-speaking Upper Silesians at 550,000, rather than the approximately 365,000 officially admitted in the 1933 German census.[108] He also mentions the Polish claims of 800,000 without challenging them. The original document from the Gestapo files in Opole, reproduced here (see p. 68), illustrates the extent of the surveillance over the use of Polish in that region of prewar Silesia.[109]

Those persons (about 1.2 million) who were able to prove their Polish extraction, background, and/or native language and declared themselves as Poles were allowed by the Polish authorities to remain in the Oder-Neisse territories.[110] However, that 1.2 million included Germans who were allowed to stay or were retained as experts (estimated by the Polish Parliament at 65,000), as well as an undetermined number of Germans who passed as Poles and, for political reasons, were not expelled or were even coerced to stay since their skills were needed for reconstruction of the economy.[111] It probably also included a sizable number of opportunists who declared themselves as Poles in order to escape the chaos of postwar Germany.

We must also consider the pattern of family ties that developed from the tradition of migrations from the Oder-Neisse area to German cities in the west and the Ruhr, as described earlier. Those family contacts were temporarily disrupted, and no visits or migrations were possible, after the World War II expulsions had been completed. Furthermore, many members of Silesian families (especially returning

German document proving police surveillance of Polish-language
religious services in Upper Silesia before World War II.

Auszugsweise Abschrift.

Bund Deutscher Osten
Landesgruppe Schlesien   Breslau, den 21. Juni 1938.
Landesleitung.
Tgb.Nr.geh.450.07/38.

Geheim

Betrifft: pp.

    In Beuthen-Stadtwald läßt die Minderheit alljährlich am
21.5. (Tag der Erstürmung des Annaberges) eine Messe für die Gefallenen aus Beuthen-Stadtwald lesen. Es handelt sich um 21
aufständische Polen die aus diesem Stadtteil stammen und bei der
Annabergschlacht gefallen sind. Obwohl es jedem Pfarrer anheim
gestellt bleiben muß, ob er je nach Bestellung deutsche bezw.
polnische Messen für verstorbene Angehörige liest, erscheint
es doch untragbar, wenn der Pfarrer in diesem Falle in seiner
Vermeldung ausdrücklich bekannt gibt, daß jene Messe für "die am
Annaberg gefallenen Aufständischen" aus Beuthen-Stadtwald gelesen
werden wird.

    pp.

Heil Hitler!
gez. Hartlieb,
Landesgruppenleiter.

An den Herrn Oberpräsidenten in Breslau.

Der Regierungspräsident.   Oppeln, den 16. Juli 1938.
I 11 Nr.58/38 g.

Geheim

    Auszugsweise Abschrift einer Meldung des Bundes Deutscher
Osten zur Kenntnis zu den Personalakten des Geistlichen, gegebe-
nenfalls weiterer Veranlassung.

In Vertretung:
gez. Wehrmeister.

Beglaubigt:

Regierungsangestellte.

An
  II 4 .
  ==========

    Sei.

(Original document is in the author's archives.)

prisoners of war) either were stranded in Germany after 1945 or for other reasons did not choose to join their families in Silesia. Hence, in 1955-59 when many people native to the area were given the relatively free choice of resuming their family contacts, they decided to join their families in the West. This group included, first of all, people who either had been forced to stay in the area after World War II or had opportunistically opted for Poland at that time. Later, because of the relatively relaxed Polish emigrating procedures of the period after October 1956,[112] many persons who did not have immediate families in Germany but rejected the Communist system and/or were lured by the German Wirtschaftwunder (economic miracle), decided to leave Poland.[113]

These persons simply asked the appropriate German authorities to issue papers stating that they had relatives in Germany.[114] Once this trend had emerged in 1957-58, it became especially pronounced in villages with a mixed population of autochthons and newcomers. When the latter were a great majority, they caused the isolation of the old population. This trend was also found, to some extent, in the industrial cities of Upper Silesia, where the system of values is typically Western European in character and material rewards are predominant in choice-making.[115]

The 1955-59 emigration wave, as it affected the Oder-Neisse areas, involved an estimated 275,000 persons. Virtually all Germans left the area, as did many persons of undetermined national consciousness who used this opportunity to emigrate in search of better economic opportunities or social system.[116] In many cases, these individuals had to learn German after they had arrived in Germany.[117]

An official West German publication of the Press and Information Office stated recently that almost 400,000 persons emigrated to that country from Poland between December 1955 and December 1970 as a result of an agreement reached between the German and the Polish Red Cross.[118] Since 579,500 Poles officially emigrated from Poland in 1955-69, it would appear that two out of three emigrants moved to West Germany, while the rest went primarily to the United States, Israel, France, and Great Britain.

The Polish-German emigration agreement, which was reached simultaneously with the West German recognition of the Oder-Neisse boundary on December 7, 1970, is now being implemented, allowing persons who have families in West Germany to leave Poland. It is estimated that by the end of 1972 about 98,000 persons in this category will join their families. Most of these people were separated by the war and its aftermath, and often the Polish and German relatives have completely lost contact. This emigration wave is essentially economic in character, since relaxed regulations allow Poles to rejoin even distant relatives. A large share of the emigrants (including all children), do not speak German, causing serious initial integration problems. However, they are following traditional westward economic migration patterns of the Poles of previous generations by supplementing the immigrant labor pool in West Germany.[119]

The autochthons in the Oder-Neisse areas are currently concentrated in several areas along the pre-1939 Polish-German border, particularly in Opole Silesia and Mazuria. In the north, they constitute 18.2 percent of the total population of the voivodship of Olsztyn (in former East Prussia), with varying strength in some of its districts (as shown in Table 10 above). In Opole Silesia, they constitute 62.7 percent of the population in the part of Katowice province lying in the Oder-Neisse territories, and 54.1 percent of the population of the voivodship of Opole. In thirteen districts of those provinces, they form the majority of the population. Outside these two compact areas of settlement—Opole Silesia and Mazuria—the autochthonous population forms strong elements of society only in some of the districts in the provinces of Gdansk, Koszalin, and Zielona Gora.[120]

Before 1945, many towns in the regions inhabited by the autochthonous Polish-speaking population had been mostly German-speaking islands. After 1945, and the expulsion or flight of the German population, they were resettled by the Polish immigrants from east or central Poland. Hence, there is a pronounced difference between the strength of autochthons in the towns and villages; for example, autochthons form 22.8 percent of the population of Opole city and 87.3 of the population of Opole county. These data illustrate and reflect a situation prevailing in Eastern Europe, where the nationality of the town population has been or still is different from that of the immediate countryside (other examples include Lvov in Galicia, Gdansk in Pomerania, Trieste in Istria, and Cluj in Transylvania). Furthermore, the town population often was composed of immigrants (some with a long history of domicile there), whereas the original ethnic group resided in the surrounding countryside. The situation was seldom reversed.

The autochthonous population of Opole Silesia and Mazuria-Warmia was bilingual, speaking Polish dialects at home and German in all the official contacts and communications. The cultural influence of the Germans (who settled in their midst and ruled these areas) upon the folk culture of the Poles native to the territories was a significant factor, not to be dismissed lightly. The Polish-speaking population thus assimilated some values of the industrial state whose territory they inhabited into their own system of values, regardless of whether they were urbanized. Their Polish dialect often was interspersed with German expressions, especially those describing technological and urban phenomena. (There is, incidentally, a direct parallel—which we know firsthand—with the situation of Polish-speaking Americans, whose vocabulary is affected in a similar way).[121]

THE IMPACT OF COLLECTIVIZATION
ON SETTLEMENT

Because of war changes and the Soviet dismantling of the industrial plants for shipment to the USSR, the rural and industrial settlement capacity of the area had been reached by 1949. Any further population increase was conditional on the economic planning of growth, rebuilding of industry (especially in small towns), and agricultural investment.

In 1949, the end of the first period in the postwar history of the Oder-Neisse areas coincided with the end of the postwar National Economic Recovery Plan and the gradual depletion of the labor reserves of the central regions of the country, which were now in the process of urbanization and industrialization. The following Six-Year Economic Plan was characterized by forced industrialization, collectivization of agriculture, expansion of heavy industry, and general administrative unification.

The social and political reforms forced on the countryside in the early 1950's contributed to the partial reversal of the rural settlement of the area, the abandonment of farms, and the lowering of agricultural productivity.[122] These processes were checked and reversed only after the events of October 1956 and the dissolution of the majority of collective farms in the area.[123]

The forced collectivization of the period 1945-49 left a more lasting impact on rural migratory trends in Poland. Since it coincided with the accelerated industrialization and urbanization of areas that were sources of migrants, it virtually stopped large-scale internal immigration to the western territories from other parts of postwar Poland.[124] Peasants from the overcrowded villages of central Poland preferred to go to the cities rather than settle in the west.

Even the voluntary dissolution of the collectives did not convince the peasants that this change of agricultural policy was permanent and would not be followed by future collectivization.* In the period beginning in 1949, the abandonment of farms and migrations to the cities could barely be replaced by land settlement and natural increase. The farming population, after the initial collectivization campaign of 1949,[125] remained fairly constant. The next period of settlement history in the western territories was influenced not by migration but by natural increase.

POST-SETTLEMENT DEMOGRAPHIC PATTERNS

There have been two distinct demographic structures in the new society of the Oder-Neisse area, one in the postwar years of 1945-49 and the other in the years since 1950. During the 1945-49 period, internal migration accounted for the major portion of population increase. In the years since 1950, the population increase can be traced to natural increase alone and the birth rate has consistently been much higher in the western provinces than in the other provinces of Poland.[126] Immediately after the war, the hardships of settling in the unfamiliar and ruined countryside were not conducive to raising families; later, the fact that the large migratory movements into the territory were composed largely of young people of reproductive age, and the progressive stabilization of the economic conditions, resulted in an increased birth rate.[127]

The demographic structure of the area's new population, and the possibilities for social and economic advancement opening rapidly with the rehabilitation and rebuilding of the area's economy have contributed decisively to the immediate and rapid growth in the birth rate of the new society of western Poland. In the short period of five years after World War II, the natural growth of population has almost completely replaced the diminishing internal and external migratory movements as a chief source of population increases.[128]

In addition, the age structure of the area's population was still affected by a constant, although small, influx of settlers.[129] They are still lured by the prospects of higher social mobility and improved economic conditions. The high birth rate in the area resulted not only from the specific age structure described above, but also from

─────────────

*After 1956, there was a remarkable growth of spending on consumers' goods and of conspicuous consumption, a phenomenon unusual for the Polish village.

the fact that women in those territories have higher fertility than in other provinces of Poland.[130] The sex and age structure showed considerable variations, depending on the territorial origin of the population and the economic characteristics of the area (see Table 12).

Thus, in 1959 more than half of the population in the areas of Opole Silesia was native-born (Katowice province, 62.7 percent, and Opole province, 54.1 percent). At the same time, the population had a much more disadvantageous age structure, with a higher percentage of older people, than in the incoming groups of settlers.[131] This was due to the relatively heavy losses that this group had suffered when its able-bodied men were drafted into the German army and war-production plants in different parts of Germany, and during the last-minute evacuation of certain groups of workers imposed by Nazi authorities during the Soviet January Offensive of 1945.

Both groups of settlers, those from the east and those from central Poland, were also characterized by specific age structures. The resettlers from the east generally arrived in family groups, and in such a group the war losses were more evenly spread.[132] The age structue of resettlers from the east was more normal than that of the other groups of settlers or the indigenous Polish population. They were resettled in the west, mostly in compact groups, and there was far more planning for their settlement. These factors accounted for the preservation of their family structure during the process of territorial settlement. Furthermore, this group was marked by higher fertility among women, which is characteristic of the less-urbanized eastern Polish countryside.[133]

The immigrants from central Poland who settled in the west had an even more unusual age structure. They were, for the most part, young enterprising men who had migrated primarily in search of economic opportunity and living conditions far more advanced than what they had known in their villages.[134] The area, with its high technical standards, was for them a powerful and impressive magnet. In view of the acute shortage of trained personnel and specialists in virtually all fields, social mobility in the west was much higher than in their places of origin. This was an additional factor to attract young men in search of a career.

As a result, the immigrants from central Poland comprised the youngest of all groups of settlers and had the highest birth rate. After they had found jobs and homes in the west, the young pioneers usually brought women from their original places of domicile. Given economic opportunities and a much higher standard of living, they started families

TABLE 12

Age Structure of Population in Selected Counties
in the Oder-Neisse Area, 1950
(percentage distribution)

| Age | Poland | Indigenous Population Agricultural County (Mragowo) | Repatriates Agricultural County (Lidzbark Warmia) | Resettlers from Central Poland | | |
				Agricultural County (Gryfice)	Industrial County (Kamienna Gora)	Large City (Wroclaw)
Total	100.0	100.0	100.0	100.0	100.0	100.0
0-2	7.8	6.7	10.4	11.6	12.3	9.2
3-6	7.8	6.2	8.5	9.3	8.8	7.3
7-14	14.1	18.0	16.5	14.0	10.6	7.8
15-18	7.6	9.9	8.5	8.0	7.0	6.8
19-29	18.8	15.3	18.4	20.0	27.6	29.7
30-59	35.5	30.2	31.3	32.1	29.9	34.8
60 and over	8.4	13.7	6.4	5.0	3.8	4.4

Source: B. Welpa, "Age Structure of the Population of People's Poland," Geographic Studies (Warsaw), No. 16, 1955, pp. 60-113.

that they probably could not have supported in their home villages and towns.[135] The psychological climate of the postwar period, and the economic stabilization that was rapidly normalizing living conditions in the western territories, favorably influenced the rate of marriages contracted and families started in the youthful society.[136] However, during the initial period of settlement, the settlers from central Poland had less favorable sex ratios because of the pioneering nature of migration as opposed to the planned transfers of the eastern Polish population.

All these factors discussed above contributed to the proportionally larger labor force in the western territories than in other parts of Poland.[137] The birth rate, which was much higher than in other parts of the country (36.7 percent in 1955) and, largely because of the immigrant characteristics of the population, the relatively low death rate (9.1 percent in 1955) resulted in a high rate of natural increase[138] (27.6 percent in 1955) which continued (19.8 percent in 1960 and 44 percent less in the following decade) despite the rapid downward trend in the natural increase in other provinces (to 8.2 percent in 1969). The rate of natural population increase in the western territories declined at a much slower rate (to 11.2 percent in 1970). Thus, even now, the natural increase in the Oder-Neisse area is high by European standards or those of Poland as a whole.

THE RESIDUAL MIGRATORY WAVE

We must also mention the effect of the secondary migratory wave of 1956-59 on the demographic situation of the Oder-Neisse areas. During those years, 344,000 persons left Poland (for Germany, Israel, and other countries), of whom 262,000 lived in the western provinces. At the same time, 263,000 Poles, predominantly from the Soviet Union, entered Poland and settled largely in the west. This wave of population exchanges also had a positive demographic influence on the population structure of the area. Although the external migrations were larger, the emigrating population was older and included a higher ratio of women than in the population domiciled in the Oder-Neisse territories. These emigrants were joining their husbands, children, or grandchildren in the Federal Republic of Germany or in the German Democratic Republic.[139] The very imbalanced age structure can be explained by the fact that many older people eligible for German pensions (such as railroad and post office workers and army veterans) decided to emigrate to Germany.[140] The immigrating population had a more evenly distributed age and sex structure.[141]

TABLE 13

Population of the Oder-Neisse Areas:
Postwar Increase and Size in Relation
to Poland's Total Population

Year	Total Population (thousands)	Born in Oder-Neisse Areas after World War II		Share of the Oder-Neisse Area's Total in Poland's Population (percentage)
		Thousands	Percentage	
1946	4,976	147.4	3.0	21.1
1947	5,228	330.0	6.3	22.0
1948	5,540	536.6	9.7	22.9
1949	5,710	759.6	13.3	23.2
1950	5,738	995.7	17.4	23.3
1955	6,737	2,183.9	32.4	24.5
1960	7,498	3,302.7	44.0	25.5
1965	8,210	4,148.4	50.5	26.0
1968	8,500	4,587.9	54.0	26.2

Sources: For 1946, 1950, and 1960, national census figures; for other years, estimates as of December 31, as quoted in Rocznik Polityczny i Gospodarczy 1969 (Warsaw: Panstwowe Wydawnictwo Ekonomiczne, 1970), p. 130.

Thus, in the final analysis, the 1956-59 external migrations affected positively the age structure of the provinces of Olsztyn, Katowice, and Opole, the areas from which most of the emigrants came.[142] These provinces had the highest percentages of native Polish population with family or economic ties in Germany, as well as the most adverse age structure.

The influx of immigrants from the Soviet Union who replaced the emigrants added relatively younger groups to the population of the Oder-Neisse area, a population whose youthfulness was already distinctive[143] in Poland, which is a generally young nation.[144] The high rate of natural increase in these areas can be expected to continue, despite the downward trend over the last decade. This rate of increase is still much higher than that of the country as a whole.[145]

The high rate of natural increase, coupled with the growing tempo of industrialization and urbanization in the Oder-Neisse area,[146] brought that area's population in 1971 to 8.9 million, a record level. It can be assumed that the area's population will grow rapidly in the following years. The cities in the area are already an average of 17 percent larger, even though some large ones (such as Wroclaw, Szczecin, Legnica) have not yet achieved previous population peaks. Future trends can be charted from the statistics on age, sex, and women of child-bearing age in the population.[147]

The current rapid growth of the urban population[148] and the above-mentioned demographic factors indicate that the urban-rural population ratios for the territory (49 to 51 percent prior to World War II), which have already changed (55 to 45 percent in 1969), will be affected further. Urbanization will proceed at an even faster pace, although the western territories are already more urbanized than the rest of Poland (55 percent and 45 percent respectively). Hence, the demographic prognosis for the Oder-Neisse areas in the near future is that of a young, growing, and highly urbanized population. Over 60 percent of the population of the western territories is composed of persons who were born there and, as Table 13 shows, 54 percent were born there after World War II.

NOTES

1. Glowny Urzad Statystyczny Rzeczypospolitej Polskiej, Rocznik Statystyczny, 1947, Vol. XI (Warsaw, 1947), Table 2, p. 33 and Table 5, p. 37. (Hereafter cited as Rocznik Statystyczny, 1947.)

2. Glowny Urzad Statystyczny Polskiej Rzeczypospolitej Ludo-wej, Rocznik Statystyczny, 1970, Vol. XXX (Warsaw, 1970), Table 2, p. 21.

3. Ibid.

4. Ibid., Table 15, p. 40.

5. Ibid., Table 2, p. 21.

6. Joanna Kruczynska, et al., Polska Zachodnia i Polnocna (Poznan: Wydawnictwo Zachodnie, 1961); information obtained from Glowny Urzad Statystyczny.

7. Rocznik Statystyczny, 1970, Vol. XXX, op. cit., Table 5, p. 380.

8. Ibid.

9. Ibid., p. 42.

10. Ibid., p. 42.

11. Herbert Feis, Between War and Peace: The Potsdam Conference (Princeton, N.J.: Princeton University Press, 1960), p. 260.

12. Ibid., p. 338-54.

13. Polish Embassy Press Office, Poland, Germany and European Peace: Official Documents 1944-48 (London, 1948), pp. 115-16.

14. Jozef Poniatowski, "Rozmiary przeludnienia rolnictwa w swietle krytyki," Rolnictwo (Warsaw), Vol. IV (1939), p. 15.

15. Glowny Urzad Statystyczny Rzeczypospolitej Polskiej, Maly Rocznik Statystyczny, 1939, Vol. X (Warsaw, 1939), Table I, p. 68. (Hereafter cited as Maly Rocznik Statystyczny, 1939.)

16. Ibid., Table 25, p. 268; Rocznik Polityczny i Gospodarczy, 1936 (Warsaw: PAT, 1936), p. 611.

17. Of 272,540 industrial establishments, only 30,509 were in categories I-VII; the rest were actually cottage industry. See Maly Rocznik Statystyczny, 1939, Vol. X, op. cit., Table 3, p. 96.

18. Ibid., Table 17, p. 52.

19. Stanislaw Antoniewski, Opisy gospodarowania w gospodarst-wach karlowatych (Warsaw: Panstwowy Instytut Naukowy Gospodarstwa Wiejskiego, 1938).

20. Ferdynand Zweig, Poland Between Two Wars (London: Secker and Warburg, 1944), pp. 117-20.

21. Ibid., pp. 77-82.

22. Ibid., p. 123.

23. Ibid., pp. 129-35.

24. Ukraine: A Concise Encyclopaedia (Toronto: University of Toronto Press, 1963), pp. 833-50.

25. Panstwowe Wydawnictwo Ekonomiczne, The Economic Development (Warsaw, 1961), p. 26.

26. See Henryk Kopec, "Zjawiska demograficzne towarzyszace zmianom granic Polski," in Biuro Studiow Osadniczo-Przesiedlenczych, Sesja Rady Naukowej dla zagadnien Ziem Odzyskanych, Vol. II (Warsaw, 1936), p. 41.

27. See Leszek Kosinski, Pochodzenie terytoialne ludnosci Ziem Zachodnich w 1950 r. (Warsaw: Instytut Geografii PAN, 1960), p. 8.

28. S. Banasiak, Dzialalnosc osadnicza Panstwowego Urzedu Repatriacyjnego na Ziemiach Odzyskanych w latach 1945-1947 (Poznan: Instytut Zachodni, 1963), p. 118.

29. U.S. Bureau of the Census, The Population of Poland, Series P-90, No. 4 (Washington, D.C.: U.S. Government Printing Office, 1954), p. 34.

30. Ibid.

31. Kopec, op. cit., p. 48.

32. The natural growth and fertility pattern among the eastern Poles was the highest in prewar Poland. See Maly Rocznik Statystyczny 1939, Vol. X, op. cit., Table 11, p. 48.

33. Ministerstwo Obrony Narodowej, Fakty i zagadnienia polskie (London, 1944), p. 179.

34. Interview with the Deputy Minister of Public Administration, Wladyslaw Wolski, in Zycie Warszawy, November 20, 1945. He expected 400,000 returnees from inside the USSR.

35. Sesja Rady Naukowej dla zagadnien Ziem Odzyskanych, Vol. II (Warsaw, 1946), pp. 71-72.

36. Leszek Kosinski, Procesy ludnosciowe na Ziemiach Odzyskanych w latach 1945-1960 (Warsaw: Panstwowe Wydawnictwo Naukowe, 1963), p. 46.

37. Atlas Narodov Mira (Moscow: Akademia Nauk SSSR, 1964), p. 16.

38. Glowny Urzad Statystyczny Rzeczypospolitej Polskiej, Rocznik Statystyczny, 1950, Vol. XIV (Warsaw, 1951), Table 8, p. 22. (Hereafter cited as Rocznik Statystyczny, 1950.)

39. Eugeniusz Romer, Powszechny atlas geograficzny (Lvov: Ksiaznica Atlas, 1934), p. 56.

40. Maly Rocznik Statystyczny, 1939, Vol. X (Warsaw, 1939), Table 33, p. 38.

41. Dziennik Zwiazkowy (Chicago), July 13, 1971, p. 2.

42. Michael T. Florinsky, ed., Enclyclopaedia of Russia and the Soviet Union (New York: McGraw-Hill, 1961), pp. 81, 320.

43. Kultura (Paris), No. 6/285, 1971, p. 147.

44. Atlas Narodov Mira, op. cit.

45. Ibid., p. 268.

46. Kultura (Paris), No. 6/285, 1971.

47. Stanislaw Lam, ed., Podreczna encyklopedia powszechna (Paris: Ksiegarnia Polska, 1954), pp. 1030-31.

48. Adam Kruczek, "W sowieckiej prasie," Kultura (Paris) No. 6/285, 1971, p. 78.

49. Atlas Narodov Mira, op. cit., p. 17.

50. Wladyslaw Pobog-Malinowski, Najnowsza historia polityczna Polski 1864-1945 (London: B. Swiderski, 1960), pp. 322-23.

51. Ukraine: A Concise Encyclopedia, pp. 886-90.

52. Pobog-Malinowski, op. cit., II, p. 329; Ukraine: A Concise Encyclopaedia, op. cit., p. 889.

53. Banasiak, op. cit., p. 15.

54. Pobog-Malinowski, op. cit., II, pp. 325-29.

55. Kruczynska, et al., op. cit., p. 328; Glowny Urzad Statystyczny Rzeczypospolitej Polskiej, Rocznik Statystyczny, 1949, Vol. XIII (Warsaw, 1950), p. 26. (Hereafter cited as Rocznik Statystyczny, 1949.)

56. Banasiak, op. cit., p. 11.

57. Kosinski, Pochodzenie terytorialne . . . , op. cit., p. 46.

58. Rocznik Statystyczny, 1950, Vol. XIV, op. cit.

59. Panstwowe Wydawnictwo Ekonomiczne, XX lat Polski Ludowej (Warsaw, 1964), p. 60.

60. Jozef Zaremba, Atlas Ziem Odzyskanych, 2nd ed. (Warsaw: Glowny Urzad Planowania Przestrzennego, 1947), Map 8.

61. Poniatowski, op. cit.

62. Pawel Rybicki, "Mozliwosci zaludnienia Ziem Odzyskanych osadnikami polskimi w grupie zawodow pozarolniczych," in Biuro Studiow Osadniczo-Przesiedlenczych, Sesja Rady Naukowej dla Zagadnien Ziem Odzyskanych, Vol. I (Warsaw, 1946), pp. 1-53.

63. Kopec, op. cit., pp. 41-42.

64. M. Olechnowicz, "Rok osadnictwa na Ziemiach Odzyskanych," in Sesja Rady . . . , Vol. II, op. cit.

65. Maly Rocznik Statystyczny, 1939, Vol. X, op. cit., Tables 17-21, pp. 52-54.

66. Jozef Szaflarski, "Zagadnienie odplywu ludnosci w ciagu ostatniego wieku z Ziem Odzyskanych a nasza akcja osadnicza na tym terenie," in Sesja Rady . . . , Vol. II, op. cit., pp. 126-42.

67. Fr. Burgdorfer, Zuruck zum Agrarstaat? (Berlin: n.p., 1933) p. 31, as quoted in Junusz Ziolkowski, "Ludnosc Ziem Zachodnich," in Polskie Ziemie Zachodnie (Poznan: Instytut Zachodni, 1959), p. 124.

68. Maly Rocznik Statystyczny, 1939, Vol. X, op. cit.

69. Hans Fulster, Volk ohne Raum (Hamburger Kulturverlag GmbH, 1947); Seweryn Wyslouch, Studia nad koncentracja w rolnictwie slaskim (Wroclaw: Ossolineum, 1956).

70. Jozef Szaflarski, Ruchy ludnosciowe (Gdansk: Instytut Baltycki, 1947); Boleslaw Olszewicz, "Sprawa reemigracji ludnosci polskiej," in Sesja Rady . . . , Vol. II, op. cit.

71. Roman Bertisch, "Osadnictwo chlopow-reemigrantow na Slasku w latach 1946-1948," Kwartalnik Opolski, II (1956) pp. 80-104, III (1957), pp. 77-100.

72. Wladyslaw Markiewicz, Przeobrazenia swiadomosci narodowej reemigrantow polskich z Francji (Poznan: Wydawnictwo Poznanskie, 1960).

73. Ibid.

74. Bertisch, op. cit

75. Ibid.

76. Rocznik Polonii 1958-59, Vol. VII (London: Tarus, 1958).

77. Rocznik Statystyczny, 1950, Vol. XIV, op. cit., Table 7, p. 22; Mikolaj Latuch, "Wspolczesne migracje zewnetrzne ludnosci w Polsce," Zeszyty Naukowe SGPS (Warsaw, 1959), Table II, p. 189.

78. Olszewicz, op. cit.

79. Rocznik Polityczny i Gospodarczy, 1936, op. cit., pp. 1150-63; Olszewicz, op. cit.

80. Andrzej Kwilecki, "Liczeblnosc i rozmieszczenie grup mniejszosci narodowych na Ziemiach Zachodnich," Przeglad Zachodni, Vol. XX, No. 4 (1964), pp. 376-87.

81. Rocznik Statystyczny, 1949, Vol. XIII, op. cit., Table 9, p. 26.

82. Kwilecki, op. cit., pp. 376-87.

83. S. Waszak, "The Number of Germans in Poland in the Years 1931-1939 Against the Background of German Losses in World War II," Polish Western Affairs, Vol. I (1960), pp. 246-90.

84. Kwilecki, op. cit., pp. 376-87.

85. Andrzej Werblan, "O genezie konfliktu," Miesiecznik Literacki, June 1968.

86. Ibid.

87. Rocznik Statystyczny, 1950, Vol. XIV, op. cit., Table 7, p. 22.

88. Banasiak, op. cit; Kazimierz Zygulski, Repatrianci na Ziemiach Zachodnich (Poznan: Instytut Zachodni, 1962), p. 19.

89. S. Pietkiewicz and M. Orlicz, "Plan regionalny przesiedlenia osadnikow rolnych na Ziemie Odzyskane," in Sesja Rady. . . , Vol. I, op. cit., pp. 11-56.

90. Sesja Rady. . . , Vol. III, op. cit., pp. III, 7-97.

91. Ibid.

92. Kosinski, Pochodzenie terytorialne. . . , op. cit., p. 22.

93. Maly Rocznik Statystyczny, 1939, Vol. X, op. cit., Table 17, p. 23.

94. Teofil Lijewski, Rozwoj sieci Kolejowej Polski (Warsaw: Instytut Geograffi PAN, 1959).

95. Stefan Golachowski, "Pierwszy rok akcji przesiedlenczo-osadniczej na Slasku O polskim," Straznica Zachodnia, Vol. XV, Nos. 1-2 (1946), pp. 47-50.

96. Glowny Urzad Statystyczny Polskiej Rzeczypospolitej Ludowej, "Narodowy Spis Powszechny z dnia 3 grudnia 1950r. Miejsce zamieszkania, ludnosci w sierpniu 1939r." (Warsaw, 1955, mimeographed.)

97. Kosinski, Pochodzenie Terytorialne. . . , op. cit., p. 8.

98. Unpublished materials of the Rada Naukowa dla zagadnien Ziem Odzyskanych.

99. Eugeniusz Romer, Polacy na Kresach Pomorskich i Poje-ziernych (Lvov: Ksiaznica Polska Tow. Naucz. Szkol Wyzszych, 1919); Kopec, op. cit.

100. Paul Weber, Die Polen in Oberschiesien (Berlin: Verlag von Julius Springer, 1919).

101. Gustaw Gizewiusz, Die Polnische Sprachfrage in Preussen, 2nd ed. (Poznan: Instytut Zachodni, 1961).

102. Ibid.; Weber, op. cit.

103. Deutschland, Die Bavolkerung des Deutschen Reiches nach den Ezgebnissen der Volkzahlung, 1933, Statistik den Deutschen Reichs Berlin, 1936 v. 451-4, pp. 31, 44, 45 (data for 1939 were only published partially).

104. Gotthold Rhode, Die Ostgebiete des Deutschen Reiches, 2nd ed. (Wurzburg: Holzner-Verlag, 1955); Bruno Gleitze, Ostdeutsche Wirtschaft (Berlin: Duncker and Humbolt, 1956), Table 7, p. 152.

105. U. S. Bureau of the Census, op. cit., Table C-B, p. 184.

106. Romer, Polacy na Kresach. . . , op. cit.

107. Stefan Golachowski, Materialy do statystyki narodowosciowej Slaska Opolskiego (Poznan: Instytut Zachodni, 1950).

108. Ibid.

109. Bund Deutscher Osten, Landesgruppe Schlesien, "Landes-leitung Tgb.nr.geh. 450.07/38 Breslau, den Juni 1938. Geheim." This document reporting on the yearly Polish minority Mass held on May 21, 1938, was found after the war in the Gestapo files in Opole. Original copy is in the author's possession.

110. Kosinski, Pochodzenie terytorialne . . . , op. cit., p. 8.

111. Wojciech Wrzesinski, "Przyczynki do problemu wschodnio-pruskiego w czasie II wojny swiatowej," Komunikaty Mazursko-War-minskie, Vol. I (1965).

112. For the extent of the post-1955 migration abroad, see Rocznik Statystyczny, 1970, Vol. XXX, op. cit., Table 41, p. 58. The yearly average since 1959 has been about 23,000.

113. H. Koenigwald, Das Dritte Probleme (Dusseldorf: Hrsg. vom Arbeits and Socialminister des Landes Nordrhein Westfalen, 1957).

114. Ibid.; Stefan Nowakowski, Adaptacja ludnosci na Slasku Opolskim (Poznan: Instytut Zachodni, 1957).

115. Ibid.

116. Private correspondence from emigrants in possession of the author.

117. Koenigswald, op. cit.; unpublished letters from emigrants in possession of the author.

118. The Bulletin (Bonn), Vol. XIX, No. 18 (May 25, 1971).

119. Alicja Zawadzka-Wetz, "Nowa emigracja," Kultura (Paris), No. 5/284, 1971, pp. 109-15.

120. Kosinski, Pochodzenie terytorialne. . . , op. cit., pp. 9-12.

121. W. Doroszewski, Jezyk polski w Stanach Zjednoczonych A.P. (Warsaw: Nakladem Tow. Naukowego, 1938); Franciszek Lyra, "English and Polish in Contact," Doctoral dissertation, University of Indiana, Bloomington, Ind., 1962.

122. Wladyslaw Misiuna, "Osiagniecia i perspektywy rozwoju rolnictwa Ziem Zachodnich," in Rozwoj gospodarczy Ziem Zachodnich w dwudziestoleciu Polski Ludowej i jego perspektywy (Poznan: Instytut Zachodni, 1964), pp. 134-36.

123. Jozef Popkiewicz, Spoldzielczosc produkcyjna na przelomie (Wroclaw: Zaklad Narodowy im. Ossolinskich Wydawnictwo, 1959).

124. Stefan Nowakowski, ed., Socjologiczne problemy miasta polskiego (Warsaw: Panstwowe Wydawnictwo Naukowe, 1964), pp. 121-51.

125. Wladyslaw Englicht, Polskie Ziemie Zachodnie. Zagadnenia rolnicze. (Poznan: Wydawnictwo Zachodnie, 1959), p. 19.

126. Adam Jelonek, "Naturalny ruch ludnosci na Ziemiach

Zachodnich," in Studia nad zagadnieniami gospodarczymi i spolecznymi Ziem Zachodnich, Vol. I (Poznan: Instytut Zachodni), pp. 133-42.

127. Ibid.

128. Kruczynska, et al., op. cit., p. 335-57.

129. Rocznik Statystyczny, 1970, Vol. XXX, op. cit., Table 39, p. 57.

130. Kruczynska, et al., op. cit., p. 345; Adam Jelonek, "Zmiany w strukturze plci i wieku ludnosci w Polsce w latach 1946-1950," Przeglad Geograficzny, Vol. XXX, No. 3 (1958), pp. 436-59.

131. Jelonek, op. cit., pp. 133-42.

132. Adam Jelonek, "Zagadnienia struktury i wieku ludnosci Ziem Zachodnich," Studia nad zagadnieniami gospodarczymi i spoleczynymi Ziem Zachodnich, Vol. I (Poznan: Instytut Zachodni), pp. 120-31.

133. Kruczynska, et al., op. cit., pp. 335-57.

134. Jan Stanislaw Los, Warunki bytowania ludnosci polskiej na Ziemiach Odzyskanych (Lublin: KUL, 1947).

135. The 227 memoirs of the settlers in the archives of the Western Institute, Poznan.

136. Kruczynska, et al., op. cit., p. 344.

137. M. Opallo, "Zmiany w uprzemyslowieniu Ziem Zachodnich," Studia nad zagadnieniami gospodarczymi i spolecznymi Ziem Zachodnich, Vol. IV, pp. 50-51.

138. B. Ziolek, "Rozwoj demograficzny Ziem Zachodnich." Studia nad zagadnieniami gospodarczymi i spolecznymi Ziem Zachodnich, Vol. IV, p. 20.

139. P. Miedzinski, "Repatriacja do NRF w ramach akcji laczenia rodzin," Przeglad Zachodni, Vol. XIV, No. 2 (1958), pp. 311-29.

140. Kazimierz Zygulski, "Wyjazdy ludnosci woj katowickiego na zachod w latach 1955-1958," unpublished manuscript, Slaski Instytut Naukowy, Katowice, p. 80.

141. Latuch, op. cit.

142. Waszak, op. cit., pp. 246-90.

143. Latuch, op. cit., Table 15; Ziolek, op. cit., Table 14.

144. Rocznik Statystyczny, 1970, Vol. XXX, op. cit, Table 10, p. 37.

145. Ziolek, op. cit. p. 31.

146. Nowakowski, Socjologiczne problemy. . . , op. cit., pp. 121-51.

147. Ziolek, op. cit., Table 20.

148. Nowakowski, Socjologiczne problemy. . . , op. cit., pp. 121-51.

4

DEVELOPMENTAL PROCESSES AFFECTING THE ECONOMIC STRUCTURE OF THE ODER-NEISSE AREAS

GEOGRAPHIC PATTERNS AND NATURAL RESOURCES

The area assigned at Potsdam is a geographic extension of prewar Polish territories.[1] The present western territories of Poland lie almost entirely in the basins of two rivers, the Oder and the Vistula, that are practically coextensive with the territory of the state (88.1 percent of the country is within the drainage basins of these rivers). The Oder basin covers 34 percent of the country's territory, and the Vistula basin 54.1 percent. The Oder basin extends far into the prewar territory of Poland through its largest tributary, the Warta, and the Warta's tributary, the Notec. It is significant that two industrial areas of prewar Poland, the textile industry area of Lodz and the heavy industry area of the Upper Silesian basin, are both centrally located on the watershed of the Oder and Vistula.

In the present geographic shape of the country, such a location of two major industrial centers affords economic advantages in distributing resources and goods. However, it also creates problems because of the increasing need for water for industrial uses. From the hydrogeographical point of view, Poland in its present territory constitutes an almost perfect unit. The Oder and the port of Szczecin, especially, provide an excellent outlet for the Silesian industrial center, as manifested by the recent growth in the volume of cargo turnover in the port of Szczecin.[2]

Furthermore, the possibility of linking the Oder basin with that of the Danube, to service the Moravian industrial center in Czechoslovakia, is being studied. Thus, the inclusion of the entire Oder basin

in Poland offers economic possibilities for both Poland and Czechoslovakia.

The unity of the Oder-Neisse areas with the rest of the country
is further underlined by the following geographic facts:

1. The western watershed of the Oder basin lies only a few
miles to the west of the Oder-Neisse line.

2. The Oder, like most Central European rivers, receives
most of its tributaries from the east, thus facilitating commercial
traffic from that direction.

3. The boundary along the Oder-Neisse rivers is the shortest
possible frontier in that area, and it also separates two water basins,
that of the North Sea (Spree and Elbe) and that of the Baltic.

Thus, the frontier along these rivers has all the elements of a
stable and natural frontier. At present, it also divides two distinct
ethnic areas, unlike all other boundaries drawn in that part of Europe
since the Middle Ages.[3]

The present territory of Poland is favored with respect to the
distribution of the natural resources located southwest of the Warta,
Vistula, and San rivers generally along the Sudetes and the Carpathian
mountains and their foothills.[4] Water and rail lines provide relative
ease of distribution. The location of natural resources determines
to a great extent the location of industries, which are largely concentrated in the same area. Hence, the coast of the Baltic and the area
east of the Vistula (except for the estuaries of the Oder and the Vistula) are industrially underdeveloped and at present offer much less
opportunity for gainful employment. Furthermore, most of the industry in that less industrialized area was badly damaged or totally destroyed during the final offensive of World War II. This contributed
considerably to the slow pace of industrialization there immediately
after the war.

The destruction of industry and the severe damage to agriculture, on which the northern regions of the country depended before
World War II, crippled the economic life of the area, hampering and
delaying the postwar reconstruction of the economy. It also postponed
industrialization, which was proceeding in other regions of the country at a relatively fast pace.[5] The lack of natural resources in the
regions north and east of the Oder and Warta rivers predetermines
the type and size of industry there. However, there are strong

indications that there are large oil deposits to be found in the area, with a geological structure similar to the recently developed north German oil fields.[6] Small-scale drilling has yielded some success, and the first oil fields in the Polish lowlands were recently brought into production (for example, in 1965 about 10 percent of oil production came from new wells).

At present, the only centers of heavy industry in the north of the Oder-Neisse area are located in or near the cities of Szczecin and Gdansk. Apart from the light industry connected with fishing and the servicing of shipping, the area contains a food-processing industry that serves the agricultural and forestry economy of the area. The southern part of the Oder-Neisse area, unlike the northern part, is relatively well endowed with natural resources. This region consists primarily of Silesia, which can be compared with the two other leading industrial regions of Europe, the Ruhr and the Don basins. The old mountain range of the Sudetes and its foothills yield a large variety of minerals, including copper, zinc, lead, nickel, arsenic, barytes, pyrites, and caolin, and there are stone quarries and hard, soft, and brown coal.

Moreover, the plentiful supply of water in the basin of the Oder, whose tributaries come from the Sudetes mountains, has been conducive to the establishment of large and varied industrial establishments, such as metal and textile plants. Industry is dominant in the area's economy and is complemented by equally well-developed intensive agriculture and food-processing.

Hence, the land uses are different in the south of the Oder-Neisse area than in the north. Urbanization is more characteristic in the south, and the villages in the foothills of the Sudetes and along the Oder are to a large extent industrialized.[7] The dense net of towns, which serve not only for trading but also as small industrial centers, helps to create additional economic opportunities for the peasants, in strong contrast to the Pomeranian areas north of the Warta-Notec rivers and in general to other parts of Poland that are less urbanized and industrialized.

WARTIME DESTRUCTION AND THE PROBLEM OF RECONSTRUCTION WITHIN THE NEW FRONTIERS

Unfortunately, large parts of Silesia were extensively demolished during the winter offensive of 1945 and during the last few

months of the war. This destruction, the flight of the German population, the chaotic postwar conditions, and the migration of masses of
people destroyed the fabric of society and the previous economic
interrelations. Despite the wartime and postwar looting and destruction, Silesia rapidly regained its economic role as soon as the migrations had ceased and the complete changeover of the population had
taken place. Its well-developed economic structure and the richness
of its natural resources were responsible for its swift recovery.[8]

The influence of war destruction on economic recovery is best
illustrated in the Sudetes area, where there was virtually no war
damage and where industry in such areas as Jelenia Gora and the
Walbrzych area, was but slightly affected by the population changeover. The light industry (glass, metal, chemical) of Jelenia Gora
and the soft coal industry of Walbrzych worked without interruption
despite the population upheaval. However, the situation was
different in the countryside along the Oder, most of which was devastated or temporarily depressed by the population expulsion and
immigration.[9]

The communication pattern of the Oder-Neisse area as a whole
was almost totally destroyed during the war. In addition, the railroad,
highway, and canal systems were all centered on Berlin in the south
and northwest and on Kaliningrad in the northeast. Thus, apart from
the destruction caused by the war, these communications systems
were not best suited to serve the new administrative centers within
the territory of the new Poland.

Immediately following the war, the government had the task of
rebuilding the railroad tracks and highways that were destroyed
during the first month of 1945 when the front rolled through these
areas. Furthermore—and far more difficult since the national
economy was near total collapse—the existing communications network had to be modified to serve the state in its new borders. Thus,
it was necessary to divert many resources from rebuilding into
reorienting the main communication routes to serve the Polish
economy. This was especially true of the roads, which had to carry
the largest share of traffic until the rebuilding of the railroad, the
heart of the Polish communication pattern.

The difficulties encountered in road reorientation were twofold:

1. All the large east-west routes were badly damaged since
they had carried the war traffic of both the retreating German and
conquering Russian armies, and were subjected to heavy bombardment.
Also, they largely skirted the territory of post-1945 Poland.

2. The north-south roads were poorly developed because of the old border alignment, and often did not continue through the territory of prewar Poland.

Thus, disjointed segments of roads of different grades had to be fashioned into new arteries to serve the economic needs of Poland in its new boundaries.

The roads to be developed were those connecting the areas rich in mineral resources and industrially well-developed (such as Silesia and Little Poland) with the major ports of Szczecin and Gdansk, the capital of Warsaw, and the regions of Pomerania in the northwest and Mazuria in the north. In particular, there were few connections between Mazuria and Warsaw. Similarily, the Wroclaw and Great Poland regions were poorly linked with Szczecin; for example, the western Polish city of Poznan was connected to Szczecin by a one-track railroad while Wroclaw was linked to Szczecin by a relatively poor road. Almost all bridges in the country had been destroyed, thus paralyzing traffic on most of the rail lines. Priorities were established, and the lines most vital to the economy of the country were the first to be rebuilt.

The enormity of the problem of reorienting the existing railroad system can be best illustrated by two examples: the changed roles of the port of Szczecin and the Olsztyn area.

Before the war, the port of Szczecin primarily served Berlin and directions west. (It was connected to Berlin by a railroad— one of the oldest in the present territory of Poland—and by an inland ship canal and an expressway.) Szczecin, Poland's westernmost port and ideally located on a river connecting it with almost half of Poland's postwar territory, was best equipped to serve as Poland's main export and transit port and long-range fishing base. Its changed role is apparent in the port statistics for the selected years 1913, 1938, 1946, and 1969 (see Table 14).[10] In its new role, the port surpassed its prewar peak transshipment figures by 80 percent and became the largest port on the Baltic (in 1968, Szczecin handled 42.8 percent of Polish sea freight, and it is approaching 15 million tons annually).

To link the port of Szczecin properly with its "new" hinterland, several one-track railroad lines were doubled and a new major highway was made from secondary roads in order to connect Szczecin with Silesia (previously, the major highway connection between Szczecin and Silesia had run along the western bank of the Oder). In order to serve the bulk and coal export of the new primary hinterland, an entirely new railroad marshalling yard was built east of the city

TABLE 14

Tonnage Loaded and Unloaded at Merchant Seaports, Selected
Years, 1949-69
(thousands of tons)

Port Commodity group	1949	1955	1960	1965	1968	1969
Total	16,907*	17,066	21,864	26,588	32,349	32,856
By port						
Gdansk	6,367	5,244	5,914	6,318	8,628	9,003
Gdynia	5,680	5,050	7,063	8,603	9,685	9,233
Szczecin	4,470	6,772	8,818	11,499	13,855	14,473
Kolobrzeg	390*	0	69	168	181	147
By commodity group						
Coal and coke	11,019	8,044	8,436	8,488	13,852	14,407
Ores	1,621	2,119	3,608	3,148	2,813	2,677
Cereals	830	1,046	2,196	3,057	1,842	1,138
Wood	329	506	677	895	812	609
Other bulk cargo	588	1,917	2,794	5,106	5,924	7,265
General cargo	1,638	3,434	4,153	5,894	7,106	6,760

*Including transshipment in Ustka, Darlowo, which were merchant ports in 1949.

Source: Concise Statistical Yearbook of Poland, 1970, Vol. XII (Warsaw: Central Statistical Office, 1970), Table 15, p. 199.

(previously, connections entered the city from the west and the trains had had to be backed up to serve the port). The huge new marshalling yard was constructed on the marshy land next to the port; it was the major building achievement of postwar construction in the area.

The changes in the communication pattern necessitated by the postwar boundary drawing were also shown by the peculiar position of Olsztyn area. Virtually all roads and railroads in the area were designed to center on two cities, Elblag and Kaliningrad. Because of economic and geographic resources, in the postwar administrative division, Elblag was allocated to the voivodship of Gdansk and Kaliningrad was alloted to the Soviet Union. Hence, the area of former East Prussia was bisected by an international border.

The new administrative unit, the voivodship of Olsztyn, had to become the new focal point of communication in the region. Thus, several roads had to be improved to higher-grade highways and made to converge on Gdansk, Olsztyn, and Warsaw, rather than on Elblag and Kaliningrad. On the other hand, the railroad network of the part of East Prussia that was assigned to Poland was too dense in the new economic-political configuration. Several of the branches either were not repaired or were dismantled, and the rails were used for rebuilding other more important lines. On some lines, the second track was removed.

Dismantling of second tracks or less important railroads by the Soviet army was especially common in the immediate postwar period. Whereas dismantling affected the economy of that particular area only marginally, such activity on major lines had more drastic economic effects. Rails were used for rebuilding Soviet home lines.[11] As a result, Polish authorities had to rebuild some of the dismantled lines after the Oder-Neisse areas were assigned to Poland. This increased the reconstruction burden of the postwar period, which lasted through early 1950.[12] After the main arteries had been rebuilt and the capacity of some lines—those that were to serve the territory of Poland in its new geographical position—had been improved or enlarged, the flow of traffic changed radically from that of the prewar days. Thus, some roads and railroads were overburdened while others were underutilized or nearly idle.

THE NEW PATTERN OF COMMUNICATIONS AND TRADE

The new pattern of communications and traffic volume was drastically different from that of 1939. This was caused not only

by the simultanous shift of both the east and the west frontiers but,
to a much greater degree, by the complete change in the economic
and political relations of contemporary Poland with its powerful
eastern neighbor.

The foreign trade between Poland and the Soviet Union had been
negligible during the period between the wars (see Table 15). Because
the political situation demanded that the Polish economy rely less on
Germany, the share of Polish imports from Germany was cut from
about 33 percent in 1928 to about 20 percent in 1934. Thus, the bulk
of Poland's prewar foreign trade was channeled through the ports of
Gdynia and Gdansk; in 1937, 77.9 percent and in 1938, 77.7 percent
of Poland's foreign trade passed through these ports.[13]

The prewar pattern of trade (75 percent by sea and 25 percent
by land) was mainly due to the temporary (in view of historical
economic development) closing of the east-west trading routes. In
the west, politics motivated a trade war between Poland and Germany;
in the east, animosity toward Communism caused complete cessation
of all contacts with Russia. The trade pattern was radically altered
when land contacts with the east were reopened and by the progressive
integration of the Polish economy within the Bloc (see Table 16).
The distribution of trade is now about 57.5 percent by land and 42.5
percent by sea.

TABLE 15

Polish Foreign Trade with USSR Before World War II

| Year | Percent of Polish | |
	Import	Export
1928	1.0	1.5
1934	2.0	2.5
1935	1.5	1.0
1936	1.5	1.0
1937	1.0	0.5

Source: Glowny Urzad Statystyczny Rzeczypospolitej Polskiej,
Maly Rocznik Statystyczny, 1939, Vol. X (Warsaw, 1939), Table 7,
pp. 166-67.

TABLE 16

Foreign Trade Turnover by Country Groups, Selected Years, 1950-69
(at current prices, in millions of exchange zlotys)

	1950	1955	1960	1965	1968	1969
Turnover						
Total	5,210	7,406	11,282	18,272	22,843	25,405
Socialist countries[a]	3,076	4,734	7,119	11,824	14,866	16,710
CMEA[b]	3,043	4,391	6,388	11,055	14,036	15,853
Other countries	2,134	2,672	4,163	6,448	7,977	8,695
Developed countries[c]	1,963	2,108	3,357	4,852	6,426	6,932
EEC[d]	549	610	1,111	1,703	2,570	2,749
EFTA[e]	1,178	1,102	1,371	1,933	2,520	2,648
Developing countries[f]	171	564	806	1,596	1,551	1,763
Imports						
Total	2,673	3,727	5,980	9,361	11,412	12,839
Socialist countries[a]	1,633	2,420	3,798	6,190	7,352	8,454
CMEA[b]	1,625	2,263	3,474	5,775	6,994	8,075
Other countries	1,040	1,307	2,182	3,171	4,060	4,385
Developed countries[c]	955	988	1,775	2,295	3,301	3,568
EEC[d]	319	376	587	882	1,436	1,504
EFTA[e]	563	504	654	888	1,330	1,422
Developing countries[f]	85	319	407	876	759	817
Exports						
Total	2,537	3,679	5,302	8,911	11,431	12,566
Socialist countries[a]	1,443	2,314	3,321	5,634	7,514	8,256
CMEA[b]	1,418	2,128	2,914	5,280	7,042	7,778
Other countries	1,094	1,365	1,981	3,277	3,917	4,310
Developed countries[c]	1,008	1,120	1,582	2,557	3,125	3,364
EEC[d]	230	234	524	881	1,134	1,245
EFTA[e]	615	598	717	1,045	1,190	1,226
Developing countries[f]	86	245	399	720	792	946

[a]Albania, Bulgaria, the Chinese People's Republic, Czechoslovakia, the Vietnam Democratic Republic, Yugoslavia, the Korean People's Democratic Republic, Hungary, and the USSR.
[b]Members of the Council of Economic Mutual Assistance: Albania, Bulgaria, Czechoslovakia, Mongolia, the German Democratic Republic, Rumania, Hungary, and the USSR.
[c]Capitalist countries of Europe as well as Japan, Republic of South Africa, United States, Canada, Australia, and New Zealand.
[d]Members of the European Economic Community: Belgium, France, the Netherlands, Luxemburg, West Germany, and Italy.
[e]Members of the European Free Trade Association: Austria, Denmark, Norway, Portugal, Switzerland, Sweden, and Great Britain.
[f]Countries of Asia, Africa, South and Central America, and Oceania, excluding countries mentioned in a and c.

Source: Concise Statistical Yearbook of Poland 1970, Vol. XII (Warsaw: Central Statistical Office, 1970), Table 7, p. 223.

These factors partially explain why the volume of Polish sea
trade expanded only moderately in the immediate postwar period
(1938, 16.3 million tons; 1949, 16.9 million tons; 1960, 21.9 million
tons, and 1969, 32.9 million tons).14 Only considerable expansion in
the total volume of exports and imports of the rapidly industrializing
country allowed for the recent increase in the volume of trade carried
by the sea (see Tables 17-20). Apart from the traditional coal exports,
manufactured goods were rapidly increasing. Furthermore, the
Polish economy's heavy dependence on the import of raw materials—
i.e., iron ore and oil, which were supplied by Sweden and Rumania
by sea before 1939 and are currently imported from the USSR—also
increased the volume of land transport from the Soviet Union.* It
has been authoritatively stated that the two transshipment railroad
stations on the eastern border, Malaszewicze near Brest and Medyka
near Przemysl,** carry as much traffic yearly as all the Polish
ports, i.e., 33 million tons.15

The annexation of the Oder-Neisse territory greatly supplemented and improved the state of the Polish communications network.
The Oder-Neisse regions have a dense communications network that
serves the industrial southwest and the coastal region of the new
Poland, and the trade patterns of both are structurally interconnected.16
Thus, a task of primary importance was the prompt rebuilding of
communication lines vital to the economy and the integration of the
acquired system of communications into one network within the new
frontiers. This task has been completed, although a few railroads
designed to link both systems are yet to be built (these lines include
the Warsaw-Mazurian Lakes, Olsztyn province-Central Poland, and
the missing link in the Wroclaw-Lodz-Warsaw line).

Construction has been delayed by costs, the pressure of the
reconstruction task in existing communication lines, and the availabil-
ity of alternative routes that could be utilized but that were indirect
and expensive in terms of fuel and time. Poland's railroads are
becoming electrified, and the plan is to build the missing Wroclaw-
Lodz connection during the electrification of the existing segments
of the line between these two cities, in the early 1970's. On the other

---

*Since 1964, pipelines have begun to carry some of the oil.

**These transshipment stations are necessitated by the differ-
ence of railroad gauge in Poland and the USSR; the gauge is 4 feet $8\frac{1}{2}$
inches in Poland and 5 feet in the Soviet Union.

TABLE 17

Freight Transport by Sea, Selected Years, 1955-69
(thousands of tons)

	Total	Of Which			
		Gdansk	Gdynia	Szczecin	Kolobrzeg
Import					
1955	5,764	1,813	1,476	2,475	0
1960	9,991	2,514	3,363	4,114	0
1965	11,275	2,086	4,326	4,798	38
1968	10,172	2,178	3,562	4,425	7
1969	10,004	2,068	3,655	4,272	9
Export					
1955*	10,059	3,326	3,106	3,627	0
1960*	11,006	3,295	3,355	4,287	69
1965	14,992	4,165	4,154	6,564	109
1968	21,671	6,382	5,955	9,194	140
1969	22,283	6,857	5,417	9,899	110

Note: Figures include transit freight.

*Excluding bunker, i.e., solid and liquid fuel for ship propulsion.

Source: Concise Statistical Yearbook of Poland, 1970 Vol. XII (Warsaw: Central Statistical Office, 1970), Table 16, p. 199.

TABLE 18

Polish Merchant Fleet, Selected Years, 1955-69
(as of December 31)

| | | | | Ships | | | | |
| | | | | | In Terms of GRT | | | |
	Total	Motor	Steam	up to 500	501- 2,000	2,001- 5,000	5,001- 10,000	Over 10,000
Number of Ships								
1955	83	40	43	6	27	29	20	1
1960	138	85	53	14	28	41	52	3
1965	196	143	53	24	29	51	81	11
1968	237	196	41	24	29	72	83	29
1969	250	210	40	24	30	78	89	29
Tonnage in Gross Registered Tons								
1955	288,203	130,541	157,662	2,927	36,756	95,102	139,131	14,287
1960	578,538	361,315	217,223	6,779	36,933	131,879	362,544	40,403
1965	885,632	642,891	242,741	11,766	36,971	162,386	544,348	130,161
1968	1,191,182	1,005,189	185,993	11,766	38,377	223,658	547,258	370,123
1969	1,261,193	1,077,034	184,159	11,766	38,317	244,448	595,082	371,580
Deadweight in Deadweight Tons								
1955	500,566	176,055	224,511	3,894	49,932	140,653	200,479	5,608
1960	824,060	517,545	306,515	9,771	51,162	188,541	536,210	38,376
1965	1,269,662	929,892	339,770	17,261	47,833	233,350	805,087	166,131
1968	1,722,837	1,476,919	245,918	17,499	51,918	323,603	826,463	503,354
1969	1,843,173	1,600,319	242,854	17,499	51,114	353,662	896,652	524,246

Source: Concise Statistical Yearbook of Poland, 1970, Vol. XII (Warsaw, Central Statistical Office, 1970), Table 12, p. 197.

TABLE 19

Import and Export Composition by Commodity
Groups Selected Years, 1950-69
(at current prices, in exchange zlotys)

Specification	Percentage of Total Imports or Exports						
	1950	1955	1960	1965	1968	1969
Imports						
Machinery and equipment	32.4	30.9	27.1	32.8	35.9	36.9
Fuels, materials, and raw materials	53.1	51.7	51.5	47.3	47.1	47.0
Agricultural products and foodstuffs	11.2	13.1	16.0	13.2	11.3	10.4
Consumer goods of industrial origin	3.3	4.3	5.4	6.7	5.7	5.7
	100.0	100.0	100.0	100.0	100.0	100.0
Exports						
Machinery and equipment	7.8	13.1	28.0	34.4	37.0	39.2
Fuels, materials, and raw materials	56.0	64.4	43.8	35.1	33.1	33.0
Agricultural products and foodstuffs	24.0	15.3	18.1	18.2	14.0	12.1
Consumer goods of industrial origin	12.2	7.2	10.1	12.3	15.9	15.7
	100.0	100.0	100.0	100.0	100.0	100.0

Source: Concise Statistical Yearbook of Poland 1970, Vol. XII (Warsaw: Central Statistical Office 1970), Table 4, p. 220.

TABLE 20

Volume Indexes of Foreign Trade by Commodity Group,
Selected Years, 1950-69
(at constant prices, in exchange zlotys)

Specification	1950	1955	1960=100 1960	1965	1968	1969
Turnover	50	63	100	164	213	236
Imports						
Machinery and equipment	44	61	100	160	201	226
Fuels, materials, and raw materials	53	71	100	186	240	281
Agricultural products and foodstuffs	46	61	100	149	199	221
Consumer goods of industrial origin	26	46	100	134	133	139
	29	49	100	208	227	257
Exports						
Machinery and equipment	57	65	100	169	227	247
Fuels, materials, and raw materials	13	32	100	210	283	330
Agricultural products and foodstuffs	85	95	100	138	180	195
Consumer goods of industrial origin	60	57	100	156	167	146
	49	43	100	219	388	422

Source: Concise Statistical Yearbook of Poland 1970, Vol. XII (Warsaw: Central Statistical Office, 1970), Table 3, p. 220.

hand, the rapid introduction of motorcycles and cars to Poland (54,000 in 1938, about 2.7 million in 1969)[17] made it necessary to allocate a larger share of communication investments into rebuilding of roads and the construction of new much-needed connections between the center of the country and the coast.[18]

It is a concomitant of the new economic and political situation of the Oder-Neisse territories that many old and much-traveled routes—such as those to points that are now within East Germany or the Kaliningrad region of the USSR—have lost their importance and serve only local traffic. The only exceptions are the supply trains of the Soviet army in Germany, which use the Kaliningrad-Berlin route extensively. The best example of the shift in use of transport routes is the Silesian Expressway, which connects Silesia with Berlin (it was built shortly before World War II and is only now being completed in Upper Silesia). The expressway segment between Wroclaw and the Polish-German border on the Neisse is falling into disuse except for light local traffic. On the other hand, the Polish government is planning to construct a super-highway between Silesia and Warsaw and the Baltic coast, following the direction vital to the national economy.

The canal connections in the area were originally constructed to serve the previous political unit, the Prussian state. The Oder and Vistula basins are connected in their lower reaches by the Bydgoszcz Canal, which was built by Prussia after the first partition of Poland. At that time, all of Pomerania was included in Prussia and the canal was designed primarily to connect East Prussia with Berlin and Brandenburg, then the center of the Prussian state. This canal allows traffic to move from the Vistula to the Oder and the port of Szczecin. At present, a much more essential connection is being planned in the upper reaches of both rivers to link Upper Silesia with Cracow. This canal is necessary to connect two areas of primary economic importance. It would facilitate the movement of raw materials and improve the distribution of finished goods. The upper reaches of the Oder and the Vistula, along which most of Poland's mineral wealth and processing plants are found, would be best served by such a canal. It also would lighten the load of the railroads, which must now carry most goods between Upper Silesia and Cracow. The construction of that canal is necessary for the easy flow of traffic within Poland's present borders. Two other canals are on the drawing boards, one connecting the Oder and the Danube through Czechoslovakia and the other linking Upper Silesia with the lower reaches of the Vistula.

The communications pattern of the western territories has now been integrated with that of the rest of Poland and serves the country in its new frontiers. The road system is adequately connected with that of central Poland, but it is in this region that the major investments must be made. Only a few segments connecting the two prewar railroad systems remain to be built.

The fact that the Oder-Neisse territories are part of the same hydrographic system as the rest of Poland is a most important factor in the current communication pattern of the area: the road and railroad systems were basically developed to serve the economics of former states and they must be adjusted accordingly. The natural condition of the interconnecting river basins of the Oder and the Vistula facilitated the tribal settlement of the area by one ethnic group, and now once again it has been included in one state organism and serves as the strong force unifying the country. Once the canal linking the upper reaches of the two basins has been built, the river transportation pattern will serve the present territory of Poland fully and adequately.

At present, the part of contemporary Poland that was Polish before 1939 requires much greater investments in all three systems: road, railroad, and canal. The difference in the density of the transportation network lies not along the 1939 Polish western border—i.e., between the Oder-Neisse territories and the rest of contemporary Poland—but primarily along the former (1914) border partitioning Poland into German and Russian holdings. The transportation network in the territories that were then part of the Russian Empire was barely developed and sorely inadequate. Even in the late 1960's, despite over fifty years of transportation investment in the eastern part of contemporary Poland (interrupted and set back by World War II), the density of the transportation network in some areas was almost three times less than in the advanced western areas.[19]

This situation explains the recent distribution of communication investment (except for rebuilding of war destruction). Much more is being allocated for this purpose in eastern Poland than in the western territories in order to alleviate the differences in density and quality of communication facilities in both parts of the country, differences easily perceived even by an untrained observer. The rapid motorization of the country, proceeding along the Italian pattern of the 1950's— i.e., stress on motorcycles to be followed by small family cars—is generating increased construction of new hard-surfaced roads and the improvement of existing ones. Thus, during the interwar period of the Second Republic 17,572 kilometers of hard-surfaced roads were constructed, mostly in the underinvested eastern part of the country,[20] and a similar rate was maintained after 1945.

At this pace, the road network will be adequately distributed across the country by the end of the 1970's. However, the emphasis on motorization will diminish the role of the railroads as the heart of the transporation system. Thus, it will be necessary to phase out several uneconomic railroad branches in the western part of Poland. This process, which can now be observed in England and West Germany (which are each closing 25 percent of their railroads), and the progressive building of new and necessary lines in the east, will equalize the railroad network across the country.[21] However, the present emphasis is primarily on the electrification of railroads. Already, a basic structure of uniformly developed electric lines connects the largest urban and industrial centers of Poland (Warsaw, Lodz, Cracow, Upper Silesia, Gdansk, Wroclaw, Lublin, and Poznan).[22]

Although there is a well-developed system of local and through roads, on the major routes road transport can only supplement the railroads. On local routes only, trucks can force the suspension of railroad branch lines where the load factor and volume of passenger traffic make road transport more profitable. Some lines are already being abandoned in the Poznan region, but the need for similar action in the western territories is not pressing since some branch lines there were never rebuilt after World War II. The general tendency to substitute road transport for traffic on branch railroads is prevailing. The branch lines in the west will be progressively closed, and such branch lines will never be built in the east, where only main lines exist (a heritage of the restrictive Tsarist policy of building railroads only on main strategic lines, whereas railroad-building in Western Europe and in western Poland, then under Prussian rule, included branches.[23]

Since the boundary between well-developed and under-developed railroad systems ran through Poland along the former Russian-Prussian partition border, the problem of integrating those two systems was difficult. After 1918, the Polish state had to link both systems and construct badly needed lines in the east. After twenty years of Polish rule, the integration of the systems was nearly adequate. However, the destruction resulting from World War II and the need to unify the railroad system again within the new borders made for a much more difficult task. This situation presented an enormous challenge to the newly established Communist administration of Poland, which on the whole has been successful in completing the task.

INDUSTRY

Although the Polish western territories generally are not heavily industrialized by Western European standards, Upper Silesia is one of the three largest industrial basins in Europe. However, the heavily industrialized areas are small in size and do not affect the basically agricultural character of the territories as a whole. The industry is located primarily in Silesia and a few large cities in the north, such as Szczecin, Gorzow, Slupsk, Gdansk, and Elblag. The fact that the concentration of industry in the area is spotty underlines the uneven economic development of these regions. The process of industrialization in the northern districts was hampered by the competitive price structure of goods produced in Silesia and other parts of Germany, as well as by the unevenly distributed resource base.

Heavy industry in the northern districts consisted only of medium-sized plants serving maritime needs and shipyards in the coastal cities.[24] Industry in the inland cities was based mainly on forest and agricultural produce.[25] The exception to the rule was the Szczecin iron foundry, established to take advantage of that city's port facilities, abundant water supply, and favorable location in the estuary of the Oder river, halfway between the Swedish ore and the Silesian coal deposits. The other center of heavy machine industry, in Elblag, was developed in the nineteenth century after its usefulness as a port located deep inside the Vistula Lagoon was nullified by the development of deep-draught streamers unable to negotiate shallow waters. Advantage was taken of the existing facilities to develop large-scale machine and locomotive factories in Elblag, to utilize the long ship-building tradition.

Apart from shipyards in Gdansk and Szczecin (cities that developed into large centers of machine industry), industry in the "northern tier" of counties is purely local and small-scale, serving the needs of the surrounding market; agriculture is the mainstay of the area economy. The small scale of operation was another characteristic of the industrial structure of the area before the war. Thus, there were small industrial firms in nearly all towns, but they were rather underinvested, ill-equipped, and relatively backward. Such firms, which accounted for a disproportionately large share of industry,[26] were essentially one-family operations geared to the scale of the local market and relying mainly on local natural resources. These firms were naturally ill-equipped to withstand competition from West German and Silesian concerns. Hence, there was relatively little industrial growth in those regions after the end of the nineteenth century.

Except in the large cities, industrial growth was virtually arrested.[27] The relative weakness of the manufacturing industry, its peculiar structural deficiencies, and the lack of an adequate resource base for manufacturing were the determining factors in the slow postwar economic recovery of the area. The heavy war destruction, the postwar looting of ownerless property in the chaotic conditions following the first wave of expulsions of Germans, and the Soviet army's removal of industrial equipment to the USSR all contributed to a much greater weakening of the industrial strength of the northern area as compared with that of Silesia.[28]

The prewar industrial structure of Silesia was far more well balanced and developed. However, the industrial development of that province also was uneven. The most developed parts of Silesia are concentrated around the coal and ore deposits in Upper Silesia and the foothills, rich in resources, of the geologically old mountain range of the Sudetes. The Upper Silesian triangle and the Walbrzych region are mainly coal-producing areas. In Upper Silesia, an extensive steel industry was developed after the discovery of coal deposits toward the end of the eighteenth century. The industry in the foothills of the Sudetes is much older. Mining activity (gold and iron ore) was recorded there in the eleventh century. The plentiful supply of water and the location of the Sudetes foothills on one of the main medieval routes linking Western and Eastern Europe caused the fast development of the textile industry. A glass industry was located in the area of Jelenia Gora and Boleslawiec, where there are deposits of the sand and clay needed in glass production.

Thus, the foothills of the Sudetes had a well-developed industry before the advent of the eighteenth century Industrial Revolution. In the following years, manufacturing industry sprang up in almost all the major cities of the province. Large-scale machine-producing factories were established in all the cities of Upper Silesia, Wroclaw (the capital of Lower Silesia), Legnica, Zielona Gora, Nowa Sol, Zagan, and other large cities in the province. The Oder River allowed fast transportation of goods and raw materials. The rich soil on the left bank of the Oder made possible the development of a food industry based on produce, and light industry served the needs of agriculture.

The relative strength of Silesian industry in relation to that of the northern parts of the Oder-Neisse territories can best be illustrated by the prewar distribution of persons gainfully employed in industry. In the Oder-Neisse areas, some 57 percent of such persons worked in Silesia, 24 percent in Pomerania and East Brandenburg, and 19 percent in East Prussia (including the part of East Prussia that was assigned to the USSR in 1945). Even if the sizable industry in and around Kaliningrad is excluded, over 60 percent of all persons in the northern Oder-Neisse area who were gainfully employed in industry were employed in Silesia. If we make the necessary corrections for the labor-intensive industries in the north (i.e., shipyards, small machine and work shops, and agricultural produce industry), the Silesian share of industry is even greater. Thus, the Oder-Neisse area as a whole was mainly agricultural; only small parts were highly urbanized and industrialized.

Nevertheless, the Oder-Neisse industry approximately equalled industry in the weak economy of prewar Poland.[29] Hence, although German sources considered these territories to be "mainly agricultural,"* for the Poles they were a very valuable addition to the Polish economy. They allowed postwar Poland to accelerate the rebuilding of its economy and provided adequate employment for landless peasants and transferees from the east. In comparing prewar and current industrial output data for the Oder-Neisse territories, one confronts difficulties, since these areas did not constitute a separate unit within Germany. Similarly, Poland administered the Oder-Neisse areas separately from the rest of the country until 1949. Furthermore, the statistics are not always comparable either for territory covered or for industries considered.

Prewar statistics compiled for eastern Germany (i.e., in general the territories east of the Oder-Neisse) almost always include the data for the Kaliningrad region, which was assigned to the USSR at Potsdam. The Kaliningrad region had a strong industrial nucleus in the city of Kaliningrad; the surrounding countryside was agricultural, but well-developed forestry yielded timber for domestic use and export. In considering comparative statistics for the Oder-Neisse territories, one must try to exclude the data for Kaliningrad. In the postwar period through 1949, data for "the recovered territories"

---

*This is best seen from the share of the industrial output of the Oder-Neisse territories in the German economy of 1937. Thus, whereas those territories then contained 21.3 percent of Germany's territory and 11.4 percent of its population, they produced only 6 percent of its industrial goods.

were compiled separately. Since 1950, when the internal territorial division took place, no data for the Oder-Neisse region as a whole have been readily available. However, the data for the seven northern and western provinces (voivodships) closely approximate those for the region as a whole in population, area, and agricultural production.

The industrial data for the area must still be approximated, since the western part of the heavily industrialized Upper Silesian basin (which was German before 1939) has now been incorporated into Katowice province, which is largely composed of the area that was Polish before the war. Thus, the western Upper Silesian industrial complex is not included in the western territories. In addition, elaborate statistical manipulation is necessary in order to compare prewar industrial output with that of the postwar period. Two factors have contributed to these difficulties. First, the prewar German census of nonagricultural employment as of May 17, 1939, did not differentiate between industry and handicrafts, thereby complicating any comparison of pre- and postwar industry. Second, the revolutionary transformation of the Polish economy, from capitalist to Communist ownership of production, not only changed the basic structure of industry but also severely restricted the postwar reconstruction of handicrafts.

HANDICRAFTS: THEIR ROLE IN REBUILDING

The handicrafts in the newly settled territories suffered an especially adverse affect as a result of the public ownership of production. Handicrafts provided a large segment of the new work force with a means of livelihood requiring little capital and thus acted as a powerful stabilizing factor in the new society. Under postwar conditions, handicrafts were the economic backbone of small towns with populations under 5,000, (such towns constituted 48.1 percent of all towns in the Oder-Neisse area). During World War II, a large part of the industry located in small towns was either merged to form larger plants, destroyed in battle, dismantled as reparations by the Soviet army after the war, or simply looted and abandoned. Thus, handicrafts had to sustain the economic life of small towns to a much larger extent than before the war.

In a subsequent wave of reorganizations directed by the Polish authorities, parts were taken from small workshops to make possible the swift rebuilding of large industrial plants whose mechanical equipment had been destroyed or removed by the Russians. The rapid rebuilding of the remaining slightly damaged workshops and industrial enterprises was accomplished by private enterprise. But on December 31, 1947, handicraft workshops in the western territories numbered only 31,723, compared to 130,000 before the wartime destructions, with total employment of 54,583. Future growth was checked by the forcible nationalization of handicraft enterprises after 1949 and by specially devised taxation that forced them out of business. Thus, by 1955 only 16,295 handicraft enterprises remained, with 22,168 employees.[30]

By December 1957, after the restrictions had been partially reversed, there were as many private handicraft enterprises as in 1947, although they employed fewer persons (31,555 shops and 41,555 employees).[31] The cooperative handicraft enterprises supplemented those figures, making the recovery from the Stalinist period nearly complete. However, despite the physical recovery of handicrafts, there are much deeper psychological effects.

The shifting attitudes of the government have greatly undermined the popular enthusiasm with which the Polish nation participated in the rebuilding of the western territories as its main national and patriotic task. The losses are difficult to assess, but the Communists' repression of the enthusiasm that permeated every civic and economic project may have set back the process of achieving social stability for many years after World War II. It wasted initiative and social energy that, if properly channeled, could have contributed greatly to a faster recovery of the economy and society from the effects of World War II.

This rather lengthy analysis of the situation of handicrafts in the area was prompted not only by their relative position in the prewar economy but also as a way of illustrating the positive role of enterprise in postwar rebuilding and the negative role of government enforcement of the new economic model through a purely mechanical and doctrinaire approach to the socioeconomic problems. However, the unnecessary—and, in the final analysis, detrimental to the economy—treatment of handicrafts in the economic model of postwar Poland should not divert our attention from the fact that the government did put all available resources into the task of rebuilding basic industry in the Oder-Neisse areas.

Sudden and drastic restriction of private enterprise had a generally negative influence on the supply of services and hence on the nation's economy. However, in the western territories the sudden changeover to a new economic model caused nearly disastrous

damage to the economic life of the region. Near economic breakdown
in small towns was the net effect of the reduction of handicraft establishments on the not yet stabilized society. The changes were imposed
on a society that was experiencing simultaneously: (1) economic
reconstruction and rebuilding, (2) large-scale migrations, and (3)
the changeover of ownership of means of production from German to
Polish.

Thus, the reversal of stated policies of mixed economy produced
a dangerous deterioration of services in the provinces as well as an
exodus of population from small towns to cities, since under the new
policy cities received added attention and priority in economic development as basic centers of industry. The disastrous effect of the
cutback in handicrafts is now freely admitted by Polish writers.[32]
The limitation imposed on private initiative in those towns, before
the economic structure was completely rebuilt, has resulted in a
large-scale migration from small towns to large cities and the virtual
stagnation of economic life in small towns.[33]

This effect was intensified by the reorganization of the distributive pattern of internal trade according to Communist economic
theories. Towns that traditionally had existed as trading intermedi-
aries between the villages and the cities were severely crippled by
the new distributive system, whereby fully developed trade outlets
were set up directly in the villages through the agricultural cooperative "Samopomoc Chlopska." The virtual monopoly of trade established
through that system, which bypassed small towns, largely limited
the village-town trade interchange and caused the outflow of traders
to other professions in the large cities.

Thus, the imposition of limitations on handicrafts along with
the transfer to villages of many of the trading functions of small
towns caused strong outward migratory movements, consequent
underpopulation, and the slow decay of unused buildings, business
places, and workshops, from which the machines were removed to
rebuild or create larger plants. The effects of that catastrophic
development on the economy and the role of small towns in Poland
have not been entirely remedied, despite the partial reversal of
economic policies after 1956. Years later, efforts were made to
check the physical deterioration of small towns and enhance their
role in the national economy by allocating new investments.

In other provinces, the decline was one of the negative effects
of the general centralization of decision-making and planning; however, in the western territories it resulted in the following developments:

1. A general exodus of recently settled population from small towns to large cities

2. Insecurity among the new settlers

3. The physical decay of half-empty small towns.

The strict application of economic dogmas to an area that had just undergone a total changeover of its population thus delayed social stability in the region for many years.[34] In addition to external factors affecting the economic and social development of the area, the incorporation of those territories into the economic sphere of a different nation-state involved substantial changes in their economic models. Some factories that were only slightly affected by war damage had to adjust their profiles of production (for example, in Kedzierzyn, the I. G. Farben synthetic gasoline plant was converted into Nitron Industry plant). But for the great majority of the plants, which were rebuilt, the changes in profile were substantial and often total. In many cases, the plants had only some buildings in common with their predecessors.

IMPACT OF THE NEW FRONTIER ON THE AREA'S ECONOMY

Changes in the economy of the Oder-Neisse area as a result of its incorporation into Poland were dictated by the following factors:

1. The needs of the new "parent" economy

2. Economies of scale involved in the cost of rebuilding some plants

3. Depletion of resources that did not warrant large-scale investments in the final years of exploitation

4. The new political geography, i.e., the location of plants vis-à-vis the new international borders and government centers.

Thus, the structure of industry in the Oder-Neisse territories in 1971 differs greatly from that of 1939. New branches of industry have been started and new resources found and developed (e.g., copper, oil, and uranium). Some existing industries were converted to produce other goods; others were not rebuilt at all because of

the cost involved or because other existing plants had easier access
to resources. Finally, some plants were located close to the present
borders (such as those on the Oder River, and in Braniewo or Goldap
in the north). In the past, such plants served areas now sliced off
by the new frontiers and drew labor from areas close by, but now
in a different country. Thus, for example, in the case of the huge
former paper industry plant in Osinki Dolne, the buildings survived
the war in relatively good order but remained idle because the border
cut the plant off from its labor supply. However, the Kostrzyn plant
has been rebuilt to speed recovery of that important railroad town.

Generally, when a factory had not suffered extensive damage,
its economic profile was continued. However, if it was necessary
for the factory to be totally reconstructed, a careful analysis of its
economic viability in the new spatial location and an assessment of
available markets and resources preceded the investment and production decisions. In order to measure the impact of the industrial
potential of the area on the economic structure of contemporary
Poland, we must examine closely the role that its industry played in
the prewar German economy and its present role in the Polish economy
of today.

According to the German economist H. Gleitze, in 1936 the
industry of all the territories east of the Oder-Neisse (i.e., including
the Kaliningrad district assigned in 1945 to the USSR) produced 6
percent of the total industrial output of Germany.[35] The situation
changed only slightly in the remaining prewar years, when many of
the industrial investments geared to a war economy were made there
(i.e., heavy industry concentration in the western part of Upper
Silesia and large communication investments). The disproportionately
small share of industry located in the Oder-Neisse territories, in
relation to their population and territory, was caused by uneven distribution of resources as well as by the restrictive Prussian investment policy, under which the Ruhr district was favored over the
Oder-Neisse areas because of the greater return on investment
there. The development of industry in Silesia faced competition
from, but was not hampered by, the simultaneous development of
the Ruhr. However, the development of marginal industries in the
northern part of the territory was hardly possible because of the
price structure of the west German products. (Oberhausen was used
as a tariff base for iron products, Essen for scrap. Both are located
in west Germany, making the Silesian products expensive because of
the distance.)

The policy by which deglomeration and strategic investments

overruled economic considerations in the years immediately preceding World War II somewhat improved the investment position of the German east.[36] Even this changed policy did not stop the phenomenon of the so-called Ostflucht, which lasted until 1939 and brought, over the period since 1870, some 4.5 million Germans from the east to the industrial west and also (by 1914 about 700,000 Poles in the industrial areas of the Ruhr, Saxony, and Berlin).[37] The Ostflucht continued until World War II, despite the increased investments allocated in the east.

This can be explained by the fact that the growth of the German economy as a whole was much greater than that in the east. In 1936, the share of the east in Germany's gross national income was only 10.8 percent, compared with 15.1 percent in 1928.

The pre-1939 investment policy, geared to the war effort, provided the east with additional plants in the heavy and chemical industries (e.g., in Upper Silesia, near Szczecin, and near Wroclaw), but it did not radically transform the industry of those regions. In 1939, those gainfully employed in industry and agriculture constituted only 7.2 percent of the German total, although the population of the area was 11.4 percent of the total.

The majority of enterprises in industry and handicrafts were rather small. They employed fewer persons per enterprise (6.5) than the German average (8.6). The averages were lower especially in the production of iron, steel, and other metal goods, machine-building and the motor vehicle industry, the electrical and optical industries, precision mechanics, and the chemical industry.

As a whole, the Oder-Neisse areas had a mixed industrial-rural character before World War II. Thus, 2.65 million or 32 percent of the population were active in industry, 2.4 million or 29 percent in agriculture and forestry, 1.1 million or 14 percent in commerce and communication, and 2.1 million or 25 percent in other occupations. Because of the different levels of economic development within the area, the occupational indexes varied widely, in accordance with the economic character of the provinces and their resource bases (i.e., the occupational index in industrialized Silesia was very different from that in the generally agricultural northern areas). The average enterprise in prewar industry and handicrafts was characterized by small size, as is evident from the large number of firms engaged in handicrafts. It is estimated that in 1939 there were about 130,000 handicrafts firms with about 518,000 employees, out of the total of 157,000 firms in both industry and handicrafts with a total employment of 877,000.[38]

This preponderance of handicrafts in the economy of the area is significant because those small-scale enterprises relied on local natural resources and thus were able to withstand the powerful competition from industry in western Germany. Furthermore, the ratio of handicrafts to industry was important in subsequent developments affecting the economy of the area. Polish economists estimate that the contraction in the number of business enterprises had already begun during the war, when the German economy was being progressively geared to the war effort. Small, inefficient, or marginal handicraft enterprises and plants were closed down or merged into larger ones. Their mechanical equipment was largely utilized in new enterprises created to serve military purposes. By 1945, the number of existing handicraft workshops had been reduced to about 100,000 and their employees had been reduced by one-half. Also, war damage and postwar looting took an especially heavy toll on handicrafts.

Damage to industry in the Oder-Neisse area was considerably higher than for Polish industry as a whole (73.1 percent of equipment and machinery destroyed as opposed to 65.7 percent). However, in view of the relatively well-developed industrial bases in key areas (such as Upper Silesia), rebuilding there could potentially have yielded results faster than did the rebuilding of scattered industrial plants in old provinces.

It is estimated that industrial capacity in the Oder-Neisse area fell to 40 percent of its prewar potential.[39] Destruction of factories in the Oder-Neisse area, by category, was as follows: blast furnaces and coke plants, 30 percent; steel plants, 40 percent; rolling and machine industry mills, 95 percent; chemical industry, 55 percent; paper industry, 94 percent; electric power plants, 60 percent. The communication network vital to industry lost 7,563 kilometers of rail lines (or 70 percent) and 33,355 kilometers of bridges (over 50 percent). The hard-surface roads were reduced by 25 percent.

The industry of the Polish western territories had been largely rebuilt by 1960. The relatively high rate of investments, averaging 25.9 percent per year in the period 1956-60,[40] was responsible for the virtually complete recovery of industry from the destruction of 1945. At present, the investment rates are constantly held at high levels because of the need to absorb numerous young workers entering the labor market of the western territories.

In 1960, there were 984,331 workers employed in industry and handicrafts (higher than the prewar figures), constituting 29.8 percent of the total industrial labor force in Poland.[41] Thus, the growth of the industrial force was much higher in the western territories than elsewhere, since the area's population was only 25.1 percent of Poland's total population.[42]

Because of the postwar Communist transformation of the economy, the comparison of data for industry and handicrafts is only partially possible, since the majority of independent handicraft enterprises were liquidated and/or merged into larger workshops now classified as industrial. Thus, the increase of employment in the electrical, clothing, and food industries, is in a sense artificial since a considerable number of the persons employed in those fields would have worked as craftsmen when the area belonged to Germany.

The accurate comparison of data would, in effect, require a separate study, a study for which the basic and full materials are inaccessible.[43] Although postwar rebuilding retained or only slightly modified the industrial structure of Silesia, it affected the productive profile of industries scattered throughout the rest of the western territories, making them conform to the economic needs of the new parent economy.

Furthermore, there has been vigorous construction of new plants. In these regions, two new major industrial centers either have been completed or are under construction: Turoszow (electric power and lignite center), now completed, and Glogow-Lubin-Legnica (copper and lignite center), under construction. Polish economists estimate the national wealth taken over in the western territories in 1945 at 37 billion prewar zlotys. By 1964, amortization had reduced that figure to an estimated 30 billion. In the postwar period, about 36 billion prewar zlotys were invested in rebuilding the area and constructing new projects that have greatly increased the productive potential of these regions.

Already 50 percent of the national wealth of the Polish western territories resulted from the investment effort of postwar Poland.[44] On a purely psychological level, this factor, which is constantly stressed in the Oder-Neisse areas, is creating intense pride in the postwar achievements in economic reconstruction. It thus is forging additional sociological links between the settlers and the area that they have rebuilt after its war devastation. In 1963, the industrial output of the area constituted 30 percent of the national total. If population (26.6 percent of the national total) and share in national output are used as a standard, the western territories' share exceeds these indexes in the production of a whole range of products (see Table 21).

Present investment effort is concentrated on alleviating the economic disproportions and relative underdevelopment of the northern provinces. This task is especially pressing because the rate of natural population increase immediately following World War II was greatest in the northern provinces, and those age groups are now reaching the labor market. Investment plans call for a large increase of labor-intensive industry to be created there under the 1965-80 long-range economic plan.

AGRICULTURE

Immediately before the war, agriculture in the Oder-Neisse regions was characterized by a war-geared intensification aimed at providing agricultural self-sufficiency in food production. This area was heavily subsidized through the Osthilfe (Help for the East), which was designed to offset the impact of labor shortages, unfavorable climatic conditions, and distance from the population centers in western Germany. While part of Germany in 1939, the area produced 25 percent of Germany's rye, 16.5 percent of its wheat, 24 percent of its potatoes, and contained 24 percent of its horses, 15 percent of its cattle, and 19 percent of its hogs. These figures reflect the autarkic tendencies of Nazi war-planning.[45]

In reality, however, the exhaustive analysis of the role of eastern agriculture in the German economy conducted in 1930 by Wilhelm Volz of the University of Leipzig reveals that those proportions are deceptive. In view of the size of agricultural imports into Germany and the price structure caused by the distance between the agricultural east and the heavily populated west, the agriculture of the region can be termed the Sorgenkind (problem child) of the Reich.[46] The agriculture of the Oder-Neisse area in reality provided only 3.3 percent of the supply of wheat on western German markets, 10.7 percent of the rye, and 4.5 percent of the potatoes. Volz comes to the following conclusions in assessing the role of eastern agriculture in the economy of the Reich:

> When one always hears that the German east is an agricultural base of Germany, it is a deceitful conclusion. . . .
> Germany does not need the [agricultural] surpluses of
> its east. . . . It is a bitter truth, but alas a truth. . . .
> It is our turn to lose the east.[47]

It has been noted that the agriculture of what was then the German eastern territories was heavily dependent on Polish labor

TABLE 21

Output of Principal Products in Western and Northern Territories,
Selected Years, 1937-64

Specification	Unit	1937	1946	1949	1963 In Absolute Figures	1963 Area Share in National Output (percentage)	1964 In Absolute Figures	1964 Area Share in National Output (percentage)
Electricity	million kilowatt-hours	3,900a	1,614	2,328	11,656	31.5	14,398	35.5
Coal								
Bituminous	thousand tons	29,911	14,478	24,247	27,771	24.5	28,310	24.1
Brown	thousand tons	4,555	1,442	4,460	10,812	70.5	14,915	73.5
Coke	thousand tons	3,944	1,595	2,831	6,035	43.5	6,103	43.0
Cooking gas	million cubic meters	251	63	144	402	49.9	422	50.8
Pig iron (in terms of open-hearth pig iron)	thousand tons	420a	144	362	748	13.9	766	13.6
Crude steel	thousand tons	520a	135	487	1,453	18.2	1,575	18.4
Rolling mill products	thousand tons	305a	–	–	383	7.0	405	7.1
Ores								
Zinc-lead, raw	thousand tons	722a	238	389	355	13.9	330	12.7
Copper, raw	thousand tons	–	–	–	2,162	100.0	2,247	100.0
Steam turbines	megawatts	–	–	–	461	100.0	474	100.0
Machine tools and woodworking machines	tons	1,320	461	2,851	15,729	30.7	17,473	32.5
Cars	number	2,127a	–	–	300	1.6	348	1.7
Trucks	number	3a	–	–	7,192	26.8	7,822	29.3
Rolling stock (excluding narrow-gauge)								
Passenger coachesb	number	106c	–	–	77	14.5	70	14.0
Good wagons	number	515b	1,736	–	13,858	89.2	14,550	92.8
Radio receivers and radiograms	thousand	–	–	90.7d	227	46.6	220	42.8
Ordinary lamp bulbs	million	0.3	–	–	30.7	40.9	38.0	45.7
Sulfuric acid (in terms of 100 percent acid)	thousand tons	58	18.3	102	368	41.4	386	38.4
Synthetic ammonia	thousand tons	–	–	–	259	57.3	291	59.0
Nitrogen fertilizer (in terms of pure nutrient)	thousand tons	–	–	–	177	53.8	192	53.3
Rayon yarn	thousand tons	6.8	0.3	–	11.8	46.4	12.3	46.5
Staple fiber	thousand tons	18.6	–	–	26.0	50.5	27.1	51.4
Cement	thousand tons	1,328	258	744	1,741	22.7	1,898	21.7

Specification	Unit	1937	1946	1949	1963 In Absolute Figures	1963 Area Share in National Output (percentage)	1964 In Absolute Figures	1964 Area Share in National Output (percentage)
Hydrated lime in lumps	thousand tons	349	81	522	919	45.8	1,039	48.0
Burned brick (excluding clinker brick)	million	1,240	—	—	755	29.7	812	29.9
Burned roofing tile	million	237	—	—	51.1	60.1	62.0	62.1
Electrical and technical porcelain	tons	2,800	—	—	8,062	56.5	8,540	57.5
Matches	million crates[e]	107	—	—	196	50.8	205	51.8
Cellulose	thousand tons	253	—	—	146	44.7	150	45.0
Paper	thousand tons	415	34	84.3	220	37.6	228	36.5
Cardboard	thousand tons	96	10	28	51.7	30.6	52.5	30.0
Cotton and imitation cotton fabrics	million meters	119[c]	40.7	99.2	212	30.5	235	30.9
Woolen and imitation wool fabrics	million meters	17.5[c]	1.4	5.0	13.0	15.5	14.7	16.4
Beet sugar (in terms of white sugar during sugarmaking season)	thousand tons	512	97.4	231	451	34.4	591	35.8
Beer	thousand hectoliters	3,100	—	—	2,868	39.5	2,955	39.0
Raw spirits (in terms of 100 percent spirits)	million liters	120	—	—	70.9	44.8	91.7	47.5
Sawn timber	thousand cubic meters	3,000	—	—	2,890	—	2,923	43.2

[a]1938.
[b]Including service wagons (restaurant cars, guard's vans, baggage vans, and mail vans.
[c]1936.
[d]1950.
[e]Crates containing 240,000 matches each.

Source: Tadeusz Derlatka and Jozef Lubojanski, Western and Northern Territories Of Poland: Facts and Figures (Warsaw: Western Press Agency, 1966), Table 9.

before 1914 and on Polish migratory harvest labor before World War
II. After World War II, many of the former migrants settled in the
area permanently, as authorized by the Allied Powers, thereby providing some continuity of rural population in areas otherwise emptied
of the former population. This was especially true of Pomerania
and former East Prussia, where such migrants previously had worked
on the large estates that comprised the majority of agricultural land.

The losses in agriculture were heavy during the battles of
January-April 1945, when the eastern front moved through the region.
Some 123,800 farmsteads in the western territories (27 percent of
the total) were destroyed or damaged by at least 15 percent; these
losses were higher than the average for Poland (22 percent). The
losses in livestock were so great that one cannot really speak of any
takeover of prewar livestock: 92 percent of the cattle, 96 percent of
the hogs, 97 percent of the sheep, and 90 percent of the horses were
killed or removed from the area.[48] In 1945, 3.8 million hectares, or
78 percent of the land, lay fallow. The decrease in the supply of natural fertilizers could be supplemented only by artificial ones, which
industry was unable to produce. Furthermore, the situation was greatly
complicated by the total exchange of the farming population in all the
parts of the region except Opole Silesia and some parts of Mazuria-
Warmia, which would have made the recovery of agriculture difficult
under any circumstances.

The exchange of industrial crews does not present as great a
problem after an initial production period. Agriculture requires not
only years of practical experience but also an intimate knowledge of
local farming methods, soil, and microclimatic conditions. The soils
of the Oder-Neisse area are generally slightly below the average for
Poland as a whole. Although soils in the western territories vary
greatly, the poorest constitute 24 percent of the total. The best soils
are those of Silesia, where good soils comprise 22 percent of the total.
In the north, good soils constitute less than 8 percent of the total. However, the Poles who transferred from the former southeastern territories of Poland (those from the northeast were a minority), settled
in large groups in the west, and formed the backbone of its new rural
population were used to much richer, better, and more fertile soils
(those of Volhynia and eastern Galicia). They were totally unprepared
for the intensive farming methods in the west, where modern agrotech-
nical methods contributed to the comparatively high yields per hectare.

In comparison, because of their backward farming methods, the
peasants who came from what had been eastern Poland obtained much
lower yields in the western territories, even in areas with considerably

better soils (see Table 22).[49] It is easy to grasp the consequences of the war losses and the settlement of a population using backward farming methods on the output of the highly advanced and mechanized agriculture of the west, which had been able to achieve high yields through the use of modern farming technology. In addition, the agriculture of the newly settled areas was unnecessarily handicapped by collectivization and the drastically changed distribution system. These "reforms" were foisted on bewildered farmers living in unfamiliar surroundings and farming under climatic conditions to which they had barely had time to adjust between 1946 and 1949. Consequently, even by 1969 yields for some crops had not regained their prewar levels (see Table 23). However, the prewar yields of major corps have been generally achieved.

The Communist system of agriculture has yet to prove its merits and achieve better results than private farming, and the juxtaposition of all these changes within such a short span of time proved nearly fatal to the agriculture of the area. Only in Silesia (in Opole province and Wroclaw) have the overall prewar yields been surpassed. In this regard, it is significant that the society of Opole province was the least disrupted by the postwar migrations. Half its population is composed of persons native to the area. Around such a stable core, the incoming settlers apparently were able to adjust more rapidly to local farming conditions. The high yield in Wroclaw province, where the population is composed of the "mix" typical for the Oder-Neisse

TABLE 22

Average Agricultural Yields, Selected Provinces
of Eastern Poland, 1934-38
(quintals per hectare)

Province	Wheat	Rye	Barley	Oats
Vilna	7.5	7.9	7.4	7.7
Nowogrodek	9.5	10.2	9.6	9.8
Volhynia	12.1	11.4	12.3	11.8
Tarnopol	11.4	11.3	10.8	11.0

Source: Glowny Urzad Statystyczny Rzeczypospolitej Polskiej, Maly Rocznik Statystyczny, 1939, Vol. X (Warsaw, 1939), Table 12, p. 78.

TABLE 23

Sowings, Production, and Yields of Main Crops in the Oder-Neisse Areas, Selected Years, 1934/38-1969

Specification	1934/38 (average)	1946	1949	1955	1961	1969
Four Major Cereals						
Sowings (thousands of hectares)	2,724	1,168	2,604	2,554	2,310	2,252
Production (thousands of tons)	4,860	876	3,255	3,455	4,216	5,057
Yields (quintals per hectare)	17.8	7.8	12.5	13.5	18.3	22.5
Wheat						
Sowings (thousands of hectares)	350	211	546	528	533	805
Production (thousands of tons)	732	161	660	760	1,126	2,044
Yields (quintals per hectare)	20.9	7.6	12.1	14.4	21.1	25.4
Sugar beets						
Sowings (thousands of hectares)	111	46	98	149	139	121
Production (thousands of tons)	3,441	819	1,617	2,458	3,613	3,273
Yields (quintals per hectare)	311	178	165	165	260	270
Potatoes						
Sowings (thousands of hectares)	814	273	572	682	622	661
Production (thousands of tons)	13,680	3,084	6,349	6,043	10,320	10,776
Yields (quintals per hectare)	168	113	111	88.6	156	163

*Wheat, rye, oats, and barley.

Source: Data for 1934/38-1961 from the Central Statistical Office and Planning Commission of the Council of Ministers, as quoted in Wladyslaw Misiuna 'Osiagniecia i perspektywy rozwoju rolnictwa Ziem Zachodnich," in Rozwoj gospodarczy Ziem Zachodnich w dwudziestoleciu Polski Ludowej i jego perspektywy (Poznan: Instytut Zachodni, 1964), Tables 2, 3, 4, pp. 150-53. Data for 1969 from Glowny Urzad Statystyczny Polskiej Rzeczypospolitej Ludowej, Rocznik Statystyczny 1970, Vol. XXX (Warsaw, 1970), Table 18, p. 222 and Table 20, p. 225.

territories as a whole, can be explained by the fact that wartime destruction was far less widespread in the areas on the left bank of the
Oder and by the generally better, fertile soils of that region.

The rural settlement was greatly helped by the destruction of
the cities (54 percent) and industry. Thus, the industrial cities were
unable to provide employment for many uprooted persons who otherwise would have moved from the villages to the cities and sought industrial jobs. Rural settlement proceeded without interruption until 1949,
when the beginning of the period of forced collectivization caused partial migrations from the farms to the cities, which, with the new
emphasis on heavy industry, were now able to absorb new workers.
Furthermore as a result of collectivization, in the years 1949-56 the
migrants from central Poland, who normally would have settled on
their own farms in the west, moved to the cities instead. Similarly,
many farmers in the area preferred to abandon their plots rather than
join the collectives.

Only after October 1956 were the collectives allowed to disband.[50]
Private farming again became respectable in the eyes of the government, and the ultimate goal of collectivization by consensus was sub-
stituted. The price of land across Poland began to rise, and all fallow
and abandoned land in the west was again put under cultivation. By
1957, considerably more persons in the western territories derived
their income from farming than in prewar days (2,760,000 as opposed
to 2,422,000). However, despite the larger farming population, there
was a shortage of workers on the state-owned farms, where employment was generally unpopular. Individual farms covered more than
3.3 million hectares and supported 2,124,000 persons, while the state-
owned farms covered 1,817,000 hectares and supported 620,000 persons.

Factors responsible for this imbalance included, in addition to
the distaste of the Polish peasant for state farms, the change in the
structure of agriculture introduced in the area at the time of settlement. As a rule, the Polish farms were smaller than the pre-1945
German farms. Farms of over 20 hectares comprised 71.9 percent
of the total acreage but amounted to only 15.7 percent of the total
number of farms. Farms exceeding 100 hectares constituted 46.6
percent of the cultivated area but amounted to only 1.8 percent of
the total number of farms.[51]

The settlement of the area was accompanied by the subdivision
of farms of over 20 hectares. Under the Communist pressure, legis-
lation defined such farms as too large for private farming and defined

the average private farm as 7-15 hectares. Two or three families were settled under one roof, immediately creating the problem of divided households. Building new farmsteads had not been made possible under the conditions of postwar destruction, and that expedient was now used to create conditions conducive to planned collectivization of agriculture. The distribution of deeds to the farms was suspended in 1949 and not resumed until 1957. The actions described above were more detrimental than any other factors to the success of the postwar rural settlement of the Oder-Neisse areas, and they contributed decisively to the feeling of instability rampant in the area until 1957.

These practices were ameliorated after 1957 when the settlers were allowed to build new farmsteads, buy new land, and finally given land titles. Even so, despite the substitution of the voluntary "rural circles" (a loose form of collective farming endowed with machinery and easy credits, as an inducement for peasants) for collectives, issuance of the titles has not been completed and has proceeded slowly. The official explanation is the existence of an acute shortage of surveyors.

The state farms were created in the west through the nationalization of large estates. In only two other provinces of the old Polish territories (Poznan and Bydgoszcz) has the share of the state farms been as large (see Table 24). In the rest of Poland, the estates have been subdivided to provide land for landless tenants or to enlarge the existing dwarf farms. The peasants' reluctance to settle on the state farms has accelerated their mechanization, but the yields of the four major cereals (wheat, rye, oats, barley) on state farms are somewhat lower than those for the privately owned farms in the western territories except in Gdansk, Opole, and Olsztyn provinces).[52]

Very poor results were obtained on the state farms, despite credit support, extensive mechanization of field work, and the assignment of trained agricultural personnel. The period of adjustment of the rural settlers, which lasted from 1945 through 1947 because of all the objective difficulties imposed either by environment or by government policies, was the period of "trial and error." Wheat yields per hectare nearly quadrupled between 1946 and 1957 in Olsztyn province and nearly tripled in Szczecin during the same period.[53]

All of the above is the best testimony to the long and difficult period of agricultural recovery caused by the following factors: (1) the wartime destruction; (2) the chaos of the postwar period; (3) the doctrinaire attitude of the government hindering recovery; and (4) the slow and painful adjustment of the new settlers to new farming methods, soil, and climatic conditions.

TABLE 24

Arable Land by Ownership and Voivodship, 1969

| Voivodship | Percentage Distribution | | |
	Individual Ownership	Agricultural Cooperative	State Ownership
Poland	83.8	1.2	14.5
Bialystok	93.1	0.2	6.5
Bydgoszcz	83.8	1.8	14.2
Gdansk	69.4	1.4	28.1
Katowice	91.4	1.3	7.1
Kielce	98.5	0.3	1.1
Koszalin	54.4	0.4	44.0
Krakow	98.2	0.2	1.5
Lublin	95.9	0.7	3.2
Lodz	96.4	0.7	2.8
Olsztyn	65.8	0.5	32.8
Opole	77.0	2.1	20.4
Poznan	77.7	4.8	17.3
Rzeszow	90.9	1.1	7.6
Szczecin	49.3	2.6	46.7
Warszawa	96.7	0.6	2.6
Wroclaw	69.5	0.8	27.9
Zielona Gora	67.4	0.7	30.0

Source: Glowny Urzad Statystyczny Polskiej Rzeczypospolitej Ludowej, Rocznik Statystyczny, 1970, Vol. XXX (Warsaw, 1970), Table 16, p. 221.

In view of these obstacles, the present results are remarkable. Because of the doctrinaire and politically motivated decisions of the government, Poland has missed its chance to radically improve its agricultural structure. The Council for the Problems of the Recovered Territories proposed such reforms[54] but had to accept imposed "solutions" that—not only in the western territories but across the country—have created uneconomical farms of 7 to 15 hectares and actually have increased the number of dwarf farms of under 5 hectares.

The debacle of the Polish Stalinist solutions for agriculture—which threatened to cause the collapse of national economy in the 1950's and thus prompted the 1956 reforms—postponed any resolution of the predicament of Polish agriculture. Currently, the Polish government hopes that a collectivistic structure will eventually be adapted to Polish agriculture, in view of the growing attractiveness of urban life and the regular exodus from the villages (a migratory wave equivalent to the natural increase). We tend to agree that this may be a solution, since the aging of the farmers is noticeable in the countryside. Over the 1960's, land was increasingly "offered" to the state by farmers because of their age, the land's decreased productivity, or unpayable tax burdens. There is also a growing lack of labor reserves in some areas of the countryside.

Although yields approximate—or even exceed, in some provinces—the prewar averages, livestock has not yet been brought to former levels in some parts of the area, despite the fact that the growth rate of livestock is higher in the western territories than in the rest of the country. However, the area's livestock, if counted per 100 hectares of farmland, corresponds to the national averages (see Table 25). This illustrates another interesting trend: the agriculture of the rest of the country, which before 1939 was generally far behind the Oder-Neisse areas, is slowly catching up with the western territories (see Table 26).

Agriculture in the Oder-Neisse area went through a period of initial decline for the reasons enumerated above, but adaptation of the new rural population to intensive farming methods is now complete. Superior farming techniques are being disseminated from the west to the rest of the country through family contacts. Those contacts are vivid and frequent, since the new society in the western territories is half composed of newcomers from central Poland who left parts of their families at their old homes. Thus, the modern agricultural techniques used in the Oder-Neisse territories serve as the model for the rest of Poland's agriculture, which is approaching these standards. Even the unpopular state farms perform an educational function

Livestock by Voivodship, 1969
(per 100 hectares of arable land)

Voivodship	Cattle		Pigs			Sheep	Horses
	Total	Cows	Total	Sows			
Poland	56.5	32.0	73.4	8.2		16.6	13.5
Bialystok	47.6	27.9	74.9	8.5		21.0	14.7
Bydgoszcz	55.4	26.3	87.3	9.4		21.8	12.7
Gdansk	56.5	26.9	65.5	7.4		18.7	10.4
Katowice	59.4	37.7	61.5	6.2		19.9	10.5
Kielce	54.4	37.6	67.5	8.5		21.7	17.4
Koszalin	49.3	20.1	53.4	5.7		16.9	7.5
Krakow	74.9	56.8	69.7	8.8		17.1	16.2
Lublin	53.6	33.3	82.4	9.5		10.5	17.6
Lodz	60.0	36.1	74.5	9.0		27.7	14.1
Olsztyn	55.0	23.0	51.4	6.0		13.7	10.2
Opole	66.8	33.2	71.6	7.1		9.2	12.7
Poznan	58.1	29.6	104.5	10.9		22.0	12.3
Rzeszow	70.6	48.2	56.4	5.6		6.5	17.4
Szczecin	49.4	20.3	50.4	5.5		17.1	7.6
Warszawa	48.2	31.7	92.0	11.0		10.0	15.0
Wroclaw	63.9	28.5	52.3	5.5		12.1	11.1
Zielona Gora	51.3	25.1	61.8	6.0		15.7	10.3

Source: Concise Statistical Yearbook of Poland, 1970, Vol. XII (Warsaw: Central Statistical Office, 1970), Table 17, p. 160.

TABLE 26

Production and Yields of Main Crops by Voivodship, Selected Years, 1955-69

Voivodship	1955 Production (thousands of tons)	1955 Yields (quintals per hectare)	1960 Production (thousands of tons)	1960 Yields (quintals per hectare)	1965 Production (thousands of tons)	1965 Yields (quintals per hectare)	1969 Production (thousands of tons)	1969 Yields (quintals per hectare)
Poland, Total	12,700	14.3	14,300	16.1	15,500	19.2	17,900	21.6
Bialystok	799	12.6	813	12.7	952	16.6	1,117	19.3
Bydgoszcz	1,032	16.4	1,206	18.3	1,362	22.9	1,534	24.6
Gdansk	326	12.4	379	15.0	459	20.5	552	22.5
Katowice	318	14.8	387	17.6	461	20.3	514	22.8
Kielce	863	14.1	927	14.9	1,121	17.4	1,280	19.9
Koszalin	460	11.4	585	14.7	585	17.0	708	20.0
Krakow	637	14.0	660	14.8	723	17.2	904	21.3
Lublin	1,146	14.0	1,178	14.7	1,418	18.7	1,596	21.2
Lodz	820	14.8	997	16.8	1,160	19.5	1,281	21.0
Olsztyn	646	12.1	689	14.1	777	18.9	905	21.3
Opole	454	16.2	606	21.2	540	21.2	661	25.4
Poznan	1,478	17.0	1,570	18.4	1,708	21.5	1,851	22.8
Rzeszow	662	12.7	717	14.4	720	17.2	894	21.5
Szczecin	435	13.9	500	17.2	490	20.0	620	22.8
Warszawa	1,440	14.9	1,463	15.0	1,667	18.6	1,859	20.1
Wroclaw	753	15.1	1,100	20.6	862	20.2	1,115	25.0
Zielona Gora	394	14.1	488	17.3	456	18.8	496	19.9

Note: Main crops are wheat, rye, barley, oats.

Source: Glowny Urzad Statystyczny Polskiej Rzeczypospolitej Ludowej, Rocznik Statystystyczny, 1970, Vol. XXX (Warsaw, 1970), Tables I and II, pp. 40*, 55*, 76.*

in the use of machinery, which is being lavished on them to offset the general effects of apathy, mismanagement, and waste inherent in those state institutions in the past. The state farms recently have begun to show profit, through appreciable increase in productivity and efficiency (see Tables 27 and 28).

Emphasis in Poland now lies on the "agricultural circles," which receive financial support and machinery. In 1969, there were 34,814 circles, with one located in 87.2 percent of all Polish villages. The agricultural circles owned 12,165 tractors. The technical modernization of agriculture also has been progressing as a result of the electrification program. 93-98 percent of the farms in the western areas (with the exception of those in the provinces of Gdansk, 90 percent, and Olsztyn, 84 percent) are now electrified, as opposed to 85.7 percent for the country as a whole. The better yields are also due to the increased use of fertilizers, which in 1969 was higher than in the rest of the country. The future of agriculture in Poland is heavily dependent on the growth of a chemical industry to provide fertilizers to further increase agricultural output.

The need to import 2 million tons of grain yearly which existed in the 1960's—a heavy burden for the Polish economy—could be decreased or eliminated altogether if the productivity of Polish agriculture increased substantially. In view of the agricultural yields that currently are being achieved in Western Europe, Poland's yield[55] easily could be raised, even doubled, if extensive industrial support and advanced technological methods were put at the disposal of Poland's agriculture (see Table 29). However, Poland's economic problems revolve around the need for the creation of a wider industrial base to provide work for the rapidly increasing labor force crowding the market. Hence, an effort to modernize agriculture would be difficult, unless there are drastic reforms in Poland's economic structure.

The proportion of those gainfully employed in agriculture (42.7 percent in 1960) is still backward compared with that of the advanced Western European economies. But since World War II the Polish village has made great strides in its economic status, perhaps the first such large-scale improvement in its history. This improvement is obscured by the current hardships, acute housing shortages, and continuing relatively low standard of living. Nonetheless, the postwar period of industrialization and urbanization gave the rural population of Poland an unprecedented opportunity for rapid social advance and brought a higher technical culture to the previously backward villages.

It may be assumed that migrants have cured some of the

TABLE 27

Production of Main Crops, 1934-38 and 1947-69
(millions of tons)

Year	Four Major Cereals[a]	Wheat	Rye	Barley	Oats	Potatoes	Sugar Beets
Total							
1934-38[b]	12.5	2.1	6.5	1.4	2.5	35.0	2.8
	13.3	2.0	6.9	1.6	2.8	38.0	6.0
1947-49[b]	10.4	1.4	5.8	1.0	2.2	29.5	4.2
1950-55[b]	11.3	2.0	6.1	1.1	2.1	30.8	6.5
1956-60[b]	13.5	2.3	7.5	1.2	2.5	36.3	7.7
1961-65[b]	14.5	3.0	7.5	1.4	2.6	43.7	11.4
1966-69[b]	16.5	4.2	8.0	1.5	2.8	47.3	13.8
1955	12.7	2.1	7.0	1.3	2.3	27.0	7.3
1956	12.1	2.1	6.6	1.1	2.3	38.1	6.4
1957	13.5	2.3	7.5	1.2	2.5	35.1	7.6
1958	13.5	2.3	7.3	1.2	2.7	34.8	8.4
1959	14.1	2.5	8.1	1.0	2.5	35.7	6.0
1960	14.3	2.3	7.9	1.3	2.8	37.9	10.3
1961	15.4	2.8	8.4	1.3	2.9	45.2	11.6
1962	13.4	2.7	6.7	1.3	2.7	37.8	10.1[c]
1963	14.5	3.1	7.1	1.5	2.8	44.9	10.7
1964	13.5	3.0	7.0	1.3	2.2	47.9	12.6
1965	15.5	3.3	8.2	1.5	2.5	42.7	12.3
1966	15.2	3.5	7.7	1.4	2.6	45.8	13.6
1967	15.7	3.9	7.6	1.4	2.8	48.2	15.5
1968	17.3	4.6	8.4	1.5	2.8	50.3	14.8
1969	17.9	4.7	8.2	1.9	3.1	44.9	11.3
Private Holdings							
1950-55[b]	9.5	1.5	5.4	0.8	1.8	27.6	5.1
1956-60[b]	11.8	1.9	6.8	0.9	2.2	32.9	6.5
1961-65[b]	12.8	2.4	6.9	1.1	2.4	40.5	9.9
1966-69[b]	14.2	3.2	7.3	1.2	2.5	43.6	12.1
1969	15.2	3.6	7.5	1.4	2.7	41.6	10.1
Cooperative Farms							
1950-55[b]	0.6	0.2	0.2	0.1	0.1	0.1	0.5
1956-60[b]	0.4	0.1	0.1	0.1	0.1	0.8	0.3
1961-65[b]	0.2	0.1	0.1	0.0	0.0	0.4	0.2
1966-69[b]	0.2	0.1	0.1	0.0	0.0	0.3	0.2
1969	0.2	0.1	0.1	0.0	0.0	0.3	0.2
State Farms							
1950-55[b]	1.2	0.3	0.5	0.2	0.2	2.1[d]	0.9
1956-60[b]	1.3	0.3	0.6	0.2	0.2	2.6[d]	0.9
1961-65[b]	1.5	0.5	0.5	0.3	0.2	2.8[d]	1.3
1966-69[b]	2.1	0.9	0.6	0.3	0.3	3.4[d]	1.5
1969	2.4	1.0	0.6	0.5	0.3	3.0[d]	1.0

[a]Wheat, rye, oats, and barley.
[b]Average annual production.
[c]Deliveries to the sugar factories amounted to 9.7 million tons; the remaining production was used to feed livestock.
[d]Including potatoes from workers' allotments (in 1969, 1.2 million tons).

Source: Concise Statistical Yearbook of Poland, 1970, Vol. XII (Warsaw: Central Statistical Office, 1970) Table 8, p. 152.

TABLE 28

Yields of Main Crops, 1934-38 and 1947-69
(quintals per hectare)

Year	Four Major Cereals[a]	Wheat	Rye	Barley	Oats	Potatoes	Sugar Beets
Total							
1934-38[b]	11.4	11.9	11.2	11.8	11.4	121	216
	13.7	14.6	12.8	15.7	14.5	138	265
1947-49[b]	11.8	11.1	11.7	11.7	12.8	121	180
1950-55[b]	12.7	13.1	12.3	13.4	13.0	117	187
1956-70[b]	15.1	16.1	14.6	16.2	15.2	131	211
1961-65[b]	17.4	19.7	16.4	19.4	17.1	154	267
1966-69[b]	20.4	23.2	18.7	22.9	20.4	174	326
1955	14.3	14.9	14.1	15.1	13.9	100	186
1956	13.7	14.5	13.2	14.6	14.2	140	177
1957	15.0	16.1	14.7	15.8	14.6	127	225
1958	14.8	15.7	14.1	16.3	15.6	126	235
1959	15.7	17.3	15.6	16.2	14.7	128	159
1960	16.1	16.9	15.4	18.3	16.9	132	256
1961	18.0	19.9	17.1	19.7	18.4	160	275
1962	16.1	19.4	14.2	19.8	17.3	130	234
1963	17.3	19.9	16.3	19.8	16.8	158	287
1964	16.2	18.7	15.8	17.0	14.2	169	283
1965	19.2	20.6	18.4	21.0	18.8	154	259
1966	19.0	21.5	17.8	20.6	18.8	169	313
1967	19.5	22.4	17.9	21.6	19.7	176	358
1968	21.4	24.8	19.8	23.6	20.7	185	357
1969	21.6	24.0	19.6	25.5	22.3	165	276
Private Holdings							
1950-55[b]	12.6	12.8	12.3	13.2	13.1	119	199
1956-60[b]	15.2	16.2	14.7	16.3	15.4	132	224
1961-65[b]	17.3	19.6	16.4	19.5	17.1	155	275
1966-69[b]	20.2	23.1	18.8	22.9	20.3	174	331
1969	21.4	23.9	19.7	25.2	22.2	166	284
Cooperative Farms							
1950-55[b]	13.6	14.4	12.9	15.0	13.4	105	158
1956-60[b]	14.8	15.9	13.7	16.8	15.2	128	138
1961-65[b]	19.7	21.6	17.8	21.6	19.5	146	239
1966-69[b]	22.6	24.0	20.1	24.3	22.7	170	301
1969	23.8	24.5	20.4	27.4	24.4	159	234
State Farms							
1950-55[b]	12.7	14.2	12.0	13.5	12.0	97[c]	153
1956-60[b]	14.3	15.7	13.5	15.7	13.5	109[c]	168
1961-65[b]	17.8	19.9	15.8	19.1	16.9	141[c]	223
1966-69[b]	21.6	24.0	18.6	23.0	21.2	165[c]	301
1969	22.9	24.6	18.9	26.6	23.3	147[c]	229

[a]Wheat, rye, oats, and barley.
[b]Average annual yields.
[c]Excluding workers' allotments.

Source: Concise Statistical Yearbook Of Poland, 1970, Vol. XII (Warsaw: Central Statistical Office, 1970), Table 9, p. 153.

TABLE 29

Yields of Wheat, Rye, Barley, and Oats in Selected
European Countries, Selected Years, 1930-69
(quintals per hectare)

Country and Product	Before World War II	1948-52	1956-60	1961-65	1966-69	1969
Belgium						
Wheat	26.9	32.2	35.9	38.3	37.8	38.2
Rye	23.9	26.1	29.2	29.9	31.0	34.8
Barley	26.3	29.8	34.5	36.9	35.2	33.0
Oats	26.8	27.9	30.9	33.5	34.6	32.5
Czechoslovakia						
Wheat	17.1	19.0	21.2	24.1	28.9	31.1
Rye	16.0	17.5	19.7	20.9	22.0	24.5
Barley	17.0	17.3	21.2	22.6	28.1	31.9
Oats	16.2	15.8	18.3	18.9	21.8	24.2
Denmark						
Wheat	30.4	36.5	39.7	41.3	45.7	45.6
Rye	17.8	23.7	26.4	29.1	32.8	36.0
Barley	29.8	34.5	35.3	38.5	38.8	39.9
Oats	26.8	31.7	32.2	37.2	38.0	38.3
Holland						
Wheat	30.3	36.4	40.4	43.7	44.5	45.1
Rye	22.7	25.9	28.9	29.1	30.8	33.4
Barley	27.9	33.4	39.0	39.8	38.1	40.1
Oats	25.5	29.4	31.1	37.8	39.8	40.7
East Germany						
Wheat	24.6	26.2	31.2	31.5	36.7	35.5
Rye	17.1	19.5	21.1	21.2	24.1	22.4
Barley	23.4	22.9	28.8	29.5	33.0	32.2
Oats	21.5	21.8	24.9	26.7	30.7	30.9
West Germany						
Wheat	22.1	26.2	31.9	33.1	39.1	40.2
Rye	18.5	22.1	26.4	26.6	31.1	33.1
Barley	21.0	23.9	29.3	30.1	35.2	37.0
Oats	20.2	22.2	26.0	28.8	33.5	34.6
Hungary						
Wheat	13.7	13.8	15.0	18.6	25.2	29.0
Rye	10.9	12.4	11.4	10.8	12.1	12.9
Barley	13.0	14.4	17.9	18.8	21.5	23.8
Oats	12.1	12.1	14.1	11.6	15.5	16.7
Poland						
Wheat	11.9	12.5	16.1	19.7	23.2	24.0
Rye	11.2	12.6	14.6	16.4	18.7	19.6
Barley	11.8	12.7	16.2	19.4	23.0	25.7
Oats	11.4	13.1	15.2	17.1	20.4	22.4

Note: Countries shown have relatively similar European climatic zones but varying levels of agricultural technology.

Source: Glowny Urzad Statystyczny Polskiej Rzeczypospolitej Ludowej, Rocznik Statystyczny 1970, Vol. XXX (Warsaw, 1970), Tables 83, 84, 85, 86, pp. 630-32.

structural malfunctions of Polish agriculture. Furthermore, the migratory movements from the backward areas to the technologically advanced western areas have had a direct bearing on the improvement of
agricultural techniques used in villages throughout Poland. Thus, the
use of fertilizers and the crop yield per hectare have shown a marked
increase since 1938.[56]

The role of the proportion of agricultural output in the western
territories in Poland's total output was measured in 1964 as follows:
four main cereals (wheat, rye, barley, oats), 30 percent; wheat, 41.7
percent; potatoes, 27.7 percent; milk, 27 percent.[57] Since the western
territories constitute about 30 percent of Polish farmland, the agricultural output of the area could be further increased if the state farms
were made more productive. They comprise, in the north, 30-40 percent of the farmland. Because the soils are generally poor but climatic conditions are ideal for rich pastures, there is a potential for an
increase in cattle-breeding.

Little has been done to promote large-scale cattle-breeding.
The perennial shortages of meat in Poland, caused by increased meat
consumption, could be alleviated if the much-discussed plans for
cattle-breeding were implemented. The industry of the area has provided Poland's great chance for recovery from the devastation of the
war and for the reallocation of its resources. If properly developed
to a level surpassing the present output, the area's agriculture could
be an equally valuable asset in solving the difficult economic situation
of contemporary Poland. Poland aspires to the Western European
standard of living, which was an unattainable prewar dream but is
now a distinct possibility—if all Poland's human and natural resources
are put to maximum productive use.

ECONOMIC RECONSTRUCTION AND URBANIZATION

The western territories came into the political framework of
Poland at a time when they and the rest of Poland had been destroyed
in almost equal proportions. The economic tasks of rebuilding thus
created grave problems for the Polish nation, but they also contributed to the formation of new ties between the settlers and the territory
they had to rebuild. This process involved sacrifices and a deeper
knowledge of the economy and history of those areas, even on the
popular level. The effort involved in the rebuilding, reorganization,
and integration of these areas into the body politic of Poland released
sociological and psychological phenomena of mass enthusiasm for
that pioneering work.

A general feeling of participation in the historic and patriotic
mission is present and evident in all written records of those early
days. The rebuilding of the economic framework was possible only
through the release of energy of such magnitude and through the active
participation of people with such powerful psychological motivation.
The integration of the areas, so devastated and disorganized that in
the early postwar days they were popularly known as the "Wild West,"
was in no small measure due to mass participation in the rebuilding
tasks.

The atmosphere of pioneering contribution, the largely selfless
initiative displayed on many occasions under difficult living conditions,
can hardly be captured by an outsider and would require a study in
itself. Documents now appearing vividly describe the pioneering days
of 1945-49 in the western territories. We can hardly omit the role
of these intangible psychosocial elements when analyzing the rebuilding
tasks of the new society. The phenomenon was too widespread to be
without consequences. The perusal, in the files of the Western Institute in Poznan, of 227 memoirs of early settlers describing early
economic problems and their solutions,[58] shows the great extent to
which this powerful psychological element then shaped life and economy

That atmosphere of dedication and mission was largely termina-
ted by the early 1950's after the introduction of rigidity and dogmatism.
A powerful source of social support for the economic rebuilding and
development of the western territories was thus destroyed, and the
changes following October 1956 were only to a small extent able to
recreate the atmosphere of the pioneering days of early 1945-49.
But these changes did rally public opinion behind the new program of
rebuilding and of rectifying past bureaucratic errors that had slowed
down the process of integration in the area.

We must also analyze the influence that the changed economic
system had on markets, distribution, and commerce. Masses of
primarily rural people were transferred into an urban environment
that was much more developed than most Polish cities.[59] The
migrants rapidly acquired new tastes and used new machines, utensils,
and household goods (see Table 30). To some extent, this also was
true of the new rural settlers since, as in most of Western Europe,
the differences between village and town life and styles were not as
sharp in the western territories as in prewar Poland.

There was a dearth of industrial products in the immediate
postwar period, when all available resources were first directed to
rebuilding and then, after 1949, to the development of basic means

TABLE 30

Estimated Selected Household Equipment in Poland, Selected Years, 1955-68
(number per 100 households, as of December 31)

Durable Consumer Goods	1955	1960	1965	1966	1967	1968
Radio sets	24	43	51	50	49	50
TV sets	0	6	24	28	32	37
Washing machines, electric	0.5	19	45	48	53	58
Refrigerators, electric	0.1	1.8	10	13	16	20
Sewing machines	6	13	21	22	23	24
Passenger cars	0.3	1.1	2.4	2.9	3.3	3.7
Motorcycles, scooters, and motorized bicycles	2	10	17	18	17	18

Source: Estimates of the Planning Commission of the Ministers' Council and the Central Statistical Office, in Concise Statistical Yearbook of Poland, 1970, Vol. XII (Warsaw: Central Statistical Office, 1970), Table 18, p. 320.

of production. For many years, there was virtually no opportunity to indulge the newly acquired tastes, values, and styles. Thus, the problem of the "buyer's explosion," even in the moderate Polish version, was postponed until the late 1950's and the 1960's (see Table 31). At that time, the changes stemming from the urbanizing effects of population transfers became evident. Until then, the available stocks of goods had to be used up or overutilized.

Since half the new population of the Oder-Neisse regions come from central Poland, frequent family reunions are staged in their old or new homes. The visitors to and from the west provide the channels of communication through which new patterns and ideas are disseminated. The growing sophistication of the "western" cousins affects the tastes of their families in the old homes. The "western" way has thus become a model.

Thus, the society of the western territories has suddenly emerged as the most progressive factor for new urban values and socioeconomic patterns. It has become the model for society in other parts of the country, a powerful market force molding values and tastes that now are eliminating the traditional and basic divisions between the cities and villages, which are becoming progressively similar in buying tastes. That social unification is the unique contribution of the western territories to contemporary Polish outlook. It forces a change of traditional production techniques and prompts the introduction of new or redesigned products to replace those of lower quality that were once acceptable to the unsophisticated consumer.

The rapid influx of the peasant population into Polish cities not only brought about the moderate—by Western standards—urbanization of Poland but also profoundly affected the cities themselves, their structure, and their role vis-à-vis the countryside. The rapid increase of urban dwellers put first-generation peasants into the cities in overwhelming numbers over a relatively short period of time, during the largely chaotic stage of postwar economic reconstruction and reorientation of the economic model.

At the same time, some cities that were deemed to have an "incorrect" social structure were to acquire a new or greatly enlarged industrial capacity (as in the case of the Nowa Huta steel mill complex near Cracow). Hence, the location of new industrial investments often was decided by extra-economic considerations. If theoretical considerations were not the sole factor determining the location of industry, they were an overriding factor in the final decision. The resulting concentration of investments in heavy industry and large-scale

TABLE 31

Savings Deposits and Checking Accounts in Polish Savings-and-Loan
Institutions, Selected Years, 1955-69
(as of December 31)

Specification	1955	1960	1965	1968	1969
Total Deposits (millions of zlotys)					
All Polish savings-and-loan institutions	2,768	20,782	61,792	104,771	120,794
Savings deposits	2,369	19,294	58,752	100,081	115,671
Checking accounts	399	1,488	3,040	4,690	5,123
National Savings Bank	1,673	15,484	44,424	76,716	90,499
Savings deposits	1,274	14,307	42,256	73,412	86,891
Checking accounts	399	1,177	2,168	3,304	3,608
Of which individual accounts	253	627	1,154	1,995	2,162
Savings-and-loan cooperatives	—	2,209	9,972	16,700	17,773
Savings deposits	—	1,898	9,100	15,314	16,258
Checking accounts	—	311	872	1,386	1,515
Workers' trade union grant-and-loan organizations	1,002	2,883	6,944	10,690	11,760
Mutual-aid funds*	93	206	452	665	762
Average per Capita (in zlotys)					
Combined savings and checking	100	695	1,958	3,231	3,697
Of which savings deposits	86	645	1,862	3,086	3,540

*In units subordinated to the Central Union of Labor Cooperatives and Central Union of Handicraft
Cooperatives for Supply and Sale.

Source: Concise Statistical Yearbook of Poland, 1970, Vol. XII (Warsaw: Central Statistical Office,
1970), Table 11, p. 336.

operations directed large portions of the rural migrants to the large cities, which grew rapidly, often at the expense of small towns. The latter slowly withered because of this strict application of the accepted economic philosophy. Later, through realistic modifications, purely economic considerations began to play their role once again.

Although thus far the population of small towns has decreased only in terms of percentages, large cities are registering rapid increases. Part of the increase still is caused by a steady influx of rural people. Consequently, the cities experience a certain amount of "rurification" (as that process is called in Polish professional literature). Not only are the cities changing the first-generation peasant, but the peasants are changing the cities, often modeling them according to village values and way of life. For example, all Polish cities now have many breeders of domestic animals and many more active small-scale farmers than before, while some rural social customs are accepted and fostered.

The inevitable transitional period brought about a certain de-urbanization of towns and cities. On the other hand, migrations increased the percentage of the total population molded by the urban style, way of life, and level of aspiration. Within the cities, migrants found educational influences and possibilities far beyond those available in the pre-1939 countryside. Thus, we can safely state that the migration influenced economic conditions and interrelations in contemporary Poland in more ways than one, reshaping traditional relationships and attitudes. Prior to 1939, the western territories (as eastern Germany) were considered part of the West and produced partly for export to Poland. By their integration into the Polish economy and political structure, these areas have reoriented Poland's economy and have become a factor in raising the standard of living and changing the values of the rural society of Poland.

NOTES

1. W. Nalkowski, Poland as a Geographical Entity (London: Allen & Unwin, 1917).

2. Glowny Urzad Statystyczny Polskiej Rzeczypospolitej Ludowej, Rocznik Statystyczny, 1970, Vol. XXX (Warsaw, 1970), Table 37, p. 311. (Hereafter cited as Rocznik Statystyczny, 1970.)

3. Heinz Quirin and Werner Trillmich, Westermanns Atlas zur Weltgeschichte (Braunschweig: Georg Westermann Verlaj, 1963).

4. Oxford Regional Economic Atlas: The USSR and Eastern Europe (London: Oxford University Press, 1956).

5. M. Opallo, "Zmiany w uprzemyslowieniu Ziem Zachodnich," in Studia nad zagadnieniami gospodarczymi i spolecznymi Ziem Zachodnich, Vol. IV, pp. 90-97.

6. Oxford Economic Atlas of the World (Oxford: Oxford University Press, 1954), p. 73.

7. Antoni Wrzosek, Bogactwa mineralne na Ziemiach Zachodnich (Katowice: Instytut Slaski, 1947); Jan Dylik, Geografia Ziem Odzyskanych (Warsaw: Ksiazka, 1946).

8. Jozef Zaremba, Atlas Ziem Odzyskanych, 2nd ed. (Warsaw: Glowny Urzad Planowania Przestrzennego, 1947).

9. Ibid.

10. Zbigniew Iwasiewicz, ed., Polskie Ziemie Zachodnie i Polnocne Zagadnienia Morskie (Poznan: Wydawnictwo Zachodnie, 1957); Rocznik Statystyczny, 1970, Vol. XXX, op. cit., Table 37, p. 311.

11. Sesja Rady Naukowej dla Zagadnien Ziem Odzyskanych, IV, VI.

12. Teofil Lijewski, Rozwoj sieci Kolejowej Polski (Warsaw: Instytut Geografii PAN, 1959).

13. Glowny Urzad Statystyczny Rzeczypospolitej Polskiej, Maly Rocznik Statystyczny, 1939, Vol. X (Warsaw, 1939), Table 6, p. 165. (Hereafter cited as Maly Rocznik Statystyczny, 1939.)

14. Ibid., Table 27, p. 204; Rocznik Statystyczny, 1970, Vol. XXX, op. cit., Table 37, p. 311.

15. Panstwowe Wydawnictwo Ekonomiczne, The Economic Development (Warsaw, 1961), p. 416.

16. Stanislaw Godowski, "Rozwoj komunikacjina Ziemiach Zachodnich," in Studia nad zagadnieniami . . . , op. cit., Vol. IV, pp. 179-96.

17. Rocznik Statystyczny, 1970, Vol. XXX, op. cit., Table 19, p. 305.

18. Godowski, op. cit.

19. Rocznik Statystyczny, 1970, Vol. XXX, op. cit., Table 2, p. 297.

20. Maly Rocznik Statystyczny, 1939, Vol. X, op. cit., Table 14, p. 197.

21. Lijewski, op. cit.

22. Atlas Polski (Warsaw: Urzad Geologii, 1963).

23. Lijewski, op. cit.

24. Zaremba, op. cit.

25. Ibid.

26. Stanislaw Smolinski, et al., "Struktura przemyslu Ziem Zachodnich w latach 1939-1959," in Studia nad zagadnieniami . . . , op. cit., Vol. IV, p. 40.

27. Jozef Kokot, Logika Poczdamu (Katowice: Slask, 1961), pp. 193-200.

28. Zaremba, op. cit.

29. Kokot, op. cit., p. 205.

30. Nowe Drogi (Warsaw), September 1956.

31. Juliusz Kolipinski, "Zagadnienia gospodarcze Ziem Zachodnich," in Polskie Ziemie Zachodnie (Poznan: Instytut Zachodni, 1959), p. 206.

32. Ibid., p. 205.

33. Jan Dangel, "O ruchach wedrowkowych ludnosci w malych miastach (Strzegom)," Miasto, Vol. VII, No. 9 (1956), pp. 32-34.

34. Ibid.; Kolipinski, op. cit., pp. 214-15.

35. Bruno Gleitze, Ostdeutsche Wirtschaft (Berlin: Duncker and Humbolt, 1956), p. 3.

36. Kokot, op. cit., pp. 193-200.

37. Jozef Szaflarski, Ruchy ludnosciowe (Gdansk: Instytut Baltycki, 1947).

38. Smolinski, et al., op. cit., p. 40.

39. Gotthold Rhode, Die Ostgebiete des Deutschen Reiches, 2nd ed. (Wurzberg: Holzner-Verlag, 1955), p. 193.

40. Opallo, op. cit., p. 61.

41. Ibid.

42. Ibid., p. 49.

43. Kolipinski, op. cit., p. 202.

44. Panstwowe Wydawnictwo Ekonomiczne, op. cit., p. 63.

45. Mysl Wspolczesna (Warsaw, 1947), Vol. I, No. 8, p. 139.

46. Wilhelm Volz, Die Ostdeutsche Wirtschaft (Langensalza, 1930), pp. 89, 90.

47. Ibid., p. 87.

48. Glowny Urzad Statystyczny Rzeczypospolitej Polskiej, Rocznik Statystyczny, 1947, Vol. XI (Warsaw, 1947), Table 18, p. 51. (Hereafter cited as Rocznik Statystyczny, 1947.)

49. Maly Rocznik Statystyczny, 1939, Vol. X, op. cit., p. 78.

50. Jozef Popkiewicz, Spoldzielczosc produkcyjna na przelomie (Wroclaw: Zaklad Narodowy im. Ossolinskich Wydawnictwo, 1959).

51. Rocznik Statystyczny, 1947, Vol. XI, op. cit., p. 39.

52. Rocznik Statystyczny, 1970, Vol. XXX, op. cit., Table 20, p. 225.

53. Rocznik Statystyczny, 1947, Vol. XI, op. cit., Table II, p. 48; Glowny Urzad Statystyczny Polskiej Rzeczypospolitej Ludowej, Rocznik Statystyczny, 1958, Vol. XVIII (Warsaw, 1958), Table 6 (11), p. 124.

54. Wincenty Stys, "Zagadnienie ustroju rolnego na Ziemiach Odzyskanych," in Biuro Studiou Osadniczo-Przesiedlenczych, Sesja Rady Naukowej dla Zagadnien Ziem Odzyskanych, Vol. I (Warsaw, 1946), pp. 7-70.

55. Rocznik Statystyczny, 1970, Vol. XXX op. cit., Table 20, p. 225.

56. Ibid., Table 107, p. 267.

57. Tadeusz Derlatka and Jozef Lubojanski, Western and Northern Territories of Poland: Facts and Figures (Warsaw: Western Press Agency, 1966), Tables 15-20.

58. 227 Memoirs, in the archives of the Western Institute in Poznan.

59. Jan Stanislaw Los, Warunki bytowania ludnosci polskiej na Ziemiach Odzyskanych (Lublin: KUL, 1947).

5

ASPECTS
OF SOCIAL INTERRELATIONS
IN THE
NEWLY CREATED SOCIETY
OF THE
WESTERN TERRITORIES

The sociological consequences of migrations are probably the
most far-reaching and the most difficult to assess over the short
term. However, enough data have been gathered in Poland by sociological research teams and individual scholars (including the author
of this study) to indicate that the migrations effected lasting changes
in Polish social structure and traditional family ties, values, institutions, leisure and work attitudes, levels of aspiration, and techniques.

Although sociological studies of these changes are conducted in
many places affected by the postwar population movements, the western territories provide an ideal social laboratory for such investi-
gations. The population there is composed of different elements from
all parts of the country and from Polish emigrant colonies aboard.
A new society is being formed, and new values and standards are
being accepted.

This is a direct result of the confrontation between the primarily
rural migrants and the economy of these areas, which is endowed
with fully developed productive facilities. Thus, the society being
created in the western territories differs from the traditional rural,
village-oriented Polish peasant society. (Such peasants still form the
backbone of Polish society as a whole, although some of them have
recently been urbanized.) The new Polish society of the Oder-Neisse
territories is characterized however by Western European economic
and social relationships, influencing and emphasizing the urban way
of life and its value for the population as a whole. Despite the initial

"rurification" of the urban centers in the western territories, the emerging new pattern of social and economic interrelations is clear. This new pattern, if only because of its quantitative aspects, must inevitably affect the village-rooted population of Poland.

THE EMERGING
SOCIOCULTURAL PATTERN

The migratory movements all over Poland, and especially in its western territories, formed a base on which a new social model has been slowly emerging. A large urbanized middle class was either ill-developed or nonexistent in most areas of prewar Poland. The emerging model accords with the median standard of living common to both the clerical and the laboring wage-earners, and the newly urbanized peasant elements derive aspiration for social mobility from it.

The migratory movements that preceded the rapid industrialization of postwar Poland have accelerated the formation of the new pattern of the middle-class way of life, leisure, and mass culture. The movement of rural masses to the cities caused the intensive interaction of these newly urbanized elements with their former villages and, in process, changed the levels of aspiration of the latter. That general influence of towns on villages still continues, breaking the social and economic barriers that previously existed between them; slowly, the life pattern of the village tends to be adapted toward that of the town.

For the first time in Polish history on such a scale, the peasants were put in direct contact with the cities (currently, virtually all peasant families have at least one member in some urban center). Because of the perennial weakness of Polish cities, this is significant for the social structure of Poland. In the past, the cities lacked deep-rooted contacts with the peasants. Large foreign colonies, only partially assimilated, were a recurring characteristic of the Polish urban scene.

Rural-urban contacts are especially noticeable in the western territories, where the good road and railroad network facilitates communication to a much larger extent than in the old provinces. Undoubtedly, the road-building investments all over the country, necessitated by the growing motorization of Poland (see Table 32) also have been influenced by such village-city contacts. Thus, the most radical and durable changes caused by the postwar migrations and the Communist revolution were wrought in the Polish villages, structurally affecting not only their economy but their social system.

The modern society taking shape in the Polish western territories already is exerting great influence on the rest of the nation through social and economic interaction within the body politic. It plays an important role in spreading the new social and cultural pattern—formed and shaped by the technologically superior and highly advanced economy of the Oder-Neisse areas—across the Polish countryside. There were two phases of socioeconomic interaction caused by the westward shift of the Polish frontiers in 1945 and the subsequent settlement of the Oder-Neisse areas by Poles:

1. The rebuilding and socioeconomic reorientation of the war-shattered area and its assimilation into contemporary Polish culture; this phase has been successfully completed.

2. The new society created through the amalgamation of various types of Polish regional culture is increasingly influencing other parts of Poland. It is cementing Polish society as a whole through the removal of the last vestiges of regional particularism. It is setting the high standard of a technical culture assimilated by the settlers as a standard to be achieved in the process of urbanizing and modernizing the way of life in the basically populist Polish society.

These characteristics of the majority of migrants who are currently adapting the urban values and way of life bring to the mind of an American researcher an analogy with the relatively recent great rural migration that flooded American cities with Southern and Eastern European immigrants. The current largely Negro and Puerto Rican population movements to the cities of the north of the United States, apart from their racial overtones, also bring somewhat similar sociological and structural changes to American cities—changes of revolutionary dimensions, regardless of the totally different political, social, and economic situations existing in the two countries.

Thus, an American perspective might provide a better understanding of the socioeconomic consequences of the great demographic revolution that currently is affecting and profoundly changing Poland. It is estimated that over 8 million persons, or 33 percent of the total population of the country at the end of the war, migrated after 1945 within the present territory of Poland or from outside it (see Table 33). There are no comparable migratory movements of proportionate dimensions to be found anywhere in Europe.

TABLE 32

Motor Vehicles in Poland, Selected Years, 1938–69
(thousands)

Description	1938	1955	1960	1965	1969
Number of automobiles	29.8	40.3	117.4	245.5	401.8
Number of privately owned automobiles	n.a	20.5	90.8	214.9	371.9
Number of trucks	8.6	73.2	120.1	183.3	240.9
Number of privately owned trucks	n.a	3.6	7.2	9.1	19.4
Number of cycles, scooters	12.1	169.7	771.4	1,464.8	1,746.3
Number of privately owned cycles, scooters	n.a	163.0	763.5	1.451.3	1,734.0
Total number of vehicles	54.0	349.8	1,113.3	2,083.0	2,668.5
Total number of privately owned vehicles	n.a	187.9	869.5	1,675.3	2,125.3

Note: n.a. = not available.

Source: Glowny Urzad Statystyczny Polskiej Rzeczypospolitej Ludowej, Rocznik Staty-

TABLE 33

Estimated Postwar Population Migrations in Poland

Year	Specification	Total
1945-49	Repatriates from west	2,282,042
1944-48	Transferees from east	2,200,000
1946-50	Peasants to the cities	2,270,000
1946-50	Poles to the Oder-Neisse	2,400,000

Sources: Glowny Urzad Statystyczny Rzeczypospolitej Polskiej, Rocznik Statystyczny, 1950, Vol. XIV (Warsaw, 1951), Table 7, p. 22; Adam Sarapata, ed., Przemiany Spoleczne w Polsce Ludowej (Warsaw: Panstwowe Wydawnictwo Naukowe, 1965), pp. 90, 92; national census of 1950.

The causal effect of migrations on the formation of the populist-oriented mass culture also bears some resemblance to American experience. Polish cities currently are facing problems similar to those faced by the American communities due to a somewhat similar influx of varying immigrant groups. In this respect, Poland's problems are close to the American rather than the European social pattern, since America also was largely molded by the "melting pot" and "varying mix."

The Polish "melting pot" abruptly brought large masses of peasants to the cities. It not only gave them increased opportunities for an improved standard of living and education but also greatly widened the social base of the Polish intelligentsia. That peculiar elite element of Polish society,[1] imbued with ideas and motivations from the past and shaped by different social and economic conditions, is currently undergoing great changes.

The sociocultural consequences of great migrations, in effect a social revolution, are most vividly manifested in the western territories. There, the newcomers did not have to conform to the values and traditions of the locality to which they migrated since the Oder-Neisse areas had been emptied of their former German population. On the other hand, the migrants arriving in cities located in the old provinces (such as Warsaw, Cracow, and Bydgoszcz) may have had to conform to the values and traditions of the population they augmented.

Apart from the physical environment, productive facilities, equipment, and resources, the new settlers in the western territories did not find any predetermined pattern of values, institutions, or way of life to which to conform. All those basic elements of the social structure had to be created outright. No pattern brought by the largely rural settlers from their previous homes could fit the economically highly advanced surroundings that they found; the new patterns had to be created by the settlers themselves. Furthermore, the composition of the newly founded society has reflected the varying mix of the major groups of settlers. It ranged from nearly complete new villages transplanted from localities cut off by the new eastern border to a bewildering mixture of elements stemming from all major groups, highly diversified in geographical, economic, sociological, and cultural origins.

The migrants to the west did not organize their social institutions strictly in accordance with the pattern of the traditionally conservative Polish peasant. This change occurred not only as a result of the leveling influence of the mixing of diverse groups; even more significant was the impact of a technical culture of a much higher order than in the settlers' previous homes. Thus, new leisure and work attitudes were fostered as a result of urbanization or easier access to the towns and cities, and through large-scale mechanization practically unknown in the Polish village of yesteryear.[2]

Sudden shifts and transfers of population brought different use of work and leisure time, that is, a change from rural to industrial tasks and pastimes. The peasant type of entertainment evolved to the urban type. Thus, the population of the area is evolving a new pattern of society approaching that of a Western society. Furthermore, because of the widespread migration of younger people to the western territories, the average age of leaders is relatively low (generally in the thirties) and social mobility is much greater than in central Poland. A change in goals of social advancement and a new level of aspirations occurred as a consequence. Old patterns of social advancement through the priesthood and marriage changed as new opportunities became available through education and Party activity.

MODIFICATIONS OF THE FAMILY PATTERN

Migrations to the cities, and especially to the western territories, have affected many a social institution and its role. Rural

family ties were reshaped by the relative independence and anonymity
that the individual found in the town or village that he selected as his
new residence. Institutions and patterns that were especially affected
included marriage, church attendance, inter-family relationships,
and parental authority. The great migrations generally involved the
loosening of social ties, especially among rural migrants in the
cities. However, prevailing customs and mores in the villages also
were affected, although to a far smaller degree.

The migration of a great mass of young people from central
Poland (as opposed to the family migrations of the eastern Polish
population) in particular led to changes in the traditional Polish family
pattern. Nevertheless, despite the loosening of family authority
and the influence of a new environment in which all people were strangers to one another, the family retained its role as the only pre-existing
organized unit of society in the western territories. The modified
pattern that emerged was shaped by the family structure of each different element of the population, from the relatively backward peasants of eastern Poland to the urbanized re-emigrant workers from
France. That pattern has elements that can be traced to each group's
place of origin, but intermarriage and unified social structure now
play the crucial role in adaptation.

Family structure plays a highly significant role in the newly
created society. We must define its influence upon the new society
and differentiate the various family patterns to be found there. Both
the settlers and the area's native Polish population were primarily
rural and thus shared the values of the Polish peasant family, but
each of these two basic groups was influenced, in a different way, by
its sex and age structure and by its family composition. Furthermore,
although the Polish peasant family has always been rigidly structured,
the war dispersal of family members, the losses, and the resulting
break-up of families, profoundly affected both new settlers and autochthons.

The group native to the area suffered chiefly because of the
large-scale conscription of its males into the German army. They
shared the fate of German soldiers throughout the war, on all the
battlefields, and suffered heavy losses. No statistics are available
on those losses. However, during our field research, we encountered
many households in Opole Silesia that had lost at least one family
member while he was serving in the Wehrmacht during World War II.
Furthermore, there was a widespread phenomenon of split families.
Many men who had survived the war in the ranks of the Wehrmacht
either were taken prisoner by the Western Allies or were evacuated

in the last months of the war and chose not to return "home" (which by then was in the Communist-controlled part of Europe).

A return movement from the Western prisoner of war camps began in the immediate postwar years. Subsequent events, which solidified the East-West ideological division of Europe in 1948-49, affected the decisions of those who remained in the West. Losses and emigration sharply reduced the age groups that were fully productive and/or of marriage age. This situation in turn resulted in a marked drop in the birth rate of the Polish native population in the postwar years. This drop can be seen from the data compiled for the counties in Opole Silesia, where the native-born population was in the majority.[3]

The absence of the men had additional and far more important sociological consequences. In many instances, the permanent or semipermanent absence of the head of the household and/or his draft-age sons forced younger male children to seek outside employment much earlier than they normally would. This dislocation was further compounded by the wartime experiences of youth, which seriously impaired the father-centered, traditional peasant family pattern. These processes—the growing independence of the younger generation and its challenge to traditional practices and values—have been further accelerated by the urbanization and industrialization of peasant society in contemporary Poland. Thus, the traditional authoritarian structure of the family in the autochthonous group was seriously impaired in the postwar period.

The same changes, although in part stemming from different causes, modified the similarly rigid code of behavior of the peasant immigrant group, which had been even more harshly treated by the war. The peasant immigrants had faced brutal experiences during the occupation, wartime expulsions, slave labor, population losses, dispersal and separation of families, and deterioration of moral values. Furthermore, although the circumstances and wartime fate of each family unit varied somewhat, the new settlers could be divided into three subgroups according to the immigration route that had taken them to the Oder-Neisse territories.

The transferees from eastern Poland generally came in family and village groups and often settled in the same village or town. Their families were the least affected by the war losses and dispersals. They retained, to a large extent, the traditional family pattern, although eventually it was modified by environment and the forces of urbanization and industrialization.

The repatriate segments of the new society also retained their family structure, but their behavior, family interrelations, and value systems had been modified by the societies in which they had lived, sometimes for decades (the repatriates included primarily Poles from France, Yugoslavia, Germany, and Rumania). Only after their return to Poland did they realize how different their attitudes were toward such issues as the role of women in the family, the upbringing of children, and the appropriate mode of behavior for teenage children and young adults.

The most vivid manifestation of changes in family values occurred among Poles who were repatriates from France.[4] They experienced, in reverse, the very same problems of adjustment to the different values that they or their parents had faced after emigration from Poland. French values and family structure, which they had once found strange and alien, had been absorbed, sometimes unwillingly; now these French values were subject to ridicule, criticism, and even ostracism in Poland.[5] The repatriates from France were further handicapped by the fact that their children almost always had adjustment problems in school because they often spoke the Polish language badly.

The behavior and values of the "French" families had been so strongly affected by Western European industrialized society that, at the beginning, such families felt alien in Poland and tended to cluster together. This also was true to some extent of the Polish repatriates from Germany. However, the animosity between Poles and Germans and the wartime experiences had deterred widespread assimilation of German values. Thus, the repatriates from Germany encountered fewer readjustment problems after their return to Poland.

Whereas the repatriates from France and Germany, as well as the much smaller groups of repatriates from Belgium, Canada, and other Western nations, actually were advanced in their social structure and system of values, the repatriates from Yugoslavia and Rumania encountered adjustment problems from the opposite side of the social development spectrum. They had lived in the societies that were more primitive, extremely rural, and highly structured. Now they suddenly had to adapt to the conditions prevailing in the areas of settlement as well as to new neighbors who were far more advanced. Their families were little affected by industrialization and their social

cohesion was much more rigid, even in comparison to the average
Polish family. In the Oder-Neisse territories, their values clashed
with those of the other more "Westernized" repatriates and the Poles
from western Poland.

With the exception of the former German residents, the repatriates had not been severely affected by war losses and dislocations.
Only the repatriates from Germany constituted an exception; they had
been severely persecuted by the Nazis, and those who had been German citizens—as many were—had been required to serve in the Wehrmacht, where losses were heavy.

However, the largest population group in the new society of the
Oder-Neisse territories was composed of settlers who immigrated
into the area from central Poland, either directly (from overcrowded
or demolished villages and cities) or after returning to Poland from
prisoner of war, concentration, and labor camps in Germany. A
large percentage of these individuals could not return to their homes
in the central provinces, since their villages and cities had been
totally destroyed.

The most compact group of urban residents displaced by the
total destruction of their city were the former residents of Warsaw
(about 143,000). They were dispersed across the western territories,
and they provided many towns and cities with their first ethnic Polish
population (as was the case, for example, in Jelenia Gora). The deportees and slave workers returning from Germany either came
directly to the Oder-Neisse area, since they knew of the destruction
of their original homes and work places in central Poland, or moved
into the western territories after returning home and finding the
destruction. A smaller group, which had been deported to Germany
from the former eastern provinces of Poland, were classified by the
Polish authorities according to their places of origin with those of
their compatriots who opted for Poland and came directly from the
east.

The former deportees shared some element of cohesion because
of their common experience as slave workers in Germany, which became an asset when they moved into the industrialized Oder-Neisse
territories: since they had worked on farms or in factories in a highly
industrialized society, they had become trained in the use of various
types of machinery. Even the settlers from central Poland had improved their skills during the war because contacts with cities became much more frequent than before 1939 and because their war
experiences imparted some technical knowledge and skills.

These two subgroups among the settlers—those who came directly from central Poland and those who came via slave labor experience—had a similar family structure. They were young and mostly enterprising, with the sex ratio shifted toward young men (women were also found in both subgroups, although not in a fifty-fifty ratio). The mobility induced by war deportations and the decision to migrate to the western territories greatly undermined the traditional peasant family pattern because of the settlers' relative independence and lack of supervision at an early age. Church authority as well as family authority was visibly weakened. Thus, the normal behavior pattern of the migrants was entirely different in their new homes in the west than in their native villages.

The major groups of newcomers—the settlers, transferees, and some of the rural repatriates (those from Yugoslavia and Rumania)—have been slowly affected by progressive industrialization and the concomitant changes. The rural migrants from the east and other Eastern European countries were least affected by those problems. On the other hand, the repatriates from the West were already largely urbanized in their behavior and mores. Thus, the traditional value systems connected with the two rigid and traditional codes—the family and the Church—were under attack, often without advance notice.

The settlement of all these groups* across the vast area of the western territories with a "varying mix" in each locality, immediately presented each new community with the daily confrontation of values, acquired or inherited, that were molded by different traditions. Thus, the ensuing problem of "mixed" marriages, which was the first indication of integration, was closely observed by students of integration in the region.[6] Since each group had a somewhat different age and sex ratio, the local inter-family ties assumed bewildering checkerboard characteristics.[7]

The differences in systems of values constituted both a positive and a negative factor in the creation of the new society in the Oder-Neisse areas after World War II. The dissimilar systems of values held by different immigrant groups and the native inhabitants made possible a relatively speedy urbanization and industrialization of the immigrants settled among the Poles native to the area, particularly in Upper Silesia. On the other hand, the differences in values were

----

*With the exception of a numerically rather insignificant group of repatriates who chose to settle in clusters.

responsible for much social friction. Generally the newly settled villages and towns were composed of many groups of settlers. It was only in Upper Silesia that the majority of the population was native to the territory and remained there following the war.

INTER-GROUP COEXISTENCE
AND ITS EFFECTS

Most of the areas of the western territories are currently populated by groups of settlers representing virtually all the regions of Poland. This admixture was caused primarily by the spontaneous and unorganized settlement of the area in the immediate postwar period.[8]

All groups have perpetuated the basic characteristic of the Polish family structure, the close contacts within the family (in reality, extended kinship relationships). These contacts have far-reaching effects on social interrelations, the flow of ideas, and the confrontation of values within the new society of the western territories and with families in France, West Germany, the USSR, and virtually all villages in other parts of Poland. Through these contacts, new values have been shaped and new ideas acquired, leading to the progressive "Westernization" of village life in other parts of Poland.

The flow of traffic to and from the area of origin is best illustrated by the direction of holiday traffic on the Polish railroads (the increased mobility is shown by the fact that the pre-1939 volume of traffic has quadrupled).[9] By studying the extra trains on various lines, one can even plot the rough relationship of preponderant "origins" of the new settlers. It has been proved beyond doubt that these exchanges have introduced an additional binding element in the social structure of the new Poland by sharing the experiences of the new society of the western areas with the rest of the country.

The adaptation of the various groups to the new place of settlement, and their amalgamation into one society, constituted a long and involved process. This process has been extensively studied by Polish sociologists since 1957. They are checking social relations between various groups, family ties, and "mixed marriages," as well as closely studying small groups. Their studies clearly demonstrate that all the groups had to adapt to one another and to the new socioeconomic conditions caused by the drastic transformation of Polish society and economy by the Communists. Various groups were brought together and had to coexist uneasily in the towns and villages.[10] The sociologists generally agree that such mixing of various groups hampered, to a considerable extent, the initial amalgamation of the population of the areas in question and retarded the formation of the new society there.

During our field research years later, we found ample evidence of the initial friction between Poles native to the territory and Poles from other regions of the country who settled there after 1945. The frictions arising from the chaotic conditions of the war-torn country and the looting by advancing Soviet armies and Polish speculators were bound to affect the social interrelations of various groups of settlers and the native population. These conflicts were further aggravated by the ideological clashes caused by the social revolution imposed on the country by the Soviet-sponsored Communist government and the differing history and traditions of various groups of settlers arriving in the western territories immediately after the military takeover of the area.

The inter-group differences appeared magnified in the microcosm of local social relations. Similarities either were not recognized or were overlooked. In their relations with the autochthonous Poles in particular, all three groups of immigrants (settlers, repatriates, and transferees) stressed similarities between themselves and overlooked their own inter-group differences. Interrelations between those two basic subdivisions of society (immigrants and autochthons) did not become frequent until some ten or fifteen years after the war. This was partially due to the Germanization of customs and mores of the autochthons, but mostly to their recent experiences. The autochthons had had to serve in the Wehrmacht, as their forefathers had served in the Prussian army since the eighteenth century, and they were thus on the other side of the great dividing line.

It is impossible to fully understand the psychological effects of the occupation without having personally experienced it; observers can have only superficial understanding. Even the most patriotic autochthons could barely grasp the reasons why they were disliked or even hated for casual actions that they found perfectly natural, such as displaying in their homes photographs of themselves and their kin in Wehrmacht uniforms, often pictures of sons, fathers, or husbands who had died in those uniforms. One who did not live throughout the nightmare of the Nazi occupation in Eastern Europe could not understand the hatred of even the ordinary Wehrmacht uniform, much less the uniform of the SS or SA. Thus, a deep cleavage developed between the autochthons and all the other groups. Thereafter, it was only natural to magnify the differences, real or imagined, and perpetuate them. From the study of youth attitudes, we found that it took almost a generation to modify those antagonisms; but they still linger on low levels, however, without disrupting social patterns.

The prewar Polish minority (the autochthons), led by a conservative rich peasant group who remained in the area, have discovered to their bewilderment that the same structural patterns that allowed them to retain cohesion and their Polish speech (Catholicism and the closely knit patriarchal family pattern) are the very institutions under attack in the new Poland. Furthermore, they had no taste for sweeping social reforms, which the peasants of central Poland, land-hungry and isolated in their villages, may have craved. Since sometimes the autochthons did not possess a clearly developed national identity, the attack on those two basic pillars of society was, in their eyes, an attack on the very essence of "Polishness." They also suffered greatly during the chaotic postwar period, when their manner of speech and behavior made it very difficult for the uneducated or ruthless elements streaming into the area from Poland to differentiate them from the Germans.

Since the autochthons did not share the immigrants' experiences of the war and occupation, the looting at the front and the postwar lawlessness, during which they suffered severely, became very negative symbols of Polish rule, adversely affecting their image of the new Poland. The newcomers, in view of their past experiences, were more philosophical and tended to dismiss those excesses as temporary phenomena. Even the leaders of the autochthons, who had hoped for Polish rule, felt themselves betrayed and their support undermined among their own people. The reality of liberation was totally different from the dream, and it also involved a social revolution, which the autochthons had come to distrust and fear under the impact of Nazi propaganda.

Furthermore, they had to adjust to living with the groups settling in their midst, who were as a rule backward at work and in social relationships. The beleaguered family and Church once again became the only redoubt for their resistance to change and their slow adaptation to the reality of the social organization of the new Poland. But even socioreligious traditions and Church membership, which enabled them to preserve, to a large extent, the Polish ethnic character that they shared with the newcomers, were burdened by different local traditions that had developed during the centuries of political separation (for example, in the churches different Polish hymns were sung and different customs observed). Thus, in the final analysis, the autochthons have had great difficulty in adapting to the new order in their transformed homeland. Although they remained in their homes, their

social adaptation to new conditions was not easier—indeed, it may
have been more difficult.[11]

The newcomers from central and eastern Poland were, of course,
faced with two basic tasks: (1) to adjust to a strange environment and
new conditions and (2) to adapt to a much higher standard of living
and aspirations in the emerging society. Since they settled primarily
in places emptied of their previous population, they could not measure
their standard of behavior or mold their pattern of social organization
after the pre-existing system of values. Instead, a system of values
was in the process of formation through the confrontation of the various
patterns brought by the settlers from their previous homes.[12]

These values clashed, coexisted, and changed; usually, although
not always, they were molded by the dominant group in each community.
Thus, the checkered pattern of social interrelations was slowly emerging. The vestiges of local and provincial differences were slowly
eliminated. For the first time, a new model of national cultural and
social interrelations is being formed on the local and provincial level,
which in the past preserved the relics of social and cultural institutions and values.[13]

In the most difficult period of postwar political and social adjustment, the settlers also found that the Church was the only immutable formal organization around which they could rally. Their traditions and values had to be unified within the Church, as there were
small differences in the religious customs of various provinces. However these differences were not as pronounced as in the case of the
Poles native to the area.

NEW ELEMENTS OF SOCIAL STABILITY

Since newcomers were a majority, they primarily carried the
burden of the reconstruction. How they fulfilled those tasks often
decided how much of the pre-existing economic structure could be
saved and utilized by the new society. Thus, the rebuilding tasks—
performed in the primitive, hazardous, unbelievably harsh, and chaotic conditions of postwar social disorganization in half-empty areas—
were a powerful determinant of the future stability of each community.

Those individuals who were actively engaged in saving and
rebuilding became the leaders of new local communities. The new
social hierarchy and scales of values that were being developed by
them became a strong bond linking the settlers with the area in which

they settled. Local initiative was channeled in two major directions:
(1) to the newly formed civic and social organizations that fostered
ties with the history of a given region, e.g., the Friends of Klodzko
Land Association (these sprang up in almost every region before
1949 and again after 1957) and (2) to the socioeconomic development
of the area.

The numerous civic and social organizations have been strongly
supported by the authorities. They are publicizing the pioneering
effort of the first settlers and, in order to create new traditions and
heritage, they are preserving for future generations the values accrued.
These organizations have been quite successful in disseminating, in
cooperation with the school systems, the body of knowledge concerning
the history of settlement in their areas. The history of each region,
often written by local civic leaders, is now being taught in schools
in the western territories.[14]

Although this settlement of the area was on a large scale and
conducted under extremely difficult conditions, it has followed, as
has been demonstrated, the traditional pattern of migrations in the
region. The new political and social pattern affected each group in
the new society and the various groups had difficulty in adapting to
one another, but historically and socially they were not strangers.
It is interesting to illustrate this observation with an analysis of the
situation that arose in Mazuria and Warmia.

The Poles native to the area are primarily the descendents of
Mazovians who migrated there during the fourteenth to sixteenth
centuries (mostly from the northwest and northeast of Mazovia, through
the Chelmno and Lomza regions respectively). In Warmia, they retained their Catholicism (since they were part of Poland until 1772),
and in Mazuria they became Protestants (in the Polish fief of Ducal
Prussia, which was under the suzerainty of Poland until 1657). Because of demographic pressures, from the fifteenth through seventeenth centuries other waves of Mazovians moved to the Grand Duchy
of Lithuania (especially in and around the Vilna region). Those members of this group who opted for Poland in 1945 had to move into its
new frontiers and were settled mostly in the north among the Mazurians
of what had been East Prussia.

The incoming landless rural resettlers were largely from
northern Mazovia just across the 1939 border. Thus, the new society
of what was East Prussia includes seemingly disparate elements of
population with previously antagonistic religious creeds. Paradoxically
enough, however, they all share the traditional folklore pattern of
peasants from the Mazovian province of Poland (around Warsaw).

The unifying pattern of traditional folklore and customs is evident in studies of the rural communities. However, we must emphasize that in East Prussia religious divergencies became the dominant feature of social interrelations and in effect hampered or prevented social integration. In contrast, in Silesia social integration was facilitated by the religious unity of settlers and autochthons.

All the groups of newcomers underwent a drastic change in outlook because of the relatively advanced state of urbanization and industrialization in the Oder-Neisse areas in comparison with rural Poland. However, they were totally unprepared for city living and its social and economic values. Thus, they initially transformed those towns into extensions of the villages from which they came. This had grave repercussions, since the migrants were unable to utilize machines that were a vital part of the economic structure.

The initial period was one of regression and waste of resources. However, since the economic framework of the society was in ruins, in some instances these resources could not have been utilized even if the settlers had known how. The period of regression has been adequately described in a study of Wroclaw by I. Turnau.[15] Turnau estimates that 40 percent of the new citizens of Wroclaw came directly from villages and another 40 percent indirectly from villages via small towns. The small towns thus acted as a "training ground" for city values and mores and for the acquisition of the skills necessary to operate the impressive technological heritage that the settlers found. The adaptation of the settlers to the area and its standards was prompted by their successful acquisition of new values and technological skills, which they have now mastered fully.

THE ROLE OF THE CATHOLIC CHURCH

The Catholic Church played a powerful role as a stabilizing factor in the new society. This fact has now been admitted in Polish literature on the subject. However, its importance is being decidedly underplayed since the Communist authorities have consistently sought to minimize and isolate the influence of the Church in contemporary Poland, both as an institution and as a social and educational force.

In the western territories, the Church also provided the only unifying force for the diverse elements comprising the settlers. This role was especially crucial in the period immediately after the war, when all other institutions, both formal and informal, were only in the process of organization. Thus, the Church performed a pioneering task in the settlement of new provinces and smoothed the process of their assimilation into the body politic of Poland; that these provinces are now a fully integrated part of the country can be attributed in no small part to that early role of the Church. The strength of the Church was traditionally based in rural communities, where for centuries the priest had been the uncontested real leader of the village. (Only after 1918, when the universal system of education spread, was another powerful factor introduced into the villages—the school and the teacher as the secular leader.) Since the Church was the first organized social unit of the new society, and often the only non-Communist social unit, it reasserted its traditional role in the rural regions almost immediately after the areas had been incorporated into Poland and reestablished its formal structure.

The Church also provided the first forum for community action and the first framework for local social structure. The original unpublished chronicle (with amateur photographs) of Church activities in the city of Szczecin within the first months of Polish rule (May-July 1945) demonstrates this fully.[16] Even then, the Church was beginning to rebuild churches, console early settlers, and reestablish the historical religious links of the region with Poland. The Church attempted to provide social as well as spiritual assistance, even in the chaotic early days of settlement.

Accurately estimating the power of the Church in the nation at that time, the Communist-dominated Polish government seldom conducted an public official function without opening it with a Mass;[17] thus, for example, the official takeover of Szczecin by the Polish authorities began with a Mass. The government thus tried to present to Polish public opinion an ostensible identity of views and actions between the Church and the state. Such an identity really existed with respect to the Polish acquisitions in the west, but the government attempted to extend this seeming unity to other aspects of life in order to gain at least part of the popular support enjoyed by the Church. Hence, the religious oath and the chaplains were retained in the Polish Army in the 1940's.

The role that the Church played in villages and towns of the area was not uniformly translated into Church attendance. Although the Church could achieve nearly 100 percent attendance by Catholic villagers once they had settled in a local community, the situation was different in the cities. The social restraints operative in the settlers' home villages did not extend to the environment of the western towns. However, as indicated in all the available Polish sources, the diminished formal participation of urban residents in the Mass has not diminished participation in other Church ceremonies. No overall

statistics have been published, but the available studies, although
limited in scope, indicate that virtually all Catholic Poles (including
the children of high Party functionaries and the functionaries themselves) do receive baptism and marry in Church ceremonies. Party
functionaries, especially in the countryside, participate in these Church
activities in churches outside their own parishes, and the Party has
been not only unable but often unwilling to antagonize its members by
suppressing such practices. The Party only ridicules them indirectly
in print—with no visible effect on the behavior of Party members.
Similarly, funerals are still conducted by the Church according to the
wishes of the families. In discussing the attitude of the new settlers
toward the Church, we should stress that the dividing line between be-
lievers and nonbelievers in the new society does not coincide with
the division between the industrialized segment of that society and
the traditionally rural segments.

Thus, the repatriates from France, who were both industrialized
and liberal in their attitudes toward religion,[18] had to a large extent
the same casual religious attitude as the young migrants from central
Poland, who had moved beyond the strict regimen of the village society of their former homes. On the other hand the highly industrialized autochthonic elements shared, on the whole, a deep attachment
to religious ceremonies with the least economically and socially developed repatriates from the east and with the highly industrialized
repatriates from Germany.

The religious attitudes of the autochthons, repatriates from
the east, and repatriates from Germany had been shaped by historical
forces. For the groups that previously lived in predominantly Protestant Germany, Catholicism was often synomymous with a national
sanctuary where the Polish language could be used.[19] The eastern
repatriates had also by and large lived among a population of a different faith (Orthodox) but, because there were no strongly established
progressive social forces (even mass education was of post-1918
date there), they were to a much greater extent dependent on Church
leadership on the local level. Thus, there existed a wide spectrum of
attitudes toward the Church and its role in the society.

In addition, the Party, through its control of all the news media
that mold public opinion, is slowly modifying the traditional attitude
toward the Church. However, strong conflict between the Party and
the Church is strengthening the support given by the people to the
Church, which, under pressure, is going through a period of revival and
rededication. During our field work, several clergymen admitted to us
that the large crowds filling their churches not only were giving an

outward sign of faith but also were present as an act of defiance toward the restrictive and oppressive policies of the government.

The attitude of the population of the western territories toward the Church is basically no different from that in other parts of Poland. It is only slightly different in the cities of the western areas because the anonymity of great masses of people makes possible change or modification of the traditional pattern of behavior. But the phenomenon is not altogether limited to the Oder-Neisse regions; attitudes toward the Church are very similar in the newly constructed cities of central Poland (e.g., Nowa Huta and Nowe Tychy) and among the postwar migrants to other cities.20

In its competition with the Communist government of Poland, the Catholic Church has been hampered by the Vatican's nonrecognition of the Polish western frontier, which is a political handicap detrimental to the hierarchy. The issue is constantly exploited by the government press and in Argumenty, the organ of the Association of Atheists and Free Thinkers. Because of the prewar concordate with Germany, the Vatican is unwilling to recognize de jure any cession of territory before the signing of the formal peace treaty. In addition, the Vatican is motivated by the practices of its diplomacy. Thus, the Catholic hierarchy in Poland has had to acquiesce to an expedient of temporary administration by which authority over sections of the former German dioceses was vested by the Pope in the person of the Primate of Poland.

However, since the religious administration of the area involves about 8 million Catholics, or 25 percent of the nation, the Polish hierarchy has been under tremendous pressure to obtain a more permanent arrangement from the Vatican. From the very beginning, the Church in Poland expressed views as to the irrevocability of the Potsdam decisions. Such views were voiced in 1945 by August Cardinal Hlond, the Polish Primate, in his pastoral letter.21 The Church attempted from the beginning to stabilize the situation on the basis of Canonical Law, that is, it sought to obtain the assent of the Bishop of Berlin for the establishment of a Polish hierarchy in the parts of the Berlin diocese that fell to Poland. This fact is documented by letters exchanged on the matter.22 The Vatican agreed to appoint Polish bishops for the area, but the residing Polish bishops were designated as bishops "in" the given apostolic administration rather than bishops "of" the given city. All documents are signed in this fashion, for example, by the archbishop "in" Wroclaw.

Another step was taken when a Polish bishop "in" Gdansk was designated bishop "of" Gdansk immediately after the death in West

Germany of the German incumbent (the last surviving German bishop from these regions). However, it was possible on technical grounds that the diocese of Gdansk was, as part of the Free City of Danzig, canonically exempt (that is, directly under the Vatican's authority), since it lies outside the prewar borders of Germany and thus was not governed by the concordate with the Reich.

The Polish Catholic hierarchy made a very strong pronouncement on the subject of the border lines in Wroclaw in 1965, during the twentieth anniversary celebrations of the establishment of the Polish Church hierarchy in the western territories. It completely and irrevocably took the position of the Polish government that the present western border of Poland along the Oder-Neisse line is final.

The recent attempts at Church-state reconciliation following the December 7, 1970, recognition by the Federal Republic of Germany of the Oder-Neisse boundary and the change of Polish leadership in December 1970 already have produced a first step. In a conciliatory move that ended a two-decade-old debate, the Polish government gave the Roman Catholic Church full title to nearly 7,000 church buildings in the Oder-Neisse area (many of these buildings former Protestant church property). Such a move was demanded by the Polish Catholic hierarchy as a first test of the Church-state rapprochement policy advocated by the new leadership of the Polish Communist Party.[23]

Furthermore, the series of Vatican-Polish negotiations that began in 1969 and continued simultaneously with the West German-Polish negotiations brought out an announcement of the Vatican's recognition of the Oder-Neisse boundary and the long-overdue ecclesiastic reorganization of church provinces in these areas immediately following the West German Bundestag's anticipated ratification of the Warsaw Treaty recognizing the Oder-Neisse boundary. The reorganization of ecclesiastic administration in the Oder-Neisse areas will bring the predicted revivial of the Polish bishoprics of Kolobrzg, Kamien, and Lubusz, which were founded in the eleventh to thirteenth centuries and later Germanized and extinguished by the Reformation.

THE ROLE OF THE COMMUNIST PARTY

The role of the Communist Party in the formation of the Polish society in the Oder-Neisse areas was dominant, but by no means as preponderant as the books published in Poland suggest. Field research conducted in the area has convinced us that the Party, although responsible for the rebuilding of the area and the organization of internal migrations and international transfers, often played an ambivalent role.

Every structure of the Party organization was haphazard and accidental. Those who held leadership roles in the rebuilding and preservation of movable property during the "heroic" period of post-war reconstruction in early 1945 were, as a rule, non-Party men or Socialists who were allowed to perform various official functions. At that time, the Party had a very limited membership (although it increased from 30,000 in January 1945 to 235,000 by December 1945[24] and, despite large-scale recruitment it could not even supply enough officials for the key positions in a nation of 24,000,000.

Furthermore, because of widespread opposition to the Communist takeover, and even armed resistance in some regions of the west, the Party could not perform its leadership functions without imposing its will by fiat. That, in turn, could not be conducive to social tranquility. However, the Party did wield tremendous power in the west. It could allocate at will, to anyone it chose, the confiscated German goods, property, and real estate. Thus, the Party immediately became the focus of power and a magnet for elements seeking social and political achievement. In fact, opportunities within the Party, on all levels, were virtually unlimited.

The existence of such vast opportunities in the Party explains the extremely rapid increase in the Party's ranks within a few years following its takeover of power in Poland. The channels of promotion were open to all who joined and conformed to Party discipline, but especially to the youth. Thus, at that time the Party was younger and more vigorous than other formal organizations. The organizational tasks of the Party were much easier in the west than in other parts of the country. From the first, the Party was a controversial factor but, because of the relative insecurity of the new settlers, it was far easier for the Party to demand and obtain support. The 1947 election districts were, however, gerrymandered in order to ensure the election of more "safe" candidates from these areas to the nation's Diet.

To effect the transition from a primitive economic pattern to the socialist model, the Party modified the revolutionary approach. The Party's attitudes were shaped by the reality of the tasks in the western territories. Thus, vast concessions were granted to private initiative, and until 1949 the Party regulated rather than controlled all the fields of economic endeavor except large industry. Generally, the Party had to appeal to national sentiment, history, and traditions, none of which were Communist in either spirit or ideology. Although

controversial on the political level, in the western areas of Poland
the Party performed well under the extremely adverse conditions of
postwar disorganization.

Even the anti-Communist observers living in the western territories at the time attested to the fact that the chaotic conditions could
have been checked only through the use of semidictatorial methods.
However, the Party role at the small group level in these territories
was definitely negative. It hindered any natural development of local
elites by claiming the monopoly of local decision-making. Even when
positive economic and social decisions were made by non-Party members in authority, they were consciously hampered so that they would
not have a positive effect on local public opinion and possibly endanger
the political dominance of the Party.

However, the fluidity of the new society imposed on the Party
a whole range of tasks that Party members normally would not have
been called upon to perform. Thus, in the words of a Polish intellectual,
"they* have proved the immense, intrinsic capacity of man to perform
any task, an ability which no one would even suspect to exist, let alone
dare to put to test." It is a moot question as to the trends that would
have developed in the society of the Oder-Neisse territories without
the dominance of the Party in economic and political decision-making.
This Party dominance has relegated all able but non-Communist leaders to pursuits other than politics, thereby furthering the flourishing
of economy, technology, arts, and other pursuits in which individuals
barred from political leadership (for which they are suited by temper-
ament and avocation) are using their energies. That civic life and
regional organizations flourish in the Oder-Neisse areas is in no
small measure due to these circumstances.

THE ROLE OF
OTHER FORMAL ORGANIZATIONS

The roles of formal organizations other than the Party and
Church in the society of the Oder-Neisse regions proved crucial in the
initial formative period and again in the period of rebuilding post-
Stalinist society. These groups were instrumental in correcting gross
errors, mismanagement, abuses, and injustices committed in the
economic and civic life of these regions. The energies of the old cadre

---

*"They" is the way Poles often refer to the Party.

of civic activists were supplemented by the zeal of younger civic leaders and were expressed in the net of well-developed local and regional societies—civic, cultural, and professional. All these groups were interested in the welfare of the western territories and their historical heritage. Until recently, these groups were centrally coordinated by the Society for the Development of the Western Territories, which was national in scope but best developed in the west. This society was disbanded after the Polish-Western German treaty was concluded in December 1970.

The Society acted, in the absence of due democratic process, as an ad hoc pressure group that was influential in removing many wrongs of the Stalinist and postwar period:

1. It corrected the abuse of the autochthonous population and stopped coercion used on the local level.

2. It was instrumental in the relaxation of emigration possibilities for those who wanted to leave.

3. It effected a partial revival of handicrafts, the rehabilitation of small towns, and the proper channeling of investments into endeavors that would yield the fastest results with the lowest input.

We observed extensively the activities of these groups at various levels up to that of the Special Ad Hoc Commission of the Diet on the Western Territories, now also defunct. These groups provided proper channels for persons who otherwise would be completely frustrated at the local political and economic level or prevented from taking part in civic affairs.

The activities of these pressure groups yielded the best results when focused on the most glaring issues, such as preventing the uneconomic utilization of existing resources or restoring production in idle plants. The regional groups have been strongly imbued with a feeling of mission and nationalist sentiment, and their activities are influenced by historical perspectives; they have placed heavy stress on renovating moments of the Polish past in the area. In the final analysis, the role of these organizations as a stabilizing factor in the new society was highly positive.

THE ROLE OF THE SCHOOL SYSTEM

Other formal institutions that exert tremendous influence on the formation of new values and social patterns are the cultural

institutions and schools at all levels. Such institutions developed
virtually simultaneously with the settlement of the area. The institutions of higher learning taken over from the Germans were few: one
university in Wroclaw, two institutes of technology (one in Wroclaw
and one in Gdansk), and a few specialized schools in art, education,
and medicine. The Wroclaw academic center, the only large one in
the area, was completely destroyed during the siege, and half a million
volumes of its library, especially rich in Slavic collections and previously inaccessible to Polish science, were burned.

The rebuilding of the university, originally merged by the Poles
with the institute of technology, in a city that had been destroyed by
70 percent, was heroic. The faculty (most of whom transferred from
the University of Lvov) and students actually rebuilt the lecture halls
while guarding precious laboratories and books that could be salvaged.

The academic schools in the west had increased to 21 by 1961.
Some are located such cities as Szczecin, which had no school at the
university level before the war and now has five colleges. The University of Wroclaw has grown into the third largest academic center
(after Warsaw and Cracow). In the academic year 1959-60, there
were 45,614 students in the area, as compared with 5,843 German
students in 1938-39. The number of students and institutions of higher
education is more than commensurate with the area's population.

On the primary and secondary levels, the Polish school system
should not be compared with the prewar German system, since the
yearly natural increase in the western territories is as large as the
total increase of the former German population in the six years between the census of 1933 and that of 1939. Thus, a huge educational
system had to be created outright. In 1945, approximately 3,000 grade
schools had already been opened. In 1960, there were 8,032 (or 31
percent of the Polish total), with 1,257,000 pupils. Secondary schools
increased from 105 in 1945 to 200 in 1960, with 44,612 pupils.

The school system educates children of settlers from all parts
of Poland. It also has a special function, that of forming a new pattern
of mass culture devoid of provincialism. It channels the best elements
of local subcultures and groups into new cultural patterns. The schools
also are instrumental in removing inter-group differences, animosities,
and stereotypes. Thus, the schools form the most powerful institution
for accelerating social amalgamation. Surveys conducted by Polish
sociologists suggests that schools have successfully developed uniform
patterns of socialization for their pupils. Hence social integration was
fostered. The impact of the youths on their parents is also being

documented. Future dissemination of the new national rather than
provincial mass culture is virtually assured in view of the size of the
area's young population (31 percent of Poland's children). This por-
tends well for the creation of a new type of Pole, reared in an industrial society and amalgamating the best elements of a diversified
traditional heritage, but geared to the tasks of modern society.

The spectacular growth of the education system is one of the
true achievements of the Communist government. Illiteracy has finally been virtually eliminated: in 1931, 22.6 percent of Poles were
illiterates; in 1960, the percentage had been reduced to 2.7. The
problem of illiteracy was especially acute in the western territories
because of the migration of eastern Poles and repatriates from southeast Europe whose standard of education was very low (in 1931, 41
percent of the population in the Polish eastern provinces was illiterate,
although the percentage for ethnic Poles was probably lower, about
30 percent).[25] Television is no longer news in the villages (there
were 5.7 million television sets in Poland in 1969) and radio ownership
is the common pattern. The sharp increases in these new trends in
communications will soon cause further changes in the traditional
village pattern of the past. It is alleviating the still existing, although
fast receding, difference between cultural patterns in town and countryside.

Education, youthful leadership, and a changed pattern of aspirations open new channels and affect the pattern of social advancement. During our stay in the area, we encountered in one western
village a scene typical of the changes in the social structure. At
dinner, the father, a typical Polish farmer, entertained three sons—
a scholar, an army major, and an attorney—all of whom were young
and, significantly, still maintained close contacts with the village
where the father farms.

Such city-village contacts were only sporadic before the war.
They are now quite common, because of the impact of education on
the villages and the changes in the social structure of the intelligentsia.

ELEMENTS OF DISORGANIZATION

Last but not least, we must stress that the migrations to the
cities and to the west caused grave social dislocations in the first
postwar period, as would any such great movements. Disorganization
occurred either toward the end of the devastating war and the savage
occupation or immediately afterward, and it was accompanied by a

TABLE 34

Adults Sentenced by Common Courts for Offenses
Prosecuted by Public Accusation, by Voivodship, 1961-69

Specification	1961	1962	1963	1964	1965	1966	1967	1968	1969	1969 Individual Cities
	Total									
Poland	302,045	276,628	253,100	182,474	207,976	248,447	231,786	220,520	150,668	94,759
Cities over 50,000	67,362	63,157	78,589	57,793	68,239	80,394	73,097	70,725	48,137	48,137
Cities up to 50,000	111,631	103,236	76,134	55,639	62,468	74,420	69,869	66,433	46,622	46,622
Villages	123,030	110,220	98,361	69,023	77,249	93,590	88,771	83,325	55,901	n.a.
Warszawa City	16,510	14,779	11,520	7,431	9,663	13,394	9,675	9,836	7,095	7,095
Krakow City	n.a.	n.a.	5,760	4,507	4,585	5,430	4,820	4,299	3,325	3,325
Lodz City	7,883	7,341	6,458	4,629	5,635	6,528	6,264	6,463	4,470	4,470
Poznan City	n.a.	n.a.	4,788	2,304	3,147	3,785	2,849	3,267	1,899	1,899
Wroclaw City	n.a.	n.a.	5,476	3,404	4,401	5,040	4,222	4,586	2,987	2,987
Bialystok	10,614	10,432	11,317	8,443	8,926	10,129	9,719	8,962	6,093	2,947
Bydgoszcz	15,097	15,683	14,388	10,022	10,394	12,592	11,882	11,531	8,055	4,962
Gdansk	15,664	13,921	12,590	9,619	10,757	11,733	11,968	10,970	7,355	5,285
Katowice	32,349	29,474	25,065	18,001	21,797	24,589	23,483	21,861	14,528	11,776
Kielce	14,431	13,588	12,144	8,235	8,944	11,678	11,290	10,556	6,888	3,363
Koszalin	8,401	7,642	6,692	4,987	5,697	6,697	7,374	6,959	4,889	2,669
Krakow	22,580a	20,506a	14,503	10,930	12,501	14,875	13,303	11,746	7,699	3,671
Lublin	14,803	12,433	12,459	9,276	9,451	11,803	11,610	11,371	8,487	3,802
Lodz	14,582	12,587	11,492	8,327	8,504	9,788	9,381	9,169	6,278	3,111
Olsztyn	14,347	13,151	11,391	7,923	10,502	10,986	10,713	9,749	7,179	3,471
Opole	10,185	8,425	9,140	8,261	8,337	8,713	7,902	7,021	4,755	2,647
Poznan	17,511a	16,614a	12,906	8,205	8,762	11,966	11,524	12,644	8,132	4,178
Rzeszow	14,326	12,153	10,883	7,790	9,824	12,238	11,141	9,229	6,123	2,584
Szczecin	9,925	10,214	7,569	6,351	8,447	8,816	9,257	7,870	5,522	4,094
Warszawa	23,664	22,171	18,811	14,490	15,704	21,251	18,792	17,729	11,263	5,278
Wroclaw	29,303a	26,675a	20,238	13,823	16,105	19,178	17,755	17,410	12,735	8,046
Zielona Gora	9,848	8,824	7,494	5,497	5,873	7,195	6,813	7,255	4,903	3,099
Not known and abroad	22	15	16	19	20	43	49	37	8	n.a.

Notes: n.a. = not available.
Offenses divided by voivodship in which they occurred.
aIncluding the voivodship-status city.
bNot divided between the cities and villages.

Source: Glowny Urzad Statystyczny Polskiej Rzeczypospolitej Ludowej, Rocznik Statystyczny, 1970, Vol. XXX (Warsaw, 1970), Table 18, p. 564.

TABLE 35

Adults Sentenced by Common Courts for Offenses
Prosecuted by Private Accusation, by Voivodship, 1961–69

Voivodship	1961	1962	1963	1964	1965	1966	1967	1968	1969
Poland	26,445[a]	21,462	18,445	9,459	14,347	15,930	14,146	11,946	7,139
Warszawa City	525	427	340	142	129	199	113	105	24
Krakow City	n.a.	n.a.	166	107	100	128	127	102	51
Lodz City	360	239	232	109	159	145	139	143	87
Poznan City	n.a.	n.a.	123	21	23	62	69	64	47
Wroclaw City	n.a.	n.a.	180	77	112	117	n.a.	n.a.	n.a.
Bialystok	1,008	795	728	336	697	595	599	506	309
Bydgoszcz	599	692	615	190	277	385	452	478	277
Gdansk	803	688	635	361	403	460	401	292	179
Katowice	1,838	1,647	1,255	557	895	1,194	1,061	883	543
Kielce	2,236	2,006	1,633	824	1,402	1,390	828	861	579
Koszalin	863	789	686	347	532	415	387	365	213
Krakow	1,695[b]	1,329[b]	922	452	609	912	826	834	457
Lublin	2,943	1,874	1,869	952	1,400	1,639	1,272	921	490
Lodz	1,422	1,276	1,136	597	983	984	897	720	446
Olsztyn	999	908	772	492	827	850	759	579	433
Opole	843	560	544	270	377	504	394	280	191
Poznan	1,039[b]	875[b]	755	410	541	614	595	542	245
Rzeszow	3,170	1,682	1,216	648	1,095	1,236	1,018	942	526
Szczecin	869	904	572	407	488	555	415	350	216
Warszawa	2,511	2,405	2,029	1,287	1,877	1,945	2,182	1,636	952
Wroclaw	1,961[b]	1,695[b]	1,349	553	868	1,041	1,260[b]	943[b]	652[b]
Zielona Gora	760	671	688	320	553	560	352	400	222

Notes: n.a. = not available.
Offenses allocated to voivodship in which they occurred.
[a]One person not allocated to a voivodship.
[b]Including the voivodship-status city.

Source: Glowny Urzad Statystyczny Polskiej Rzeczypospolitej Ludowej, Rocznik Statystyczny, 1970, Vol. XXX
(Warsaw 1970) Table 23, p. 566.

backwash of demoralization and total disregard for human life and
values. The revolutionary changes caused by the radical remolding
of the society and economy on the Communist model brought further
elements of disorganization and pressure. A new system was being
forced on the established system of values, which was already weakened by the brutal experiences of war and postwar chaos.

The young peasants who left their home environments to migrate
were subject to great pressures. The elements of disorganization in
the western territories—crime, alcoholism, juvenile deliquency—
were especially rampant during the period of migrations before 1949.
The disintegration of the old value system and political and social
alienation took their toll. The West German propaganda (aimed to
spread insecurity among autochthons), the political pressure of Communism, and the attacks on the Church—all these conflict situations
blocked the creation of a unified society and the amalgamation of
various groups.

Most of these problems are now receding from the social scene.
The violence and crimes of the "pioneer" period, which were much
higher than elsewhere in Poland, have been overcome with the stabilization of society accomplished after 1957. Now the statistics for
the western territories do not show trends different from those in
other parts of the county.[26]

Alcoholism and juvenile delinquency are growing and have become a national problem. But here again, although there are some
variations in pattern, the picture in the western territories is not
markedly different from the national scene (see Tables 34 and 35).[27]

The growing stability of society accounts for the decrease in
the intensity of disintegrating elements. In fact, in this respect life
in the western territories is no different from that in other parts of
Poland. Each year cements new ties in the society of the Oder-Neisse
areas. This society is western in outlook, progressively unified, and
accepts the national standard language and mores, but at the same
time it preserves variations conditioned by the specific admixtures
of values brought into that society by the "melting-in" groups.[28]

NOTES

1. Jozef Chalasinski, Przeszlosc i przyszlosc inteligencji
polskiej (Warsaw: Ludowa Spoldzielnia Wydawnicza, 1958).

2. Zygmunt Dulczewski, ed, Tworzenie sie nowego spoleczenstwa na Ziemiach Zachodnich (Poznan: Instytut Zachodni, 1961).

3. Stefan Golachowski, Ruchy ludnosciowe na Opolszczyznie (Opole: Instytut Slaski, 1948).

4. Wladyslaw Markiewicz, Przebobrazenia swiadomosci narodowej reemigrantow polskich z Francji (Poznan: Wydawnictow Poznanskie, 1960).

5. Ibid.

6. A. Olszewska, et al., "Malzenstwa mieszane na Slasku Opolskim," Przeglad Socjologiczny, Vol. XIII, No. 1 (1959), pp. 89-105.

7. Bozenna Chmielewska, Spoleczne przeobrazenia srodowisk wiejskich na Ziemiach Zachodnich (Poznan: Instytut Zachodni, 1965).

8. Zygmunt Dulczewski, Spoleczne aspekty migracji na Ziemiach Zachodnich (Poznan: Instytut Zachodni, 1964).

9. Glowny Urzad Statystyczny Polskiej Rzeczypospolitej Ludowej, Rocznik Statystyczny, 1970, Vol. XXX (Warsaw, 1970), Table 1, pp. 42-43. (Hereafter cited as Rocznik Statystyczny, 1970.)

10. Leszek Kosinski, Pochodzenie terytorialne ludnosci Ziem Zachodnich w 1950 r. (Warsaw: Instytut Geografii PAN, 1960).

11. Stefan Nowakowski, Przeobrazenia spoleczne wsi opolskiej (Poznan: Instytut Zachodni, 1960).

12. Zygmunt Dulczewski and Andrzej Kwilecki, Spoleczenstwo wielkopolskie w osadnictwie Ziem Zachodnich (Poznan: Wydawnictwo Poznanskie, 1962).

13. Zygmunt Dulczewski and Andrzej Kwilecki, Z zycia osadnikow na Ziemiach Zachodnich (Warsaw: Pantswowe Zaklady Wydawnictw Szkolnych, 1961).

14. Andrzej Kwilecki, Rola spoleczna nauczycielana Ziemiach Zachodnich (Poznan: Instytut Zachodni, 1960).

15. Irena Turnau, Studia nad struktura ludnosciowa polskiego Wroclawia (Poznan: Instytut Slaski, 1960).

16. Manuscripts in possesion of the author.

17. Ibid.

18. Markiewicz, op. cit.

19. Stefan Golachowski, Materialy do statystyki narodowosciowej Slaska Opolskiego (Poznan: Instytut Zachodni, 1950); Gustaw Gizewiusz, Die Polnische Sprachfrage in Preussen, 2nd ed. (Poznan: Instytut Zachodni, 1961).

20. Results of author's field research.

21. Jozef Kokot, Logika Poczdamy (Katowice: Slask, 1961), p. 9.

22. Manuscripts and letters, photostatic copies of which are in the author's possesion.

23. The New York Times, June 24, 1971.

24. M. K. Dziewanowski, The Communist Party of Poland (Cambridge, Mass.: Harvard University Press, 1959), pp. 192, 346.

25. Glowny Urzad Statystyczny Rzeczypospolitej Polskiej, Maly Rocznik Statystyczny, 1939, Vol. X (Warsaw, 1939), Tables 23, 24, pp. 28-29.

26. Rocznik Statystyczny, 1970, Vol. XXX, op. cit., Tables 18, 23, pp. 564, 566.

27. Ibid., Tables 26, 27 (810), p. 567.

28. Adam Sarapata, ed., Przemiany spoleczne w Polsce Ludowej (Warsaw: Pantswowe Wydawnictwo Naukowe, 1965).

6

CONCLUSIONS AND IMPLICATIONS
FOR THE FUTURE
INTERNATIONAL RELATIONS
OF EAST-CENTRAL EUROPE

Our study of the history and effects of the post-World War II population and boundary shifts in Poland has been an ambitious and very difficult task. It has not been possible to closely examine all aspects and implications of these events. Such difficulties were inevitable because these dramatic events affected virtually all phases of life in Poland.

The direct and indirect results of this shift of a medium-sized nation—unique in the history of modern Europe—were enormous and mutually interrelated and intertwined. Thus, we have retraced their impact on the nation's entire economic and social structure. It would have been a far less formidable task to present only one byproduct of these movements.

However, from the very beginning we have been fascinated by the idea of a much more complete presentation of this mass phenomenon, especially in view of the lack of studies on the subject published in the United States. It is hoped that even this tentative collection of data, previously scattered or unavailable in this country, will have some lasting value.

Our investigation required years of field research and the accumulation of a veritable library of relevant materials, collected from a multitude of sources. Even if no other purpose had been served, the results justify the effort by providing an adequate scholarly base for further studies of this interesting, yet so little researched, topic.

Hence, this study is of intrinsic interest for several disciplines of the social sciences—history, demography, economics, sociology, and international relations. But we did not undertake our investigation exclusively within the methodological framework of any one of these disciplines. In this fact lies the study's advantage as well as its main handicap. The study seeks to provide a broad view of interrelations affecting data of interest to each of these disciplines. If we had taken the perspective of any single one discipline, we should have found it virtually impossible to attempt to advance and fully illustrate the basic tenet of the study.

Our proposition is that the basic transformation and modernization of Poland, currently occurring on a scale unprecedented even in the turbulent history of that nation, were essentially predetermined by the events described in this study. To explore this set of interrelations, we have used all the general tools of the social sciences.

GENERAL CONCLUSIONS

The data contained in this study support most of the original hypotheses and assumptions formulated. However, adequate treatment of some of these hypotheses would require separate studies for which this study could serve only as a beginning. We have proved that these drastic population and boundary shifts provided Poland with a much more viable territorial base and enabled Poland to reallocate its human and natural resources. However, the hypothesis on the priority of these elements over the simultaneous changes in Poland's socioeconomic model would have to be demonstrated by a separate study in depth.

We have been shown that Poland's industrialization and modernization would have been delayed or hampered if it had not been for the new territorial and economic base acquired with the Oder-Neisse areas. Our hypothesis concerning the links between the migrations and the socioeconomic development of Polish society at large has been demonstrated and analyzed. However, further studies are required to document the degree and number of changes induced in the process of modernization of the Polish social structure.

We have succeeded in demonstrating that the basic misgivings of the Western Allies as to postwar Poland's capacity to absorb such an extension of its western border were premature. We have shown that the arguments against the transfer to Poland of the territory between the Western and Eastern Neisse rivers, the only territory questioned at the time, were not valid. We have documented this issue with previously unpublished materials that we consider a valuable and lasting historical contribution of this study. Furthermore, we have proven that the Great Powers consciously decided on the boundary changes in order to provide Poland with a viable structure, within the realities of power and the postwar status quo, without impeding Poland's national integrity, independence, and cultural identity. They have carried within themselves the seeds of permanency.

The data assembled support our basic assumptions on the demographic aspects of the study. Thus, the high birth rate observed in the new society of the western territories has been traced to the impact of migrations and the characteristics of the migrants. The colonization process, it has been demonstrated, was by and large haphazard and spontaneous. The role of the tradition of westward migratory movements in the success of colonization has been indicated.

The data supporting the economic hypotheses demonstrate that the rebuilding and revolutionary changes in the ownership of means of production were a heavy burden for the economy of these regions. The effects of the change in ownership of means of production delayed the achievement of social stability for many years.

The data assembled show that the industrial potential of the areas is being realized and also project further growth. However, these data underline the inadequate development of the area's agricultural potential. The relationship between the failure of the Communist agricultural model and the slow results in agriculture has been established. We have indicated the links between yields, postwar destruction, and the difficult adjustment of the settlers to farming conditions in the western territories. The impact of the advanced techniques of Western agriculture on Poland as a whole, although suggested, requires more study in depth.

We have shown the elements present in the social integration processes now in progress in the western territories. We have proved that the integration processes between various immigrant groups are well advanced, in contrast to those between the immigrants and the autochthons. The emergence of a new sociocultural pattern free of the vestiges of provincial characteristics has been demonstrated. The positive social role of the Church in the integration process has been demonstrated by field research and documents. The positive role of the Party, as the force responsible for organizational tasks, has been shown by the data on the scale of changes involved in the total restructuring of the area. The Party's negative role on initial social integration and stability has been well documented. The growing role of education and the school system in the formation of new values and mass culture has been shown against the background of former group diversity and the favorable age structure of the new society. Finally, we have shown that current data on social disorganization do not suggest a continuation of the postwar trends associated with migrations and social dislocations.

HISTORICAL BACKGROUND AND POLITICAL FRAMEWORK

We analyzed in detail the position taken by each government concerned with the boundary changes during and immediately after World War II. We have documented the fact that the Polish government attempted to preserve the status quo on the 1939 Polish-Soviet border and achieve substantial changes in the 1939 Polish-German frontier. These claims were based primarily on strategic and economic considerations. At the same time, the program of incorporation in the west was hampered and modified by the fact that such incorporations might unfavorably affect the possibility of preserving the status quo in the east.

We have illustrated this hypothesis through the use of hitherto unpublished documents from the archives of the Polish government in exile in London, indicating the basic unanimity of views on the subject between the Polish government in London and the Polish resistance movement in Poland. Although politically unrealistic and untenable, the position of the Polish government on the question of the eastern frontiers was solidly supported by the underground in Poland.

This proposition was demonstrated by the use of hitherto unpublished position papers prepared by the underground authorities. We have seen that this rigid attitude precluded the Polish government from achieving a much better settlement in the east, and that the Polish government did not believe that the extensive changes in the Polish western frontier were possible and would be supported by the Western Powers. Thus, whereas the rigid maximalist position was maintained on the issue of the inviolability of the eastern frontier, only a minimalist program of corrections was advanced for the west.

Hence, it was assumed that no alternative program had been prepared and no political preparations had been made in anticipation of the least favorable eastern boundary solution along the Curzon Line, which would inevitably cause a large-scale migration from the lost territories. As the documentation shows, the last-minute attempts to save the city of Lvov for Poland, if undertaken earlier, might have at least reduced the scale of migrations. Because the Polish government concentrated on a policy on the boundary issue that would have been realistic only if there had been general acceptance of the Polish view, it was totally unprepared for the boundary solutions that were imposed on Poland during and after World War II. By its rigidity on the issue of the eastern frontier, the Polish government failed to win full Allied support for the western acquisitions.

To a large extent, the no-alternative stand of the Polish government on the eastern boundary issue, when such an alternative was still possible, preempted for the Communists the role of champions of the Oder-Neisse boundary solution. We have shown that, by adopting as a goal this western border delimitation of post-World War II Poland, the Communists followed a highly popular policy that is emotionally appealing to national sentiments and historical traditions. This policy has enabled them to avoid accusations of being traitors to Polish public interests in the east.

Furthermore, we have demonstrated, with the aid of recently published materials, that the Curzon Line, which was widely claimed to be an ethnographic border, was not really based on such considerations. Despite the large-scale migrations of eastern Poles, the ethnographic situation in the northeastern areas of prewar Poland has remained essentially unchanged since 1931, as indicated by comparisons of ethnographic maps of the area.

Although the Polish government agreed only to one-sided changes in the Polish western borders, the Western Allies approached the problem of Polish borders differently. Faced with the reality of Soviet power and claims in Eastern Europe—a situation they were unable to reverse politically—they planned to compensate Poland for the forcible cession of the eastern territories with granting it the western territories, which would guarantee Poland's political and economic viability.

Since the planned western compensations were considered by the Allies to be of primary importance, they were extensive and economically valuable. This proposition was proved by use of the hitherto unpublished and formerly classified American document "Postwar Poland: Economic and Political Outlook," which was prepared by the Research and Analysis Branch of the U.S. Office of Strategic

Services following the Yalta Conference. This document generally paralleled the British position on the matter.

We have also shown that the unwillingness of the Western powers to include the area between the Western and Eastern Neisse rivers in postwar Poland caused the weakening of the language used to describe the territorial cessions to Poland in the compromise formula that was finally accepted at Potsdam. However, the Western powers authorized and cooperated in the transfer of Germans from the contested area, thus creating a fait accompli that seriously undermined their previous position and stablized the Oder-Neisse Line as the de facto frontier of Poland.

Thus, the provisions for the transfer of population, to which all the parties subscribed, differentiated the Oder-Neisse issue from typical jurisdictional boundary conflicts, which involve sovereignty over both territory and population.

Although population transfers were used in the past as a means of boundary settlements (most notably the Greek-Turkish exchanges conducted under the League of Nations after World War I), we have assumed that this was the first case, in international affairs, of assigning to one country the territory of another after it had been emptied of its former population. Former German inhabitants who had fled or been expelled after the war were barred from returning to their former domiciles in these territories.

We have proved that the wartime decisions of the Allies, although not finalized, carried within themselves the seeds of permanency. The hitherto unpublished documents used by the author in this study throw a new light on the problem of the Polish boundary changes during World War II, and we believe that their use is a valuable and lasting historical contribution.

DEMOGRAPHIC ASPECTS

We have established that the westward shift of Polish ethnic and national territory profoundly and permanently affected Polish social structure generally and that of the Oder-Neisse territories in particular. The migration involved 4.5 million Poles, mostly young, who moved to the newly acquired western territories. There were obvious demographic consequences to the fact that these relatively young people came into the possession of a far more advanced and well-developed economic infrastructure than that of prewar Poland. The better living conditions that the settlers found, and their age structure, were factors in the rapidly increasing birth rate in the 1950's and 1960's. At the same time, the migration of many rural people from parts of Poland that had been largely destroyed during the war directly affected social and economic conditions by relieving the population pressure and removing the redundant labor force from the villages of central Poland.

Since the migrants came from several distinct population groups, we described the characteristics and social history of each and its impact on the new society created in the western territories. The differences between the migrants and the autochthons also were analyzed, since it was assumed that their varied demographic characteristics differently affected the emerging society.

We have shown that the migration of small farmers and landless rural residents from other parts of Poland into the western areas was facilitated by the fact that it duplicated the traditional westward migratory trends toward industry in the nineteenth and twentieth centuries. The scope of the secondary migrations that followed can be assessed by the fact that migrants from central Poland, rather than re-emigrants or transferees from the former eastern Polish territories, currently constitute the largest portion of the population in the Oder-Neisse regions.

We also demonstrated that the primarily peasant characteristics of all the migratory groups affected the high birth-rate pattern in the western provinces.

Furthermore, with data drawn from both Polish and Soviet sources, we proved that the eastern Polish component of the new society—the group for whose transfer the idea of territorial compensation was primarily formulated—was only partially able to move into the new Poland.

Several deductions were made concerning the mode of settlement of the Oder-Neisse areas by the Poles:

1. Despite the existence of the planning and colonizing machinery, the overall settlement process was spontaneous rather than organized.

2. The plans for organized colonization were formulated too late or were not applicable in view of the spontaneous influx of settlers.

3. The situations arising out of the spontaneous colonization were legalized ex post facto.

4. Although haphazard, the general settlement pattern largely conforms to earlier formulated plans. However, this was accidental and due to the direction of the communication lines.

5. Only the eastern Poles and some groups of central Poles were systematically resettled.

We decided that the area was largely settled in two phases: first the spontaneous migrations of the postwar period, followed by the planned transfers designed to modify the emerging settlement pattern. We further concluded that the progressive assimilation of Poland into the Communist system and the impact of the cold war precluded any large-scale return of Polish emigrants from Western Europe. This limited the potential supply of skilled immigrants needed in the western territories.

We have shown that one of the groups comprising the new society in the western territories was especially valuable to the Poles for political, national, and economic reasons. That group was made up of the autochtonous population of Upper Silesia and the Mazurian Lake region. They numbered over one million and, although heavily Germanized, retained their Polish dialects and customs. However, we have pointed out that the grave excesses committed against that group during the chaotic postwar periods, the relative inexperience of the new Polish authorities with their problems, and, especially, frictions between the settlers and the native population neutralized that group and eventually caused it to diminish through emigration.

In addition, we concluded that the political pressures accompanying collectivization in the early 1950's were by far the most destructive force that adversely affected all components of the population in the western areas. These political pressures disrupted the newly established social ties and considerably slowed down or reversed the stabilization process. In addition, the political pressures partially obliterated the results of the rural settlement policy by causing peasants to abandon their farms and move to the cities. They also diminished the new flow of immigrants to the area.

The demographic makeup of the settlers was postulated to have the most lasting effect on the new society in the Oder-Neisse areas. Since 1950, the natural growth of population has nearly completely replaced the diminishing internal and external migratory movements as a source of population increases. It is further established that the high birth rate in the area is due not only to the specific age level of the settlers but also to the higher fertility of women, which is characteristic of the rural origin of the majority of settlers.

Thus, we may anticipate that on the whole the high rate of natural population increase will continue, despite its decrease over the 1960's. It is because of the high birth rate that, in 1971, the population in the Oder-Neisse areas again reached its prewar peak, despite the extensive depopulation of those provinces immediately following the war. Furthermore, in view of the high birth rate in the cities and the continuous village-city migrations, we are convinced that the urbanization of the Oder-Neisse areas will continue.

ECONOMIC ASPECTS

We believe that the economic integration of the western territories within Poland was facilitated by its geographic location in relation to the rest of Poland: the area is set within the basins of two major rivers, the Oder and the Vistula, which are nearly coextensive with the territory of the Polish state. In addition to location, the much more developed industrial base of the Oder-Neisse territories in relation to the rest of the country is considered of prime economic importance.

The wartime destruction and postwar looting drastically reduced the economic potential of the area to a fraction of its prewar output. However, in view of the fact that most of the former residents either fled or were expelled, that small share of the area's industrial capacity which was undamaged was put immediately at the disposal of the Polish economy. There would not have been initially enough labor force to activate production had more industries survived the war. The subsequent expulsions of the remaining Germans in 1946-47 did not greatly affect the economy because of the simultaneous influx into these territories of migrants from other parts of Poland and Poles returning from Germany and other Western European countries.

Moreover, the destruction that ruined wide stretches of the area did not affect Upper Silesia and the Sudetic coal and industrial regions. This was considered of primary importance for the future ability of Poland to utilize the industrial resources of the area. Furthermore, despite the destruction of the communications system, the road and railroad networks serving those areas were much denser than those in other parts of Poland. Hence, we have shown that it could serve the new economic area much more rapidly than would appear from analysis of war destruction.

However, we agreed that the rebuilding and reorientation of the industry, trade, and communication toward the new economic markets constituted a formidable task that required considerable investment to be allocated to this purpose during the first postwar years. We have illustrated the complexity of problems involved in the rebuilding and reorientation of the Oder-Neisse economic infrastructure and in the forging of new interrelations. Such illustration was deemed important, since initially those tasks diverted a significant portion of Poland's postwar investment capital.

Furthermore, the revolutionary transition of the Polish economy from capitalist to state ownership of production particularly hampered the rebuilding of the economic structure of the western territories. This was especially true of the rebuilding of handicrafts, which had provided a large segment of the new work force with its means of livelihood and thus acted as a powerful stabilizing factor in the new society.

Thus, we assumed that the forcible introduction of the new economic model of ownership caused a drastic reduction in the number of handicraft establishments and had nearly disastrous results on the economies of smaller towns in the area. The role of handicrafts in small towns of the region was disproportionately greater in view of the destruction of large industrial enterprises during or after the war and the removal of productive equipment from small industries to replace machinery in larger industrial centers. Thus, it was assumed that the doctrinaire approach of the planners was responsible for the serious economic conditions in the small towns. The negative impact of these reforms was further compounded by the simultaneous reorganization of the distributive pattern of internal trade through the establishment of direct trade outlets in the villages.

We believe that the economic changes described above had a catastrophic impact on the economy and role of small towns in Poland generally, and in the western areas particularly. The negative effects of those reforms were especially far-reaching because they occurred in a region that was not yet stabilized. Thus, strong outward migratory movements caused grave economic dislocations and, as a consequence, the underpopulation and slow decay of small towns.

We assumed that the partial reversal in 1956 of economic policies in relation to handicrafts and private enterprise in small towns of the Oder-Neisse area did not entirely remove the effects of the former policies. We believe that the strict application of economic dogmas to an area that had just undergone total population changeover delayed social stability in the region for many years. Through this example, we sought to show the negative role of government enforcement of the new economic model through a purely mechanical and doctrinaire approach to socioeconomic problems, as opposed to the positive role of private enterprise in the postwar rebuilding.

Despite the temporary economic reversals caused by the narrow application of political doctrines, we believe that the investment effort of the Polish government, although concentrated primarily in heavy industry, resulted in the rebuilding of the full economic potential of the area. This proposition has been illustrated with data showing the production totals of the area both in absolute terms and as ratios of the national output.

However, the concentration of past investment efforts in selected sectors of the economy, especially in Silesia, has created economic disproportions and relative underdevelopment of the northern provinces. The consistently high rate of natural increase and relatively limited investment in labor-intensive industry were bound to produce mounting economic difficulties in those regions as the labor supply increased. We assumed that the Oder-Neisse area's economic problems do not lie in the industrial framework, which has been sufficiently strong to allow for added efforts to alleviate the economic disproportions described above, but, rather, in agriculture.

The wartime destruction, postwar migrations, and settlement of farmers who had no knowledge of local farming methods, soil, and microclimatic conditions all have had a lasting impact on the state of agriculture. New farmers came from areas where the intensive farming methods of the West were generally unknown. We believe that they were further hampered by the collectivization policy pursued by the Polish government in the years 1949-56. Thus, the collectivization efforts proved nearly fatal to the area's agriculture.

Although prewar yields have been generally achieved, the agricultural potential of these areas is far from fully exploited. In view of the disproportionately large share of investments directed to state farms, they should have achieved much better yields than private farms. However, overall state farm yields have been higher than those on private farms only since 1966-69, and only on the average. In view of the central role of state farms in the area, a considerable increase in state farm yields could close the yield gap that still exists between Polish and Western European agriculture (see Table 29, Chapter 4).

It was also stipulated that the political decisions predetermining the extent of state farm holdings in the western territories prevented a more rational distribution of farm land among the new settlers. These policies were designed to facilitate the planned collectivization, which was delayed for reasons of expediency. Nevertheless, we have shown that the superior agricultural techniques adopted by the settlers and now widely used serve as an advanced model for farmers in other parts of Poland. This model is communicated through the family links maintained by farmers in the western areas with their families elsewhere in Poland.

SOCIAL INTERRELATIONS

Although all groups of settlers, as well as the autochthons, shared the values of the Polish peasant family, we have shown that each was influenced in a different way by recent history, the dispersal of family members, the war losses, and postwar migrations. We analyzed those differences and their impact on the family structure within each group of migrants. Furthermore, we felt that it was significant to trace the relationship between the wartime experiences of the groups and their relative ability to adjust to the social conditions in the newly acquired western areas.

In view of the diversity of groups settling in the same communities within the area, we assumed that the daily confrontation of acquired or inherited values, customs, and traditions presented a serious barrier to social amalgamation and creation of a unified social pattern.

We considered that the ensuing problem of "mixed" marriges was the first indication of integration, and "mixed" marriages have been widely accepted throughout the western territories. However, some settlers are still reluctant to marry autochthons and vice versa. We have indicated that these prejudices were influenced by wartime experiences that remain vivid and by the Germanization of the customs and mores of the autochthons.

The experiences of settlers in the area are apparently being shared with their families in other parts of Poland through the flow of traffic to and from "the area of origin" or family domicile. Through these contacts, new values shaped by the higher standard of living in the western areas are influencing village life in other parts of Poland.

We also have shown that the coexistence of various groups interspersed throughout the provinces leads to the elimination of vestiges of local or provincial characteristics. Thus, a national pattern of cultural and social interrelations is being molded on the provincial level where, in the past, the relics of local social and cultural institutions and values were preserved.

We have stated that, throughout the postwar period in the western territories, settlers found in the Catholic Church the only immutable formal organization around which they could rally. Thus, the Church played a powerful role as a stabilizing factor in the new society by providing the first form of community action and the first framework for local social structure. Moreover, although the Church in the western areas has often been the leader of social forces, the religious attitudes of the population there are not basically different from that of other parts of the country.

We considered that the role of the Communist Party in the formation of the Polish society in the Oder-Neisse areas was dominant but by no means preponderant; although the Party has been responsible for the rebuilding of the area and the organization of internal migrations and international transfers, it often played an ambivalent role.

In view of the Party's very limited initial membership, the early leadership roles usually were filled by non-Party men. Furthermore, because of the widespread resistance to the Communist takeover, the Party often could not perform leadership functions without using force— and they used it often. That, in turn, could not be conducive to achieving social tranquility. Furthermore, in the early postwar period the Party had to appeal to national sentiment, history, and traditions that were not Communist in either spirit or ideology, as well as maintain a modus vivendi with the Church. It is only since 1949 that the Communist Party has been in complete control of the social forces in the western areas.

We also found that schools at all levels, as well as various cultural institutions, are exerting a tremendous influence on the formation of new values. The system comprising primary and secondary schools as well as all types of university schools has been fully developed and performs a special function in forming a new mass culture devoid of provincialism. Because of the coexistence of various groups, the school system stresses the best elements of local subcultures and group values.

Finally, we found that the elements of disorganization in the western territories that were widespread during the period of migrations—due to the disintegration of the old value systems, lack of contact with old communities, and alienation in a strange place of settlement— are slowly receding from the social scene. We have proved this proposition by showing that statistics on court sentences for criminal acts for the western territories do not show trends different from comparable regions in other parts of the country.

FUTURE IMPLICATIONS

The postwar realignment of social and economic resources in Poland has vast implications for the future relationships in East-Central Europe. The failure of the West (with the exception of France) to accept the de jure status of Poland's western border is an issue of diminishing importance, in view of present East-West rapprochement. Thus, it is assumed that such recognition will soon be obtained, especially in view of the impact of the historic Warsaw Treaty of December 7, 1970, in which the Federal Republic of Germany pledged the inviolability of the Oder-Neisse boundary and recognized it de facto. The pending ratification of this treaty may close the darkest chapter in the tragic history of Polish-German relations and truly open a new era.

The Potsdam decisions removed the economic handicaps that prevented Poland from playing its role in the political configuration of East-Central Europe. By their long-range nature, these decisions laid the foundation for the economic modernization of a country whose political structure was, in the twentieth century, endangered as much by the narrowness of its economic base as by power relationships. The shift of borders transformed Poland's chances for future prosperity and internal tranquility, regardless of present contingencies. The Potsdam decisions also cut the Gordian knot of minority squabbles in a vital area of Europe and laid the foundations for better future relations. The recent growth of Polish economic potential, which has contributed to the steady elimination of the glaring disparities between Poland and Germany—which were a possible cause of international disequilibrium and tensions—came about largely as a result of the integration of the Oder-Neisse areas into Poland.

Thus, the totally new socioeconomic pattern molded by the huge migratory movements began taking shape. Regardless what the future has in store for Poland, the post-World War II demographic revolution wrought durable changes in its social structure and economy. The urbanizing and industrializing trends continue, although on a smaller scale, and contemporary Poland, its economy, and its social structure bear less and less relationship to the Poland of thirty years ago. Industrialization and urbanization also have strengthened Poland's political and international potential, regardless of the present system of ideological blocs and binding alliances. The political balance of power in East-Central Europe has been affected by the drastic economic and structural changes wrought in Poland by migrations, the forced pace of capital accumulation for rebuilding of war-desolated old provinces, the reactivation of the war-shattered economy in the newly-acquired western territories, and industrialization.

Although currently obscured by existing Communist Bloc inequities and considerations, Poland's potential as a political power has been enhanced by the newly redistributed social structure and recently developed economic capacity, despite the unfinished nature of urbanization and the existence of unused or underdeveloped resources (as in agriculture, with its relatively backward techniques, organization, and output). If further developed, Poland's present territory could provide an adequately balanced base of agricultural, industrial, and natural resources and, as a result, a high national standard of living.

Thus, the social distribution caused by the migrations could be considered conditio sine qua non of current economic advances. However, it should be noted that the need for more investments requiring huge capital resources will slow any appreciable increases in the Polish standard of living. Such investments are necessary for petro-chemical industry in Plock; lignite and electricity in Belchatow in central Poland; iron ore, lignite, potash, and electricity in the Konin-Leczyca-Turek industrial triangle; natural gas resources in Lubaczow; sulfur in Tarnobrzeg; all these areas are industrially backward but well endowed with labor and natural resources. Unless the annoying economic mismanagement and waste inherent in centrally directed, highly theoretical, and cumbersome planning machinery is eliminated or vastly redressed, it obviously will cause a heavy drain on economic resources, which at this stage remain limited.

Nevertheless, Poland's economic resources and hence political power have been greatly developed and argumented during the recent years. The present unused potential is considerable, despite the present lack of the large quantities of oil and iron ore that are needed for large-scale industrial development. It must be stressed that the distribution of population and the modernization of Polish social structure laid the foundations for future economic development of and the growth of Poland's political power and international influence. If used in the national interest, Poland's growing international influence could increasingly contribute to the peace and prosperity of East-Central Europe as well as the entire continent.

In analyzing the Polish demographic revolution and the subsequent urbanization, growth, and development that reshaped economy, society, and power relationships, it is necessary to underline the role played by the integration of the Oder-Neisse areas into the body politic of Poland. This was an overriding factor in enabling relatively rapid rebuilding of Poland's economic potential despite the simultaneous sociopolitical experiments that retarded growth. The integration of the Oder-Neisse areas helped Poland to finally solve the perennial problem of agricultural labor surpluses and unemployment. Finally, the assimilation of the western territories provided Poland with a large resource base and offered the chance of achieving a higher national standard of living in the future.

More than 25 years after Potsdam, the Oder-Neisse area forms an integral part of the Polish economy. Settlers rebuilt the area's economic capacity from war devastation and put it back into productive use. The rebuilding, carried out by a war-decimated nation, created a lasting bond between the area and its settlers. It became in turn a powerful political and emotional argument especially in view of the destruction by the Nazis of 38 percent of the Polish national wealth during World War II.

There can be no doubt that without the Oder-Neisse areas Poland would have no hope of standing on its own economically and would sooner or later become completely dependent on the USSR. The recent growth of Polish economic potential came about largely through the integration of those areas with Poland.

Today, the western territories represent 33 percent of Poland's area and contribute, on the average, 28 percent of the country's industrial output (by comparison, in 1936 they contributed 6.4 percent of Germany's industrial output). Some 50 percent of Poland's export capacity is located in the western territories. Some 8.9 million Poles, or 28.8 percent of Poland's population, live there, and the natural rate of population increase there remains 35 percent higher than in Poland as a whole (the population in the western territories increases by about 150,000 per year).

Whereas in economic terms the western territories were of marginal value to 1939 Germany, they are vital for modern Poland and its future development. Their share of national industry is an indication of their importance, and that share will increase in the near future as the demographic outlook for the territories necessitates further capital investment. The total population of the western territories was 25.4 percent of Poland's total population in 1960, but 31 percent of all Polish children up to 10 years of age lived in the western territories. The area's resources, which remain underdeveloped and currently are receiving substantial investments (currently 26.2 percent of Poland's development capital), may be an answer to the present Polish agricultural shortages.

The integration and assimilation of the Oder-Neisse areas within the national body politic, which considerably strengthened Poland's socioeconomic structure, also profoundly affected international relations by the change in power ratios in that part of the continent, whose weakness has often tempted expansionists. It also brought a challenge: the rapid adjustment of Poland to the highly developed technical culture in the western territories and the rapid development of the area's economic resources.

Thus, in the final analysis, the western territories provided Poland with a historical opportunity for social redistribution through migrations and for the raising of the standard of living for a quarter of the population. The western territories enabled Poland to shorten its period of economic development and to overcome the economic backwardness caused by the eighteenth-century partitions. But the highly developed technical culture in the western territories necessitated rapid adjustment. Thus, in the long-term view, the westward shift of Polish national territory will enable Poland to become the intermediary between the West and East, partaking of both systems and traditions. Poland's swift modernization will be its contribution to the stability and economic strength of East-Central Europe.

POLAND'S EASTERN BOUNDARY: THE
ORIGIN OF THE CURZON LINE

The Curzon Line was originally designed as an armistice line between the Soviet and Polish armies. When it was proposed, it was specifically suggested that the acceptance of this line would not prejudice Polish claims to the territory east of the line; however, the acceptance of the line would empower the Polish government to establish a Polish administration to the west of the line. Since the armistice was never agreed upon, the line never materialized. However, there were important discrepancies in the actual description of the Curzon Line; these stemmed from loose usage of the term "Curzon Line" in discussions and conferences.

The confusion originated in the erroneous and ambiguous description of the line in the telegram sent above Lord Curzon's signature from Spa on July 11, 1920. The "Curzon Line" proposed by that telegram was composed of two parts: the northern, which passed through the territory of the former Russian Empire, and the southern, through the former Austro-Hungarian Empire (Galicia). Future disagreement was based upon an apparent contradiction contained in the description of the southern section of this line. The first part of the telegram that gave birth to the Curzon Line reads:

That an immediate armistice be signed between Poland and Soviet Russia whereby hostilities should be suspended.
The terms of this armistice should provide on the one hand

that the Polish army shall immediately withdraw to the line
provisionally laid down last year by the Peace Conference
as the eastern boundary within which Poland is entitled to
establish a Polish Administration. This line runs approximately as follows: Grodno, Vapovka, Niemirov, Brest-
Litovsk, Dorogusk, Ustilug, east of Hrubieshov, Krilow
and thence west of Rava Ruska, east of Przemysl to the
Carpathians. . . . On the other hand, the armistice should
provide that the armies of Soviet Russia should stand at a
distance of fifty kilometers to the east of this line: in
Eastern Galicia each army will stand on the line they occupy at the date of the signature of the armistice.[1]

Since the line dividing the two belligerent armies on July 10 ran
outside the territory of East Galicia, the wording describing the proposed delimitation of the southern section of the Polish-Soviet armistice line was misleading and offered in effect two variants of the line
in that section. One actually divided the former Austrian province of
Galicia east of Przemysl. The other, "the line they (the armies)
occupy at the data of the signature of the armistice," lay outside the
territory of East Galicia. Even at the high point of the Soviet offensive in early August, that line was only about thirty miles east of
Lvov.

We must mention that there are divergent opinions as to the
origin of this seeming contradiction in the description of the southern
section of the Curzon Line. W. Sworakowski ascribes it to an error
caused at the time that the telegram was drafted.[2] L. Kirkien,[3]
quoting Harold Nicolson,[4] observes that this misleading wording was
purposely introduced by the "back-room boys" of the British Foreign
Office in order to secure East Galicia for the future when Tzarist
Russia would be restored, in return for the latter's abandonment of
its traditional territorial ambitions in the Dardanelles and the Per-
sian Gulf area.

The southern segment of the Curzon Line, described in Lord
Curzon's telegram as running east of Przemysl, was to coincide with
the November 20, 1919, line that delimited the western frontier of
the autonomous East Galician territory in the event that that territory were subsequently assigned to Poland by the peace conference.
Thus, by incorporating in his telegram two versions of the southern
segment of the proposed armistice line, the British Foreign Secretary
originated the ambiguous description of that segment. This formed
the basis for formal Soviet claims in that area during World War II.[5]

The East Galician area between the two possible southern segments of the Curzon Line contained 1,875,000 Poles (39 percent of the population at the time of the 1931 census).[6] By the wording of the telegram, these Poles were added to the approximately 2 million Poles living in other areas behind the Curzon Line who faced a change of nationality or westward migration in 1945.[7]

The failure to save the city of Lvov made the southeastern border of Poland in 1945 almost identical with the so-called "Line A" proposed, on April 26, 1919, by the Commission on Polish Affairs to the Supreme Allied Council as the boundary of an autonomous territory of East Galicia inside the Republic of Poland. At the same time in 1919, "Line B," which included within the Polish Republic the city of Lvov and the oil wells of Drogobych, was suggested as a boundary in the event of the creation of an independent state of Eastern Galician Ukrainians.[8]

Line A became the "Line of November 20, 1919" included in the resolution of the Supreme Allied Council that divided Galicia into two parts. By this resolution, Polish sovereignty was definitely acknowledged in the western part, while the eastern part was given to Poland for 25 years, as a mandate of the League of Nations. However, the resolution of November 20 was rescinded by the Supreme Allied Council on December 22, 1919; Poland was authorized to assume control of the whole of East Galicia, and thus neither Line A nor Line B was put into effect. The Line of November 20, 1919, was revived by Lloyd George in 1920 as the southern section of the "Curzon Line"; and it reappeared again during the Teheran Conference of World War II, which determined the present eastern boundary of Poland.

POLAND'S WESTERN BOUNDARY:
POLISH VIEWS

Polish Views Following World War I

The Oder-Neisse boundary did not constitute the Polish national goal during World War I. The maximal extension of the western border demanded by the Polish delegation during the Paris Peace Conference of 1919 was basically the 1939 border, with the addition of ethnically Polish Opole Silesia and a slight correction in the Slupsk area in Pomerania.[9] The demand was largely approved by the peace conference, without the inclusion of the Slupsk area.

That decision of the Paris Peace Conference, presented to the German delegation on May 7, 1919, was subsequently changed, under German protest with English support, to include a provision for the conducting of a plebiscite in Silesia. The changes modifying the original decision on the East Prussia and Gdansk area were more drastic, and Polish border demands with regard to that area remained unfulfilled. Originally, Poland demanded a line strikingly similar to the current Polish-Soviet border across former East Prussia from the vicinity of Braniewo to Goldap, with the provision that north of that line an autonomous Konigsberg region would be created as a League of Nations mandate in a customs union with Poland.[10]

The provisions accepted by the Paris Peace Conference for that region created the Free City of Danzig and called for a plebiscite in the southern and western parts of East Prussia. The plebiscite area covered a population that spoke predominantly in a Polish dialect but was heavily Germanized because of the religious factor (Protestant majority) and long political and cultural ties with Prussia.[11] Both plebiscites were conducted July 11, 1920, under conditions very unfavorable to Poland. Apart from ethnic loyalties, the population was asked to choose between its past experience of the German social order and an uncertain future if it chose the untried social and political system of the newly emerging Polish state, a state whose independence was at that very time endangered by the Soviet army advance toward Warsaw.

Polish territorial demands during and after World War I basically included only ethnically Polish territories and such predominantly German areas as were deemed economically essential to the Polish state (such as Gdansk) or were claimed to provide Poland with a larger coastline (such as the areas east of Slupsk in Pomerania and around the city of Elblag and to its east in East Prussia).

The areas allocated to Poland on the basis of the Versailles Treaty were only the territories that had been Polish before the partitions of Poland at the end of the eighteenth century, with the minor exception of the corrections in the border regions of Lower Silesia and East Prussia (adjudicated to Poland to provide it with unimpeded access to Dzialdowo). The more important frontier modification was the allocation of part of Upper Silesia to Poland following the plebiscite and three uprisings of the Polish population there.

The ethnographically Polish areas in Silesia and East Prussia, which remained in Germany after World War I, were the only terra

irredenta areas to which Poland made any serious claims.[12] After
the ratification of the Versailles Treaty, these claims were put forward only by various political parties (such as the National Party) and
not by the Polish Foreign Office. After the Polish-German nonaggres-
sion treaty of 1934, even these unofficial claims were dropped in order
to establish some kind of rapprochement between Poland and Germany.[13] In reality, the existence of large minorities on both sides of
the Versailles Treaty border was used by both states to win sociocultural and political concessions for these groups. (According to
Polish sources, there were 1.4 million Poles in Germany, 741,000
Germans in Poland;[14] according to German sources, there were
705,000 Polish-speaking citizens in Germany and about 1.4 million
Germans in Poland.[15])

Only in the late 1930's after the Anschluss did Polish propaganda
begin a campaign designed to remind the public of the territories
beyond Poland's western border that were inhabited by Poles and had
been during the time of the Piast dynasty (tenth through fourteenth
centuries) when the territorial extension of the Polish tribes was
broadly delimited in the west along the rivers Oder, Bober (a left
tributary of the Oder parallel to the Western or Lusatian Neisse,
about twenty miles east), and Queis. Large parts of the area between
that original border and the Versailles Treaty border of contemporary
Poland were Germanized during the thirteenth through nineteenth
centuries. Before 1939, some parties claimed for Poland the Polish-
speaking areas in the easternmost parts of Silesia, which were the
only Germanized parts of that vast region included in medieval
Poland.[16] However, in view of the area's integration with Germany,
any irredentist claims put forward by Polish nationalist groups were
more propagandist in nature than real.[17]

Polish Views During World War II

The Polish Council of Ministers took a formal stand on the
issue of the postwar border of Poland in "The Resolution of the
Council of Ministers Concerning the Method of Proceeding in Matters
Connected with Our Frontier with Germany," passed on October 7,
1942.[18] Article 1 of that resolution states:

It is our aim to incorporate Danzig, East Prussia and
Oppeln Silesia into the Polish State as well as shifting the
border westward with Germany generally and securing
freedom of access to the Baltic.

Furthermore, Article 2 states:

> The program of incorporation of Danzig and East Prussia
> should be argued on the basis of the necessity for liqui-
> dating that main staging base of Germany against Poland
> and generally against Eastern Europe and the necessity
> of securing for Poland a broad and secured access to the
> sea. . . . It is also now necessary to impress the Anglo-
> Saxon political circles with the need for shortening the
> Silesian "wedge" of the Reich by taking away Opole
> Silesia with certain additions in Poland's favor. . . . In
> the case of Opole Silesia one should not limit one's self
> to stressing the one-sided interest of the Polish state
> but underline the necessity for lengthening the Polish-
> Czech border to prevent the Polish-Czechoslovak Con-
> federation and the whole Mid-European Confederation
> from hanging in mid drift. . . . One should limit one's
> self at present in this matter [of defining the border,
> from the Baltic south] to the general formula of the neces-
> sity for shortening the western Polish-German border . . .
> and moving it westward; this is indispensable to the inter-
> ests of the Polish state and its harbors.[19]

In addition, Article 4 states:

> It is detrimental in the highest degree to make fantastic
> territorial demands, up to the Lusatian Neisse or
> Bober . . . such unlimited demands disqualify Poles, in
> the eyes of Anglo-Saxon public opinion, as an irrepressibly
> greedy nation—which would totally harm our realistic aspi-
> rations and territorial claims. Furthermore, pressing for
> excessively broad Polish claims in the West could foster,
> things being as they are at present, designs to deprive
> Poland of part of her eastern territories in exchange for
> the western acquisitions.[20]

Thus, the Polish government's plans for shortening the future
Polish-German border were based mainly on strategic and ethnic
considerations and did not involve a program of broad territorial
acquisitions up to the Oder-Neisse. These plans were primarily
motivated by the desire to strengthen Poland's future military position in the west without prejudicing, through excessive western
territorial claims, the 1939 eastern frontier.[21] The Oder-Neisse

line in these projects was defined only as the limit of the postwar "strict occupation."

In the secret memorandum of the Polish government, "Measures To Be Applied to Germany Immediately after Cessation of Hostilities," Article 11a specifies:

A line following the left bank of the river Gorlitzer Neisse and the left bank of the Oder, including the necessary bridgeheads; the estuary of the Oder, including Stettin, the islands of this estuary and the Isle of Rugen. The occupying power should be Poland and in the southern area bordering Czechoslovakia—Poland and Czechoslovakia.[22]

The same formulations can be found in the confidential memorandum of the Polish Ministry of Preparatory Work Concerning the Peace Conference, "Principles of Preliminary Settlement Concerning Relations with Germany after the End of the Hostilities."[23]

A similar attitude, motivated by the apprehension that overly extensive territorial claims in the west might endanger the 1939 frontier with the USSR, is also manifest in the secret instructions sent (through the Office of the Prime Minister) by Marian Seyda, the head of the Ministry of Preparatory Work Concerning the Peace Conference, to the government's delegate in Warsaw on April 28, 1943. These secret instructions read:

We persist in the great program of territorial revindication in the West, but within the realistic appraisal of what Poland will be able to digest, developing herself as a strong and cohesive state. We aim with our program of incorporation at the Oder along its entire course. However, setting the bolder goal of incorporating the Lusatian Neisse would be actually detrimental to Poland, since we are not able to digest the whole Lower Silesia on the left bank of the Oder after the removal, apart from the five to six million of an additional 2.5 million rabidly inimical Germans, and to man all the economic posts. To put forward such an incorporation program would compromise us in the Anglo-Saxon world on the ground of glaring imperialism and could make inroads in the cause of the eastern territories.[24]

The next top-secret communication of the Polish government in London to its delegate in Poland, dated March 20, 1943, repeats the territorial postulates cited above, which:

> were accepted by the Council of Ministers and also unanimously by the National Council, that included East Prussia, Danzig and Oppeln Silesia, if it is possible to enlarge it somewhat, and the Oder line. Considering that the full Oder Line as the frontier of incorporation is encountering great difficulties, the Ministry of Peace Conference Affairs is secretly preparing for yet different contingencies, first of all a line from the environs of Kolberg in the southern direction in such a way as to include half the territory between the former border of Poznan (region) and the Oder.[25]

The answer of the Political Coordinating Committee (PKP) of the resistance movement in Warsaw in the same document specifies the following localities, through which such an alternative contingent line should run:

> Stary Dab, Santok, Notec, Warta, the western border of the districts (powiat) of Skwierzyna, Miedzyrzecz, Babimost and then directly to the Oder through Kleinitz and along the Oder channel to the mouth of the Olawa and finally along that river and the northern watershed of the Nissa Klodzka to the Sudetic border, leaving the Klodzko county to the Czechs, and, of course, incorporating East Russia and the Free City of Danzig into Poland.[26]

This line, proposed as a negotiable alternative to the "Oder Line" mentioned as the territorial political goal of Poland, was somewhat corrected again by the Polish Government in London to run through the following places:

> Gorzow, Gorzowskie Holendry on the Warta, toward the Oder to the east of Krosno, Radnitz. The southern section is identical but the General Staff insists on Zielona Gora. Alternatively: from the environs of Kolobrzeg south toward Lobes, Drawsko, Choszczno, Kurzig, Gorzowskie Holendry, perhaps Lobes, Drawsko, Choszczno, Santok, possibly Radnitz.[27]

Thus the official incorporation program of the Polish government in London, correlated with and approved by the Polish underground movement, aimed at the areas whose incorporation was thought to be attainable, whose extent would not jeopardize the defense of Poland's pre-1939 eastern borders.

This last precondition was the most important factor in determining and modifying the extent of the territorial program of incorporation in the west. Both the Polish government and the civil authorities of the Polish resistance treated the incorporation from the point of view of future military security and as a compensation for huge material losses suffered during World War II, not as compensation for the eastern territories. All the political factions, both in exile and in the underground, with the exception of the Communists, insisted on the inviolability of the eastern frontiers of Poland, which were drawn at the Riga Peace Conference of 1921 and in existence until 1939.

In essence, the postwar western border of Poland, postulated as above, in conjunction with the status quo ante in the east, would have divided Germany and Poland roughly along the line drawn almost due south from Kolobrzeg to the Oder and then along the western border of the province of Opole. The additions between that line and the former Polish-German frontier would thus enlarge Poland's pre-1939 territory by almost two-thirds of the present western territories (plus the northern part of East Prussia, which was later assigned to the USSR at Potsdam). This was not to be.

This political program of incorporation of western areas and retention of the status quo ante in the east was doomed by the positions on the matter of both the Western Powers and the Soviet Union as early as the Teheran Conference of November 28-December 1, 1943.[28] In effect, the shifts of the Polish western border were designed by the Great Powers to provide Poland with territorial compensation for areas behind the Curzon Line that were to be given to the USSR and to give the new Poland a viable economic and strategic base against any future German incursions. Therefore, the planning for territorial expansion done by the Polish Government in London is of only historical interest.

It was the Polish Communist leadership that advocated the westward shift and the abandonment of the eastern territories. The Communists became the decisive political element in Poland toward the end of World War II, and were so at the time of the Potsdam Conference which assigned the Oder-Neisse territories to Poland. However, it is significant that former Prime Minister Mikolajczyk (who attended the Potsdam Conference as the Vice-Premier of the new Provisional Government of National Unity) vehemently supported

the Communist arguments for the Oder-Neisse frontier when the loss
of the eastern territories resulted in a de facto westward shift of
the territory of the Polish state.[29] The necessity of providing territory for those former Polish inhabitants of eastern Poland who had
opted for Poland changed Mikolajczyk's moderate position on incorporations.

In essence, the Communist program for the westward shift of
Poland was a throwback to the conception of ethnic Poland as it had
existed under the Piast Dynasty, 966-1340 (the latter date marks the
beginning of the eastern expansion of Poland into the Ruthenian lands),
as opposed to the multinational Poland of the time of the Polish-
Lithuanian Commonwealth, 1386-1795.[30]

The establishment of the western frontier on the Oder-Neisse
at the approximate site of the original Polish ethnic borders was
also a political necessity for the Polish Communists, who advocated
the cession of eastern Poland to the USSR. Such an unpopular stand
had to be bolstered by a far-reaching western incorporation program,
if the Communists were to achieve some measure of support for their
social and political goals. Thus, the Communist position on the
western frontier along the Oder-Neisse rivers in effect repeated the
claims that had long been made by various Polish nationalist groups
before World War II and during that war, in exile and in the underground press.[31]

We should mention that such a recovery of the lands lost before
and during the fourteenth century was sporadically advocated by
various Polish leaders and scholars through the ages, including
Dlugosz (an eminent fifteenth-century historian),[32] Kollataj (a fore-
most eighteenth-century political writer),[33] and Pawlowski (a leading
turn-of-the-century geographer). Even during World War I, when
the political future was yet not certain, a book published in 1918
advocated such an outline of the Polish border.[34] Although such
exaggerated territorial claims were at that time thoroughly unrealistic
and theoretical—none of the Polish leadership centers or parties
demanded such borders—they were subsequently presented in a 1930's
German historical atlas as official Polish claims.[35]

NOTES

1. Quoted in W. Sworakowski, "An Error Regarding Eastern
Galicia in Curzon's Note to the Soviet Government," Journal of
Central European Affairs, Vol. IV, No. 1 (April 1944).

2. Ibid.

3. Leszek Kirkien, Russia, Poland and the Curzon Line, 2nd ed. (London: Caldra House, Ltd., 1945).

4. Harold Nicolson, Curzon: The Last Phase, 1919-1925 (London: Constable, 1934), p. 204.

5. William O. Leahy, I Was There (New York: McGraw-Hill, 1950), p. 210.

6. Kirkien, op. cit., p. 50.

7. Stanislaw Mikolajczyk, The Rape of Poland (New York: McGraw-Hill, 1948), p. 143.

8. Encyclopaedia Britannica, Vol. VIII, article entitled "Poland" (1966), p. 133.

9. Roman Dmowski, Polityka polska a odbudowanie Panstwa, Vol. II, 3rd ed. (Hanover: n.p., 1947), pp. 161-66; Josef Engel, Grosser Historischer Weltatlas, Vol. III, 2nd ed., (Munich: Bayerischer Schulbuch-Verlag, 1962), p. 157.

10. Dmowski, Vol. II, op. cit., p. 166.

11. Paul Weber, Die Polen in Oberschlesien (Berlin: Verlag von Julius Springer, 1919).

12. Eugeniusz Romer, Powszechny atlas geograficzny (Lwow: Ksiaznica Atlas, 1934).

13. Marian Wojciechowski, Stosunki polsko niemieckie, 1933-1938 (Poznan: Instytut Zachodni, 1965).

14. Glowny Urzad Statystyczny Rzeczypospolitej Polskiej, Maly Rocznik Statystyczny, 1939, Vol. X (Warsaw, 1939), Table 17, p. 22.

15. S. Waszak, "The Number of Germans in Poland in the Years 1931-1939 Against the Background of German Losses in the Second World War," Polish Western Affairs, Vol. I (1960), p. 266; Bruno Gleitze, Ostdeutsche Wirtschaft (Berlin: Duncker and Humbolt, 1956), p. 152, quoting Die deutschen Vertreibungsverluste: Bevolkerungs-bilanzen für die deutschen Verteibungsgebrete 1939-1950.

16. Heinz Quirin and Werner Trillmich, Westermanns Atlas zur Weltgeschichte (Braunschweig: Georg Westermann Verlag, 1963).

17. Ibid. and W. Fuchs, Poland's Policy of Expansion (Berlin: Deutscher Ostmarken-Verein, 1932).

18. Archives of the General Sikorski Polish Institute and Museum in London, MSS A-XII-23/42. (Hereafter cited as Sikorski Archives.)

19. Ibid., PRM-K, 105, "Most Secret."

20. Ibid.

21. Ibid.

22. Sikorski Archives, op. cit., A-XII-23/42.

23. Sikorski Archives, op. cit., A-XII-1/88.

24. Acts of the Civil Chancellary of the President of the Polish Republic in London, No. 29.

25. Ibid.

26. Ibid.

27. Ibid.

28. Winston S. Churchill, Closing the Ring (London: Cassell, 1954), pp. 320, 403.

29. Herbert Feis, Between War and Peace: The Potsdam Conference (Princeton, N.J.: Princeton University Press, 1960), pp. 209, 230.

30. Cambridge History of Poland, 2 vols. (London: Cambridge University Press, 1950 and 1942).

31. Tadeusz Bielecki, "Zagadnienia glowne," Mysl Polska (London), December 15, 1942.

32. Jan Dlugosz, Dziejow Polskich Ksiag dwanascie (Krakow: 1870, pp. 445-46).

33. Hugo Kollataj, Uwagi nad terazniejszym polozeniem Saksonii i Polski z nia zjednoczonej (Lipsk, 1808), and Uwagi nad terazniejszym polozeniem tej czesci ziemi polskiej, ktora od pokoju tylzyckiego zaczeto zwac Ks. Warszawskim (Lipsk, 1808), pp. 133-34.

34. Msciwoj Jahoda, Zachodnia granica Polski, 2nd ed. (Warsaw: Komitet Obrony Narodowej, 1918).

35. Richard Andree, Andrees Allgemeiner Handatlas (Bielefeld: Velhagen wrd Klasings, 1924-25).

B

BASIC ECONOMIC
AND POLITICAL ASSUMPTIONS
IN
PREVIOUSLY UNPUBLISHED DOCUMENT
PRESENTING UNITED STATES VIEW
OF POSTWAR POLAND

A document entitled "Postwar Poland: Economic and Political Outlook," prepared by the Research and Analysis Branch of the Office of Strategic Services and dated March 9, 1945—after Yalta but before Potsdam—reflects the position of the United States delegations to both of those conferences. In the case of Poland's western and eastern borders, it outlines alternatives for bargaining purposes. However, the eastern alternatives are far less flexible since the American representatives had already accepted the Curzon Line at the Teheran Conference.[1] Thus it states:

2. . . . that the Curzon Line, or a fairly close approxima-
tion to it, will constitute Poland's eastern frontier. This
result leaves open the possibility that Lwow, or even the
Galician oil fields, as well as Bialystok and the Suwalki
triangle may remain within its territory.[2]

The western border alternatives are much broader, since inter-
allied discussions and pronouncements on the issue used rather
loosely worded proposals such as "Oder Line" and "East Prussia"
(where substantial Soviet claims were subsequently accepted).[3] The
document in question states precisely two well-defined alternatives
for the new western border of Poland and makes detailed area and
population analyses of the new Poland under both assumptions. The
document assumes:

3. That Polish-German frontier will follow one of two
alternative versions: a) In addition to the restoration of

her prewar frontiers with Germany, Poland to receive the
Opplen District of Silesia [i.e., all of Upper Silesia as
originally envisaged at Versailles] as well as a large part
of East Prussia (the area west of the strategic Konigsberg-
Insterburg-Kaunas Railway) which is estimated to comprise
72.7 percent of East Prussia; b) Poland to expand to the
Oder River and to receive the part of Silesia which lies
west of the Oder (as far as Gorlitz).

As for the future population transfers stemming from the new
frontiers described above, the document assumes that:

The total German population to be dealt with after the war
may amount thus to 5.7 million people or 7.9 million
people depending on the way the frontiers are drawn. It
is clearly impossible to predict how many Germans will
leave Poland during and after the end of hostilities; some
will go to rump-Germany, some may be forcibly deported
to Russia. . . . On the other hand it may be assumed that
a considerable number of Germans, possibly a million,
will turn out to be of Polish nationality. Another problem
is that of the number of Poles who may wish to cross the
Curzon Line from the east and settle in post-war Poland.
It has been estimated that before the war about four
million ethnic Poles lived in parts of Poland located east
of the Curzon Line.[4]

This document also contains a very realistic appraisal of the
economic situation and the chances of economic growth in the new
territorial extension of postwar Poland. It makes the basic assumption that the problem of rural overcrowding would be insoluble without speedy industrialization even within the new Polish frontiers. It
states that there would be insufficient land for a comprehensive land
reform that would satisfy all the landless peasants. It continues:

As remote as the possibility of solving the problem of land
scarcity may be even if the most generous allotment of
German land to Poland is assumed, the possibility does not
exist at all if the narrower frontiers (2 and 3a) should
become a reality [i.e., if only East Prussia west and east
of Kaliningrad and Opole Silesia were added to the area
of pre-1939 Poland west of the Curzon Line.][5]

Furthermore, the document assumes:

That Poland will remain an independent state. This fact
does not preclude the possibility that its foreign policy may

create close political and economic links to some other
country or combination of countries. It implies only that
it will represent a political and economic entity within
well-defined frontiers and in control of its own currency,
its own custom tariffs, etc.[6]

Thus, although the allocation of farmland in the new western
provinces was assumed sufficient to ease the pressure on land that
had existed in prewar Poland and had rendered any economic reforms
unworkable, a vast program of postwar industrialization was considered the key to economic rehabilitation and an improved standard
of living.[7] However, the feasibility of the enforced program of
industrialization necessary to double the prewar standard of living
was dependent upon either foreign loans or a severe restriction of
consumption that would result in forced domestic savings. The document considers the choice of free or forced methods for the country's
economic development as determinants of the fate of democracy in
postwar Poland. It states:

The only means by which investment could be financed
without a drastic tightening of the belts of the population
would be foreign aid. Sizable American capital exports
may be directed to Poland. This development, however,
would be possible only if such investments were sponsored
by the government. For many years Poland will presum-
ably remain an area politically too uncertain to be re-
garded as an attractive outlet for foreign capital inves-
tors. . . . The methods by which Polish leaders approach
industrialization will decide the character of Polish life in
the decades following the war. If the investments required
to provide Poland with heavy industry and with the technology necessary for productive farming have to be financed
exclusively by domestic forced savings, there is little
prospect for a democratic government in Poland. Severe
restrictions of consumption necessitating drastic controls
of production and distribution may be incompatible with
democratic representative government, particularily in
a country such as Poland, where the standard of living is
very low. Under such circumstances, the time preference
of the population differs from the one imposed by the
administration, the necessity of forcing people to save
becomes tantamount to the necessity of forcing them politically to obey. It is doubtful that any Polish administration embarking on a large-scale program of economic
reconstruction without far-reaching foreign support would
be able to muster a sufficiently large popular support for
its economic policy. The execution of the land reform and

the resettlement of Polish peasants on territories conquered
from Germany might provide a temporary political breath-
ing spell, but even this would probably soon come to an end.
The necessity of severely taxing the peasants and the in-
ability to provide them with sufficient quantities of industrial consumer goods are likely to turn the political sentiments of the village away from the urban administration.
Even the allegiance of the industrial workers would be un-
reliable. Since real wages would have to be kept down, the
short-run position of industrial workers is not likely to
improve. This fact would demand a considerable effort to
explain to the urban population the rationale of their situation. Property-owning classes and generally well-to-do
citizens would not be among the supporters of an administration pledged to such an accumulation program. Their
immediate sacrifice would be largest and their resistance
accordingly strongest. A rigorous dictatorship would be
thus the most likely political framework of an economic
policy involving changes as radical as may be necessary to
lead Poland out of its pre-war stagnation. Such a dictatorship would, under normal conditions, result only from
social revolution and civil war. However, probable upheaval following the liberation of Poland may create conditions in which political changes unimaginable before will
become a matter of course. The social revolution in
Poland, instead of being fought in the streets of Warsaw
and Lodz, may be decided in the chancelleries of Moscow,
London and Washington. The outlook for Polish democracy would probably be considerably brighter if the industrialization of the country were financed by foreign loans.
Spared the privations of "initial accumulation," the Poles
may find much easier ways and means of organizing a
democratic political structure.[8]

The position document closes with the following statement:

Whether other foreign support will be available will depend
upon the maintenance of a democratic regime in Poland,
and, more important, upon the general international
situation. If the world after this war should enter a period
of comparative tranquility and confidence, the chances for
Poland to secure important international cooperation in its
economic efforts are excellent. Good relations between
the United States and the USSR is the most important single
condition. Very little can be predicted about Poland's

economic future at the present time. Poland's fate after the war will not be decided in Poland. In this fundamental sense Poland never was and never will be a "Great Power," the assertions of its former rulers notwithstanding. The way in which the country will live and develop in the decades to come will depend on factors and circumstances involving complexes much larger and much more impor- tant than the Polish issue. How these crucial determinants of Poland's future will behave can hardly be charted yet.[9]

NOTES

1. U. S. Department of State, Historical office, The Conference at Cairo and Teheran, 1943 (Washington, D.C: U. S. Government Printing Office, 1961), p. 594.

2. U.S. Office of Strategic Services, Research and Analysis Branch, "Postwar Poland: Economic and Political Outlook" (Wash- ington, D.C., 1945, mimeographed), p. 22.

3. Winston S. Churchill, Closing the Ring (London: Cassell, 1954), pp. 309-403.

4. U. S. Office of Strategic Services, Research and Analysis Branch, op. cit., pp. 24-25.

5. Ibid., p. 29.

6. Ibid., p. 22.

7. Ibid., p. 37.

8. Ibid., pp. 38-39.

9. Ibid., p. 40.

C

TREATY BETWEEN
THE REPUBLIC OF POLAND
AND THE
GERMAN DEMOCRATIC REPUBLIC
CONCERNING THE DELIMITATION
OF THE ESTABLISHED AND EXISTING
POLISH-GERMAN STATE FRONTIER

(Zgorzelec, July 6, 1950)

The President of the Republic of Poland and the President of the German Democratic Republic, guided by the desire to give expression to the will to consolidate universal peace and wishing to contribute to harmonious cooperation between peace-loving nations,

recognizing that this cooperation between the Polish and German nations has been made possible by the destruction of German fascism by the USSR and by the growth of democratic forces in Germany—and

wishing, after the tragic experience of Hitlerism, to create unshakable foundations for peaceful and good-neighborly relations between both nations,

desiring to stabilize and consolidate mutual relations on the basis of the Potsdam Agreement which established the frontier on the Oder and the Lusatian Neisse,

implementing the decisions of the Warsaw Declaration of the Government of the Republic of Poland and of the Delegation of the Provisional Government of the German Democratic Republic of 6 June 1950,

recognizing the established and existing frontier as the inviolable frontier of peace and friendship which does not divide, but unites the two nations—

have decided to conclude the present agreement and named as their plenipotentiaries:

for the President of the Republic of Poland, Mr. Jozef Cyrankiewicz, Chairman of the Council of Ministers, Mr. Stefan Wierblowski, Head of the Ministry of Foreign Affairs;

for the President of the German Democratic Republic, Mr. Otto Grotewohl, Chairman of the Council of Ministers, Mr. Georg Dertinger, Minister of Foreign Affairs;

who, after exchanging their full powers, which were found to be in due and proper form, have agreed to the following decisions:

Article 1

The High Contracting Parties are agreed that the established and existing frontier running from the Baltic Sea along a line west of the locality of Swinoujscie and then along the River Oder to the confluence of the Lusatian Neisse and along the Lusatian Neisse to the Czechoslovak frontier, constitutes the state frontier between Poland and Germany.

Article 2

The Polish-German state frontier, drawn in accordance with the present Agreement, also divides in a vertical line the air and sea space as well as the subterranean area.

Article 3

In order to carry out the marking on the spot of the Polish-German state frontier mentioned in Article 1, the High Contracting Parties are establishing the Mixed Polish-German Commission with its seat in Warsaw. This Commission is consisting of eight members, of whom four are to be appointed by the Government of the Republic of Poland and four by the Provisional Government of the German Democratic Republic.

Article 4

The Mixed Polish-German Commission will meet not later than 31 August 1950, to carry out the activities indicated in Article 3.

Article 5

After the completion of the delimitation on the spot of the state frontier, the High Contracting Parties shall draw up an instrument recording the demarcation of the state frontier between Poland and Germany.

Article 6

In carrying out the delimitation of the Polish-German state frontier, the High Contracting Parties shall conclude agreements on the questions of frontier crossings, of local frontier traffic, and of navigation on the waters of the frontier-zone.

These agreements shall be concluded within one month after the coming into force of the instrument recording the delimitation of the state frontier between Poland and Germany mentioned in Article 5.

Article 7

The present Agreement is subject to ratification which shall take place within the shortest possible time. The Agreement will come into force at the moment of the exchange of ratification documents which take place in Berlin.

In witness thereof the plenipotentiaries have signed and affixed their seals to the present Agreement.

Article 8

Executed on 6 July 1959, at Zgorzelec in two copies, both in the Polish and German languages, both being equally binding.*

---

*Dziennik Ustaw Rzeczypospolitej Polski [Official Gazette of the Republic of Poland], 1951, No. 14, p. 106.

D

TREATY BETWEEN
THE POLISH PEOPLE'S REPUBLIC
AND THE
FEDERAL REPUBLIC OF GERMANY
CONCERNING THE BASES
OF NORMALIZATION
OF THEIR MUTUAL RELATIONS

(Warsaw, December 7, 1970)

The Polish People's Republic and Federal Republic of Germany:

considering that more than 25 years have passed since the termination of World War II of which Poland was the first victim and which brought grave sufferings upon the peoples of Europe,

mindful that during that time in both countries a new generation has grown up which must be secured a peaceful future,

desirous of creating lasting bases for peaceful coexistence and development of normal and good relations between them,

aiming at consolidation of peace and security in Europe,

aware that the inviolability of the frontiers and respect for the territorial integrity and sovereignty of all states in Europe within their present frontiers are the basic condition of peace,

have agreed as follows:

Article I

1. The Polish People's Republic and the Federal Republic of Germany unanimously affirm that the existing border line, the course

of which was established in Chapter IX of the decisions of the Potsdam Conference of 2 August 1945 as from the Baltic Sea immediately west of Swinoujscie and thence along the Oder River to the confluence of the Lusatian Neisse River and along the Lusatian Neisse to the Czechoslovak frontier, constitutes the Western State Frontier of the Polish People's Republic.

2. They confirm the inviolability of their existing frontiers, now and in the future, and mutually pledge to respect unreservedly their territorial integrity.

3. They declare that they have no territorial claims against one another nor shall they advance such claims in the future.

Article II

1. The Polish People's Republic and the Federal Republic of Germany shall be guided in their mutual relations as well as in matters concerning the safeguarding of European and world security by the Purposes and Principles set forth in the Charter of the United Nations.

2. Accordingly, in conformity with Articles 1 and 2 of the Charter of the United Nations they shall settle all their disputes exclusively by peaceful means and in questions of European and international security as well as in their mutual relations they shall refrain from the threat of force or the use of force.

Article III

1. The Polish People's Republic and the Federal Republic of Germany shall undertake further steps aimed at full normalization and all-round development of their mutual relations, the lasting basis of which shall be the present Treaty.

2. They agree that the expansion of their cooperation in the fields of economic, scientific, scientific-technical, cultural, and other relations is in their common interest.

Article IV

The present Treaty does not affect bilateral or multilateral international agreements previously concluded by the Parties or concerning them.

Article V

The present Treaty is subject to ratification and shall come into force on the date of exchange of the instruments of ratification which will take place in Bonn.

In witness whereof the Plenipotentiaries of the Contracting Parties have signed this Treaty.

The present Treaty was drawn up in Warsaw on the seventh day of December 1970 in two originals, each in the Polish and German languages, both texts being equally authentic.*

For the Polish People's Republic	For the Federal Republic of Germany
Jozef Cyrankiewicz Stefan Jedrychowski	Willy Brandt Walter Scheel

---

*Legal and Treaty Department of the Ministry of Foreign Affairs of the Polish People's Republic.

MAP I

Contemporary Poland
Administrative Map (1968)

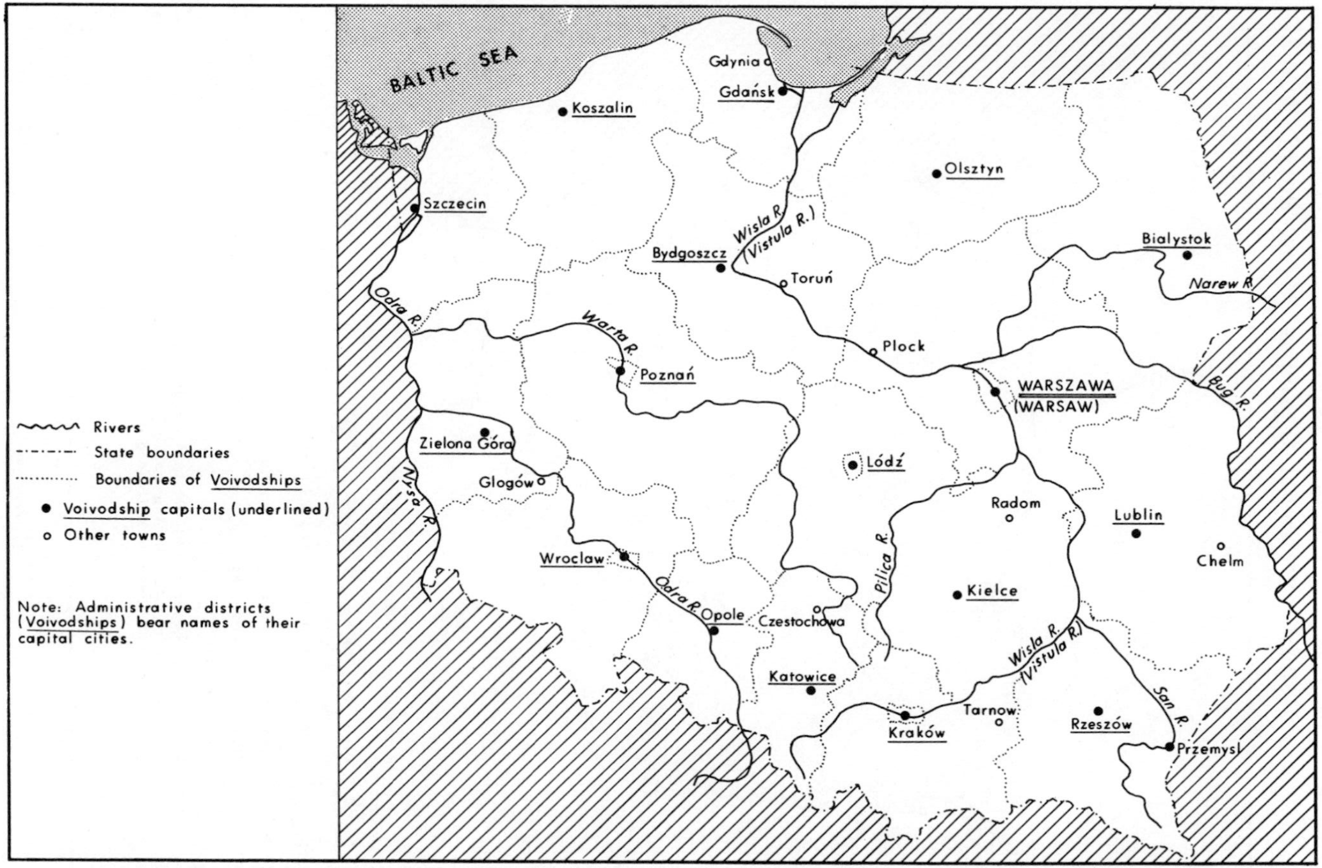

BALTIC SEA

Gdynia
Gdańsk
Gdańsk

Koszalin

Szczecin

Słupsk

Toruń

Bydgoszcz

Poznań

Wrocław

Zielona Góra

Głogów

Opole

Częstochowa

Katowice

Kraków

Tarnów

Rzeszów

Przemyśl

Kielce

Radom

Łódź

Płock

WARSZAWA
(WARSAW)

Olsztyn

Białystok

Lublin

Chełm

Wisła R. (Vistula R.)

Odra R.

Warta R.

Nysa R.

Pilica R.

San R.

Bug R.

Narew R.

Wisła R.

Lublin

Rivers
State boundaries
Boundaries of Voivodships
● Voivodship capitals (underlined)
o Other towns

Note: Administrative districts
(Voivodships) bear names of their
capital cities.

225

MAP 2

Poland—Territorial Changes After World War II

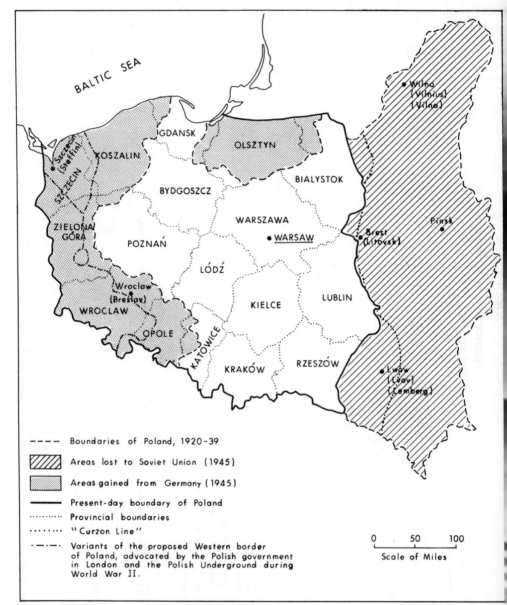

- - - - Boundaries of Poland, 1920-39

///// Areas lost to Soviet Union (1945)

▓▓▓ Areas gained from Germany (1945)

——— Present-day boundary of Poland

········ Provincial boundaries

········ "Curzon Line"

·—·—· Variants of the proposed Western border
of Poland, advocated by the Polish government
in London and the Polish Underground during
World War II.

```
0        50      100
```

Scale of Miles

MAP 3

Polish Ethnic Areas in the Vilna Region in 1936 and 1964

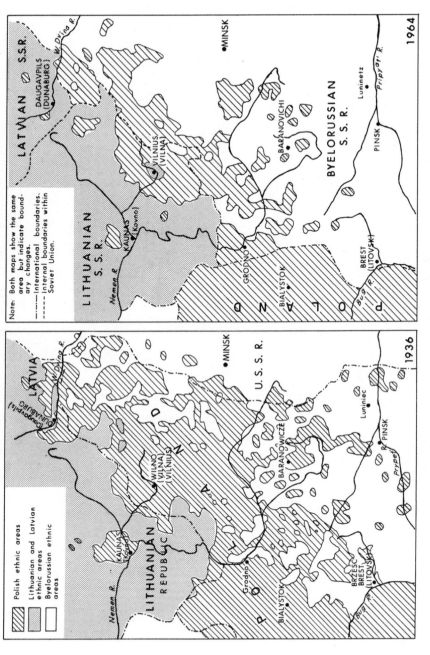

Note: Both maps show the same area but indicate boundary changes.
—•—•— International boundaries.
- - - - - Internal boundaries within Soviet Union.

Legend:
- Polish ethnic areas
- Lithuanian and Latvian ethnic areas
- Byelorussian ethnic areas

Sources: Map for 1936—data from E. Romer, Atlas Powszechny (Lwów, 1936); Map for 1964—data from Atlas Mira (Moscow, 1964).

227

SELECTED BIBLIOGRAPHY

Acts of the Civil Chancellery of the President of the Polish Republic in London, No. 29.

Anders, W. An Army in Exile. London: MacMillan, 1950.

Antoniewski, Stanislaw. Opisy gospodarowania w gospodarstwach karlowatych. Warsaw: Panstwowy Instytut Naukowy Gospodarstwa Wiejskiego, 1938.

Apter, David E. The Politics of Modernization. Chicago: The University of Chicago Press, 1965.

Archives of the General Sikorski Polish Institute and Museum in London, MSS A-XII-23/42.

Atlas Narodov Mira. Moscow: Akademia Nauk SSSR, 1964.

Atlas Polski. Warsaw: Urzad Geologii, 1963.

Atlas Statystyczny. Warsaw: Glowny Urzad Statystyczny Polskiej Rzeczypospolitej Ludowej, 1970.

Banasiak, S. Dzialalnosc osadnicza Panstwowego Urzedu Repatriacyjnego na Ziemiach Odzyskanych w latach 1945-1947. Poznan: Instytut Zachodni, 1963.

Barcinski, F. Bogactwa kopalne Polski. Warsaw: n.p., 1949.

Bertisch, Roman. "Osadnictwo chlopow-reemigrantow na Slasku w latach 1946-1948." Kwartalnik Opolski. Vols. II (1956), III (1957).

Bielecki, Tadeusz. "Zagadnienia glowne." Mysl Polska (London), December 15, 1942.

Biuro Studiow Osadniczo-Przesiedlenczych. Sesja Rady Naukowej dla Zagadnien Ziem Odzyskanych. Vols. I-IV. Warsaw, 1946.

Bor-Komorowski, T. The Secret Army. London: Victor Gollancz, 1951.

Bystron, Jan. Etnografia Polski. Warsaw: Czytelnik, 1947.

_____. Kultura ludowa. Warsaw: Nasza Ksiegarnia, 1936.

231

Cambridge History of Poland. 2 vols. London: Cambridge University Press, 1942 and 1950.

Chalasinski, Jozef. Przeszlosc i przyszlosc inteligencji polskiej. Warsaw: Ludowa Spoldzielnia Wydawnicza, 1958.

Chmielewska, Bozenna. Spoleczne przeobrazenia srodowisk wiejskich na Ziemiach Zachodnich. Poznan: Instytut Zachodni, 1965.

Churchill, Winston S. Closing the Ring. London: Cassell, 1954.

Cienkowski, W., et al. Straty Wojenne Polski w latach 1939-1945. Poznan: Wydawnictwo Zachodnie, 1962.

Concise Statistical Yearbook of Poland, 1970. Vol. XII. Warsaw: Central Statistical Office, 1970.

Concise Statistical Year-Book of Poland, September 1939-June 1941. London: Polish Ministry of Information, 1941.

The Conference at Cairo and Teheran, 1943. Foreign Relations of the United States. Diplomatic Papers. Washington, D.C.: U. S. Government Printing Office, 1961.

Czaplinski, Wladyslaw, and Ladogorski, Tadeusz, eds. Atlas historyczny Polski. 2nd ed. Wroclaw: Panstwowe Przedsie-biorstwo Wydawnictw Kartograficznych, 1970.

Czarnecki, Feliks. Bibliografia Ziem Zachodnich 1945-1958. Poznan: Instytut Zachodni, 1962.

Dahl, Robert A. Modern Political Analysis. 2nd ed. Englewood Cliffs, N.J.: Prentice-Hall, 1971.

Dangel, Jan. "O ruchach wedrowkowych ludnosci w malych miastach (Strzegom)," Miasto, Vol. VII, No. 9 (1956).

Derlatka, Tadeusz, and Lubojanski, Jozef. Western and Northern Territories of Poland: Facts and Figures. Warsaw: Western Press Agency, 1966.

Dmowski, Roman. Polityka polska a odbudowanie Panstwa. Vol. II. 3rd ed. Hanover: n.p., 1947.

Doroszewski, W. Jezyk polski w Stanach Ziednoczonych A.P. Warsaw: Nakladem Tow. Naukowego, 1938.

Dulczewski, Zygmunt. Spoleczne aspekty migracji na Ziemiach Zachodnich. Poznan: Instytut Zachodni, 1964.

_____, and Kwilecki, Andrzej, eds. Pamietniki osadnikow Ziem Odzyskanych. Poznan: Wydawnictwo Poznanskie, 1963.

_____. Spoleczenstwo wielkopolskie w osadnictwie Ziem Zachodnich. Poznan. Wydawnicwto Poznanskie, 1962.

_____. Tworzenie sie nowego spoleczenstwa na Ziemiach Zachodnich. Poznan: Instytut Zachodni, 1961.

_____. Z zycia osadnikow na Ziemiach Zachodnich. Warsaw: Panstwowe Zaklady Wydawnictw Szkolnych, 1961.

Dybowski, Roman. Poland in World Civilization. New York: J. M. Barrett, 1950.

Dylik, Jan. Geografia Ziem Odzyskanych. Warsaw: Ksiazka, 1946.

Dziennik Polski i Dziennik Zolnierza (London). January 18, 1944.

Dziewanowski, M. K. The Communist Party of Poland. Cambridge, Mass.: Harvard University Press, 1959.

Dziewonski, K., et al., eds. Studia na aktywizacja malych miast. Warsaw: Panstwowe Wydawnictwo Naukowe, 1957.

Encyclopaedia Britannica. Vol. XVIII. Article entitled "Poland" (1966).

Engel, Jozef. Grosser Historischer Weltatlas. Vol. III. 2nd ed. Munich: Bayerischer Schulbuch-Verlag, 1962.

Englicht, Wladyslaw. Polskie Ziemie Zachodnie. Zagadnienia rolnicze. Poznan: Wydawnictwo Zachodnie, 1959.

Feis, Herbert. Between War and Peace: The Potsdam Conference. Princeton, N.J.: Princeton University Press, 1960.

Finkle, Jason L., and Gable, Richard W. Political Development and Social Change. New York: John Wiley and Sons Inc., 1966.

Florinsky, Michael T., ed. Encyclopedia of Russia and the Soviet Union. New York: McGraw-Hill, 1961.

Fuchs, W. Poland's Policy of Expansion. Berlin: Deutscher Ostmarken-Verein, 1932.

Ginsburg, Norton. Atlas of Economic Development. Chicago: The
University of Chicago Press, 1961.

Gizewiusz, Gustaw. Die Polnische Sprachfrage in Pruessen. 2nd ed.
Poznan: Instytut Zachodni, 1961.

Gleitze, Bruno. Ostdeutsche Wirtschaft. Berlin: Duncker and Humbolt, 1956.

Glowny Urzad Statystyczny Polskiej Rzeczypospolitej Ludowej. "Narodowy Spis Powszechny z dnia 3 grudnia 1950r. Miejsce zamieszkania ludnosci w sierpniu 1939r." Warsaw, 1955 (mimeographed).

_____. Rocznik Statystyczny, 1958. Vol. XVIII. Warsaw, 1958.

_____. Rocznik Statystyczny, 1962. Vol. XXII. Warsaw, 1962.

_____. Rocznik Statystyczny, 1965. Vol. XXV. Warsaw, 1965.

_____. Rocznik Statystyczny, 1966. Vol. XXVI. Warsaw, 1966.

_____. Rocznik Statystyczny, 1970. Vol. XXX. Warsaw, 1970.

Glowny Urzad Statystyczny Rzeczypospolitej Polskiej. Maly Rocznik
Statystyczny, 1939. Vol. X. Warsaw, 1939.

_____. Rocznik Statystyczny, 1947. Vol. XI. Warsaw, 1947.

_____. Rocznik Statystyczny, 1948. Vol. XII. Warsaw, 1948.

_____. Rocznik Statystyczny, 1949. Vol. XIII. Warsaw, 1950.

_____. Rocznik Statystyczny, 1950. Vol. XIV. Warsaw, 1951.

Godowski, Stanislaw. "Rozwoj komunikacji na Ziemiach Zachodnich."
In Studia nad zagadnieniami gospodarczymi i spolecznymi Ziem
Zachodnich. Vol. IV.

Golachowski, Stefan. Materialy do statystyki narodowosciowej Slaska
Opolskiego. Poznan: Instytut Zachodni, 1950.

_____. "Pierwszy rok akcji przesiedlenczo-osadniczej na Slasku Opolskim." Straznica Zachodnia, Vol. XV, Nos. 1-2 (1946).

_____. Ruchy ludnosciowe na Opolszczyznie. Opole: Instytut Slaski, 1948.

Great Britain. Parliamentary Debates. (Commons) Vol. CMVI (1944).

Gross, Feliks. The Polish Worker. New York: Roy, 1945.

Hartleb, Kazimierz. Kultura Polski od zarania dziejow do dni ostatnich. New York: Roy, n.d.

Hertz, Aleksander. "The Case of an Eastern European Intelligentsia." Journal of Central European Affairs, January 1951.

History of Poland. Warsaw: Polish Scientific Publishers, 1968.

Holt, Robert T., and Turner, John E. The Political Basis of Economic Development. Princeton, N. J.: D. Van Nostrand Company, 1966.

Hull, Cordell. The Memoirs of Cordell Hull. Vol. II. London: Hodder and Stoughton, 1948.

Instytut Historyczny imienia Generala Sikorskiego. Documents on Polish-Soviet Relations 1939-1945. Vol. I: 1939-43. London: Heinemann, 1961.

Instytut Zachodni. Polish Western Territories. Poznan, 1959.

_____. Ziemie Staropolski. Vols. I-VI. Poznan, 1948-59.

International Labor Office. International Migration. 1945-1957. Geneva, 1959.

Iwasiewicz, Zbigniew, ed. Polskie Ziemie Zachodnie i Polnocne Zagadnienia Morskie. Poznan: Wydawnictwo Zachodnie, 1957.

Jahoda, Msciwoj. Zachodnia granica Polski. 2nd ed. Warsaw: Komitet Obrony Narodowej, 1918.

Jelonek, Adam. "Naturalny ruch ludnosci na Ziemiach Zachodnich." In Studia nad zagadnieniami gospodarczymi i spolecznymi Ziem Zachodnich. Vol. I.

_____. "Zagadnienia struktury i wieku ludnosci Ziem Zachodnich."
In Studia nad zagadnieniami gospodarczymi i spolecznymi Ziem
Zachodnich. Vol. I.

_____. "Zmiany w strukturze plci i wieku ludnosci w Polsce w
latach 1946-1950." Przeglad Geograficzny, Vol. XXX, No. 3
(1958).

Jordan, J. Oder-Neisse Line: A Study of the Political Economic and
European Significance of Poland's Western Frontier. London:
Polish Freedom Movement "Independence and Democracy,"
1952.

Kaczkowski, Sylvester. Stosunki ludnosciowe Szczecina w latach 1945-
1955. Warsaw: Ksiazka i Wiedza, 1968.

Kaps, Johannes. Die Tragedie Schlesiens 1945-46 in Dokumenten
unter besonderer Berucksichtigung des Erzbistums Breslau.
Munich: Christ Unterwegs, 1952-53.

Karski, Jan. Story of Secret State. Boston: Houghton Mifflin, 1944.

Kielczewska, Maria. O podstawy geograficzne Polski. Poznan:
Instytut Zachodni, 1946.

Kirkien, Leszek. Russia, Poland and the Curzon Line. 2nd ed. London:
Caldra House, Ltd., 1945.

Koehl, Robert. German Resettlement and Population Policy 1938-1945:
A History of the Reich Commission for the Strengthening of
Germandom. Cambridge, Mass.: Harvard Historical Monographs,
Vol. XXI, 1957.

Koenigwald, H. Das Dritte Probleme. Dusseldorf: Hrsg. vom Arbeits
und Social-minister des Landes Nordrhein Westfalen, 1957.

Koerber, Hans Joachim. Die Bevolkerung der deutschen Ostgebiete
unter polnischer Verwaltung. Berlin: Osteuropa Institut an der
Freien Universitat Berlin, 1958.

Kokot, Jozef. The Logic of the Oder-Neisse Frontier. Poznan-Warsaw:
Western Press Agency, 1959.

_____. Logika Poczdamu. Katowice: Slask, 1961.

_____, and Brozek, Andrzej. Polityka dezinformacji w wydawnic-twach Statistisches Bundesamt. Opole: Instytut Slaski, 1965.

Kolaja, Jiri. "Polityczne konsekwencje cech narodowych." Kultura (Paris), No.11/61 (1952).

Kolipinski, Juliusz. "Zagadnienia gospodarcze Ziem Zachodnich." In Polskie Ziemie Zachodnie. Poznan: Instytut Zachodni, 1959.

Kollataj, Hugo. Uwagi nad terazniejszym polozeniem Saksonii i Polski z nia zjednoczonej. Lipsk: n.p., 1808.

_____. Uwagi nad terazniejszym polozeniem tej czesci ziemi polskiej ktora od pokoju tylzyckiego zaczeto zwac Ks. Warszaw-skim. Lipsk, 1808.

Kopec, Henryk. "Zjawiska demograficzne towarzyszace zmianom granic Polski." In Biuro Studiow Osadniczo-Przesiedlenczych, Sesja Rady Naukowej dla zagadnien Ziem Odzyskanych, Vol. II. Warsaw, 1946.

Kosinski, Leszek. Pochodzenie terytorialne ludnosci Ziem Zachodnich w 1950r. Warsaw: Instytut Geografii PAN, 1960.

_____. Procesy ludnosciowe na Ziemiach Odzyskanych w latach 1945-1960. Warsaw: Panstwowe Wydawnictwo Naukowe, 1963.

_____, and Pudlo, Krystyna. "Liczba i rozmieszczenie ludnosci na Ziemiach Zachodnich w latach 1939-1958." Problemy rozwoju gospodarczego i demograficznego Ziem Zachodnich w latach 1945-1958. Poznan: Instytut Zachodni, 1960.

Kot, Stanislaw. Listy z Rosji do Generala Sikorskiego. London: Sklad Glowny Jutro Polski, 1955.

Kowalski, Wlodzimierz T. Walka dyplomatyczna o miejsce Polski w Europie (1939-1945). 2nd ed. Warsaw: Ksiazka i Wiedza, 1967.

_____. ZSRR a granica na Odrze i Nysie Luzyckiej 1941-1945. Warsaw: Wydawnictwo MON, 1965.

Kruczynska, Joanna, et al. Polska Zachodnia i Polnocna. Poznan: Wydawnictwo Zachodnie, 1961.

Kulischer, Eugene M. Europe on the Move. New York: Columbia University Press, 1948.

Kwilecki, Andrzej. "Liczebnosc i rozmieszczenie grup mniejszosci narodowych na Ziemiach Zachodnich." Przeglad Zachodni, Vol. XX, No. 4 (1964).

_____. Rola spoleczna nauczyciela na Ziemiach Zachodnich. Poznan: Instytut Zachodni, 1960.

Ladas, Stephen P. The Exchange of Minorities. Bulgaria, Greece and Turkey. New York: MacMillan, 1932.

Lam, Stanislaw, ed. Podreczna encyklopedia powszechna. Paris: Ksiegarnia Polska, 1954.

Lane, Arthur Bliss. I Saw Poland Betrayed: An American Ambassador Reports to the American People. Indianapolis: Bobbs-Merrill Co., 1948.

Latuch, Mikolaj. "Wspolczesne migracje zewnetrzne ludnosci w Polsce." Zeszyty Naukowe SGPS. Warsaw, 1959.

Leahy, William O. I Was There. New York: McGraw-Hill, 1950.

Lednicki, W. Life and Culture of Poland. New York: Roy, 1944.

Lehr-Splawinski, T. O pochodzeniu i ojczyznie Slowian. Poznan: n.p., 1946.

Lesniewski, Andrzej, ed. Western Frontier of Poland: Documents, Statements, Opinions. Warsaw: Polish Institute of International Affairs and Western Press Agency, 1965.

Lewicki, A., and Friedberg, J. Zarys historii polskiej. London: Wydawnictwo Swiatowego Zwiazku Polakow z Zagranicy, 1947.

Lijewski, Teofil. Rozwoj sieci kolejowej Polski. Warsaw: Instytut Geografii PAN, 1959.

Los, Jan Stanislaw. Warunki bytowania ludnosci polskiej na Ziemiach Odzyskanych. Lublin: KUL, 1947.

Loth, J., and Cichocka-Petrazycka, Z. Geografia gospodarcza Polski. Warsaw: n.p., 1947.

Lubojanski, Jozef. The Polish Language in Opole Silesia in the Years 1910-1939. Poznan-Warsaw: Western Press Agency, "German Testimonies" Series, 1957.

Lyra, Franciszek. "English and Polish in Contact." Doctoral dissertation, University of Indiana, 1962.

Markiewicz, Wladyslaw. Przeobrazenia swiadomosci narodowej reemigrantow polskich z Francji. Poznan: Wydawnictwo Poznanskie, 1960.

Miedzinski, P. "Repatriacja do NRF w ramach akcji laczenia rodzin." Przeglad Zachodni, Vol. XIV, No. 2 (1958).

Mikolajczyk, Stanislaw. The Rape of Poland. New York: McGraw-Hill, 1948.

Ministerstwo Obrony Narodowej. Fakty i zagadnienia polskie. London, 1944.

Misiuna, Wladyslaw. "Osiagniecia i perspektywy rozwoju rolnictwa Ziem Zachodnich." In Rozwoj gospodarczy Ziem Zachodnich w dwudziestoleciu Polski Ludowej i jego perspektywy. Poznan: Instytut Zachodni, 1964.

Le Monde (Paris). March 27, 1959.

Nalkowski, W. Poland as a Geographical Entity. London: Allen and Unwin, 1917.

Nicolson, Harold. Curzon: The Last Phase, 1919-1925. London: Constable, 1934.

1939-1950 Population Movements Between the Oder and Bug Rivers. Collective work. Poznan-Warsaw: Western Press Agency, "Studies and Monographs" Series, 1961.

Nowakowski, Stefan. Adaptacja ludnosci na Slasku Opolskim. Poznan: Instytut Zachodni, 1957.

_____. Narodziny miasta. Warsaw: Panstwowe Wydawnictwo Naukowe, 1967.

_____. Przeobrazenia spoleczne wsi opolskiej. Poznan: Instytut Zachodni, 1960.

_____, ed. Socjologiczne problemy miasta polskiego. Warsaw: Panstwowe Wydawnictwo Naukowe, 1964.

Olechnowicz, M. "Rok osadnictwa na Ziemiach Odzyskanych." In Biuro Studiow Osadniczo-Przesiedlenczych, Sesja Rady Naukowej dla Zagadnien Ziem Odzyskanych, Vol. II. Warsaw, 1946.

Olszewicz, Boleslaw. "Sprawa reemigracji ludnosci polskiej." In Biuro Studiow Osadniczo-Przesiedlenczych, Sesja Rady Naukowej dla Zagadnien Ziem Odzyskanych, Vol. II. Warsaw, 1946.

Opallo, M. "Zmiany w uprzemyslowieniu Ziem Zachodnich." In Studia nad zagadnieniami gospodarczymi i spolecznymi Ziem Zachodnich, Vol. IV.

Osteuropa Handbuch. Cologne-Graz: Herausgegeben von Werner Markert, Band "Polen," 1959.

Oxford Economic Atlas of the World. Oxford: Oxford University Press, 1954.

Oxford Regional Economic Atlas: The USSR and Eastern Europe. London: Oxford University Press, 1956.

Panstwowe Wydawnictwo Ekonomiczne. The Economic Development. Warsaw, 1961.

_____. XX lat Polski Ludowej. Warsaw, 1964.

Peikert, Paul. Kronika dni oblezenia. Wroclaw 22.I.-6V. 1945, Karol Jonca and Alfred Konieczny, eds., "Annales Silesiae," Suppl. II, Wroclaw-Warsaw-Krakow, 1964.

Pietkiewicz, S., and Orlicz, M. "Plan regionalny przesiedlenia osadnikow rolnych na Ziemie Odzyskane." In Biuro Studiow Osadniczo-Przesiedlenczych, Sesja Rady Naukowej dla Zagadnien Ziem Odzyskanych, Vol. I. Warsaw, 1946.

Pobog-Malinowski, Wladyslaw. Najnowsza historia polityczna Polski 1864-1945. London: B. Swiderski, 1960.

Poland 1969: Facts and Figures. Warsaw: Interpress Publishers, 1969.

Polish Embassy Press Office. Poland, Germany and European Peace: Official Documents 1944-1948. London, 1948.

Polska Akademia Nauk, Komitet Badan nad Kultura Wspolczesna, Mlode pokolenie wsi Polski Ludowej: Pamietniki i Studia. Vol. IV. Od chlopa do robotnika. Warsaw: Ludowa Spoldzielnia Wydawnicza, 1967.

Poniatowski, Jozef. "Rozmiary przeludnienia rolnictwa w swietle Krytyki." Rolnictwo (Warsaw), Vol. IV (1939).

Popiolek, Kazimierz, and Sobanski, Waclaw. The Last Attempt to Germanize Opole Silesia. Poznan-Warsaw: Western Press Agency, "German Testimonies" Series, 1959.

Popkiewicz, Jozef. Spoldzielczosc produkcyjna na przelomie. Wroclaw: Zaklad Narodowy im. Ossolinskich Wydawnictwo, 1959.

Pospieszalski, Karol Marian. "Hitlerowskie prawo okupacyjne w Polsce." 2 parts. In Documenta Occupationis Teutonicae, Vols. V, VI. Poznan: Instytut Zachodni, 1952 and 1958.

_____. "Niemiecka lista narodowa Kraju Warty." In Documenta Occupationis Teutonicae, Vol. IV. Poznan: Instytut Zachodni, 1949.

_____. "Sprawa 58,000 Volksdeutschow." In Documenta Occupationis Teutonicae, Vol. VII. Poznan: Instytut Zachodni, 1959.

Pounds, Norman J. G. Divided Germany and Berlin. Princeton, N. J.: Van Nostrand, 1962.

_____. Poland Between East and West. Princeton, N.J.: Van Nostrand, 1964.

Pruszynski, K. "Wobec Rosji." Wiadomosci Polskie (London), October 4, 1942.

Putrament, Jerzy. Pol wieku. Warsaw: Czytelnik, 1962.

Putzger, F. W. Historischer Weltatlas. 83rd ed. Bielefeld: Velhagen und Klasing, 1961.

Pye, Lucian W. Aspects of Political Development. Boston: Little, Brown and Company, 1966.

Quirin, Heinz, and Trillmich, Werner. Westermanns Atlas zur Weltgeschichte. Braunschweig: Georg Westermann Verlag, 1963.

Raczynski, Edward. W sojuszniczym Londynie. London: Polish Research Centre, 1960.

Rada Ochrony Pomnikow Walki i Meczenstwa. Przewodnik po upamietnionych miejscach walk i meczenstwa lata wojny 1939-1945. Warsaw: "Sport i Turystyka," 1966.

Rhode, Gotthold. Die Ostgebiete des Deutschen Reiches. 2nd ed. Wurzburg: Holzner-Verlag, 1955.

Rocznik Polityczny i Gospodarczy 1936. Warsaw: PAT, 1936.

Rocznik Polityczny i Gospodarczy 1969. Warsaw: Panstwowe Wydawnictwo Ekonomiczne, 1970.

Rocznik Polonii 1958-59. Vol. VII. London: Taurus, 1958.

Rocznik Statystyki Miedzynarodowej 1970. Seria "Statystyka Miedzynarodowa," Nr. 5. Warsaw: Glowny Urzad Statystyczny Polskiej Rzeczypospolitej Ludowej, 1970.

Romer, Eugeniusz. Polacy na Kresach Pomorskich i Pojeziernych. Lvov: Ksiaznica Polska Towarzystwo Szkolne Wyzszych, 1919.

_____. Powszechny atlas geograficzny. Lvov: Ksiaznica Atlas, 1934.

Rozmanit, Tadeusz. "Czy Mikolajczyk zaprzepascil Lwow?" Horyzonty (Paris), Vol. X, No. 107.

Rozwoj gospodarczy Ziem Zachodnich i Polnocnych Polski. Warsaw: Polskie Wydawnictwa Gospodarcze, 1960.

Russett, Bruce M. "Inequality and Instability: The Relation of Land Tenure to Politics." World Politics, Vol. XVI (April 1964).

Rutkowski, Jan. Historia gospodarcza Polski. do (1864r). Warsaw: Ksiazka i Wiedza, 1953.

Rybicki, Pawel. "Mozliwosci zaludnienia Ziem Odzyskanych osadnikami polskimi w grupie zawodow pozarolniczych." In Biuro Studiow Osadniczo-Przesiedlenczych, Sesja Rady Naukowej dla Zagadnien Ziem Odzyskanych, Vol. I. Warsaw, 1946.

Sarapata, Adam, ed. Przemiany spoleczne w Polsce Ludowej. Warsaw: Panstwowe Wydawnictwo Naukowe, 1965.

Schechtman, B. Joseph. European Population Transfers 1939-1945. New York: Oxford University Press, 1946.

Schieder, Theodor, ed. The Expulsion of the German Population from the Territories East of the Oder-Neisse-Line. Federal Ministry for Expellees, Refugees and War Victims. Bonn: Federal Ministry, n.d.

Schimitzek, Stanislaw. Truth or Conjecture? German Civilian War Losses in the East. Warsaw-Poznan: Zachodnia Agencja Prasowa, 1966.

Seyda, Marian. Poland and Germany and the Post-War Reconstruction of Europe. New York: Polish Information Center, 1943.

Sherwood, R. E. The White House Papers of H. Hopkins. Vol. II. London: Eyre and Spottiswoode, 1949.

Smolinski, Stanislaw, et al. "Struktura przemyslu Ziem Zachodnich w latach 1939-1959." In Studia nad zagadnieniami gospodarczymi i spolecznymi Ziem Zachodnich, Vol. IV, 1964.

Studia nad zagadnieniami gospodarczymi i spolecznymi Ziem Zachodnich. No. 1. Problemy rozwoju gospodarczego i demograficznego Ziem Zachodnich w latach 1945-1958. Poznan: Instytut Zachodni, 1960.

_____. No. 4. Rozwoj gospodarczy Ziem Zachodnich w dwudziestoleciu Polski Ludowej i jego perspektywy. Poznan: Instytut Zachodni, 1964.

Stys, Wincenty. "Zagadnienie ustroju rolnego na Ziemiach Odzyskanych." In Biuro Studiow Osadniczo-Przesiedlenczych, Sesja Rady Naukowej dla Zagadnien Ziem Odzyskanych, Vol. I. Warsaw, 1946.

Sworakowski, W. "An Error Regarding Eastern Galicia in Curzon's Note to the Soviet Government." Journal of Central European Affairs, Vol. IV, No. 1 (April 1944).

Szarflarski, Jozef. Ruchy ludnosciowe. Gdansk: Instytut Baltycki, 1947.

_____. "Zagadnienie odplywu ludnosci w ciagu ostatniego wieku z Ziem Odzyskanych a nasza akcja osadnicza na tym terenie." In Biuro Studiow Osadniczo-Przesiedlenczych, Sesja Rady Naukowej dla Zagadnien Ziem Odzyskanych, Vol. II. Warsaw, 1946.

Szafranski, Jan. "Poland's Losses in World War II." In 1939-1945 War Losses in Poland. Poznan-Warsaw: Wydawnictwo Zachodnie, Studies and Monographs of Western Press Agency, 1960.

Szczepanski, Jan. Polish Society. New York: Random House, 1970.

Szturm de Sztrem, Edward. Statistical Atlas of Poland. London:
    The Polish Ministry of Information, n.d.

Taylor, J. The Economic Development of Poland 1919-1950. Ithaca,
    N. Y.: Cornell University Press, 1952.

Thorwald, Jurgen. Es begann an der Weichsel. 5th ed. Stuttgart:
    n.p., 1952.

Turnau, Irena. Studia nad struktura ludnosciowa polskiego Wroclawia.
    Poznan: Instytut Slaski, 1960.

Ukraine: A Concise Encyclopaedia. Toronto: University of Toronto
    Press, 1963.

U. S. Bureau of the Census. The Population of Poland. Series P-90,
    No. 4. Washington, D. C.: U. S. Government Printing Office,
    1954.

U. S. Department of State. The Conferences of Malta and Yalta. Wash-
    ington, D. C.: U. S. Government Printing Office, 1955.

U. S. Department of State, Historical Office. The Conference of Berlin:
    The Potsdam Conference, 1945. Vol. II. Washington, D. C.:
    U. S. Government Printing Office, 1960.

U. S. Office of Strategic Services, Research and Analysis Branch.
    "Postwar Poland: Economic and Political Outlook." Washington,
    D. C., 1945 (mimeographed).

Volz, Wilhelm. Die Ostdeutsche Wirtschaft. Langensalza, 1930.

Waszak, S. "The Number of Germans in Poland in the Years 1931-1939
    Against the Background of German Losses in the Second World
    War." Polish Western Affairs, Vol. I (1960).

Weber, Paul. Die Polen in Oberschlesien. Berlin: Verlag von Julius
    Springer, 1919.

West German Federal Statistical Office. Statistical Pocket-Book on
    Expellees in the Federal Republic of Germany and West Berlin.
    Wiesbaden, 1953.

Wielka encyklopedia powszechna PWN Polska. Warsaw: Panstwowe
    Wydawnictwo Naukowe, 1967.

Wiewiora, Boleslaw. Polish German Frontier from the Standpoint of International Law. Poznan-Warsaw: Wydawnictwo Zachodnie, 1959.

Wiskemann, Elisabeth. Germany's Eastern Neighbours, Problems Relating to the Oder-Neisse-Line and the Czech Frontier Regions. London-New York-Toronto: Oxford University Press, 1956.

Wojciechowski, Marian. Stosunki polsko niemieckie 1933-1938. Poznan: Instytut Zachodni, 1965.

Wojciechowski, Z., ed. Poland's Place in Europe. Poznan, 1947.

Wrzesinski, Wojciech. "Przyczynki do problemu wschodniopruskiego w czasie II wojny swiatowej." In Komunikaty Mazursko-War- minskie, Vol. I. Olsztyn, 1965.

Wrzosek, Antoni. Bogactwa mineralne na Ziemiach Zachodnich. Katowice: Instytut Slaski, 1947.

Zaremba, Jozef. Atlas Ziem Odzyskanych. 2nd ed. Warsaw: Glowny Urzad Planowania Przestrzennego, 1947.

Zaremba, Piotr. Pierwszy szczecinski rok 1945. Poznan: Wydawnictwo Poznanskie, 1966.

Ziolek, B. "Rozwoj demograficzny Ziem Zachodnich." In Studia nad zagadnieniami gospodarczymi i spolecznymi Ziem Zachodnich, Vol. IV, 1964.

Ziolkowski, Janusz. Urbanizacja. Miasto. Osiedle. Studia sociolog- iczne. Warsaw: Panstwowe Wydawnictwo Naukowe, 1965.

Zweig, Ferdinand. Poland Between Two Wars. London: Secker and Warburg, 1944.

Zycie Warszawy. November 20, 1945.

Zygulski, Kazimierz. Repatrianci na Ziemiach Zachodnich. Poznan: Instytut Zachodni, 1962.

_____. "Wyjazdy ludnosci woj katowickiego na zachod w latach 1955-1958." Manuscript, Slaski Instytut Naukowy, Katowice.

Z. ANTHONY KRUSZEWSKI is currently Associate Professor of Political Science, The University of Texas at El Paso, where he is also co-director of the university's Cross-Cultural Southwest Ethnic Study Center and Chairman of the Interdisciplinary Program for Soviet and East European Studies.

Before coming to The University of Texas in 1968, Professor Kruszewski was Assistant Professor of Political Science and Coordinator, Political Science Department, State University of New York at Plattsburgh and an Instructor in the U.S. Air Force Institute's Political Science Program at Plattsburgh Air Force Base. He has been a guest lecturer at the Universities of Warsaw and Wroclaw in Poland.

Born in Poland and educated in England, Dr. Kruszewski studied at Northwestern University and received a Ph.D. from The University of Chicago.